THERE'S CORPSES EVERYWHERE

Yet Another *Liō* Collection

by Mark Tatulli

Andrews McMeel
Publishing, LLC

Kansas City • Sydney • London

LIŌ is distributed internationally by Universal Uclick.

There's Corpses Everywhere copyright © 2010 by Mark Tatulli. All rights reserved. Printed in China. No part of this book may be used or reproduced in any manner whatsoever without written permission except in the case of reprints in the context of reviews. For information, write Andrews McMeel Publishing, LLC, an Andrews McMeel Universal company, 1130 Walnut Street, Kansas City, Missouri 64106.

ISBN-13: 978-0-7407-9733-0
ISBN-10: 0-7407-9733-6

Library of Congress Control Number: 2010922407

10 11 12 13 14 WKT 10 9 8 7 6 5 4 3 2 1

www.andrewsmcmeel.com

───── **ATTENTION: SCHOOLS AND BUSINESSES** ─────

Andrews McMeel books are available at quantity discounts with bulk purchase for educational, business, or sales promotional use. For information, please write to: Special Sales Department, Andrews McMeel Publishing, LLC, 1130 Walnut Street, Kansas City, Missouri 64106.

TO TERRI--

LOVE-- MT.

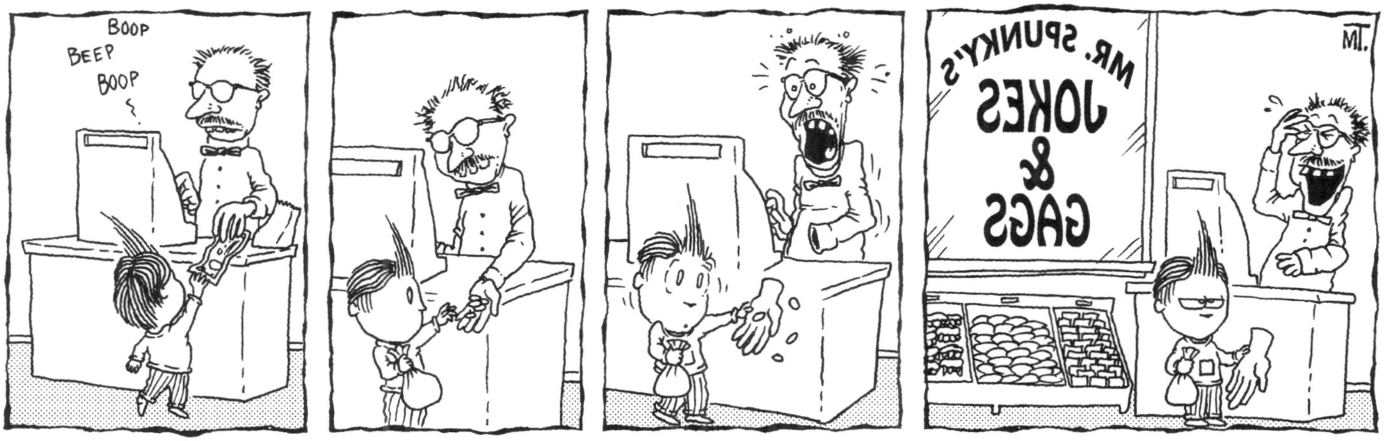
BOOP
BEEP
BOOP
MR. SPUNKY'S
JOKES
&
GAGS
MT.

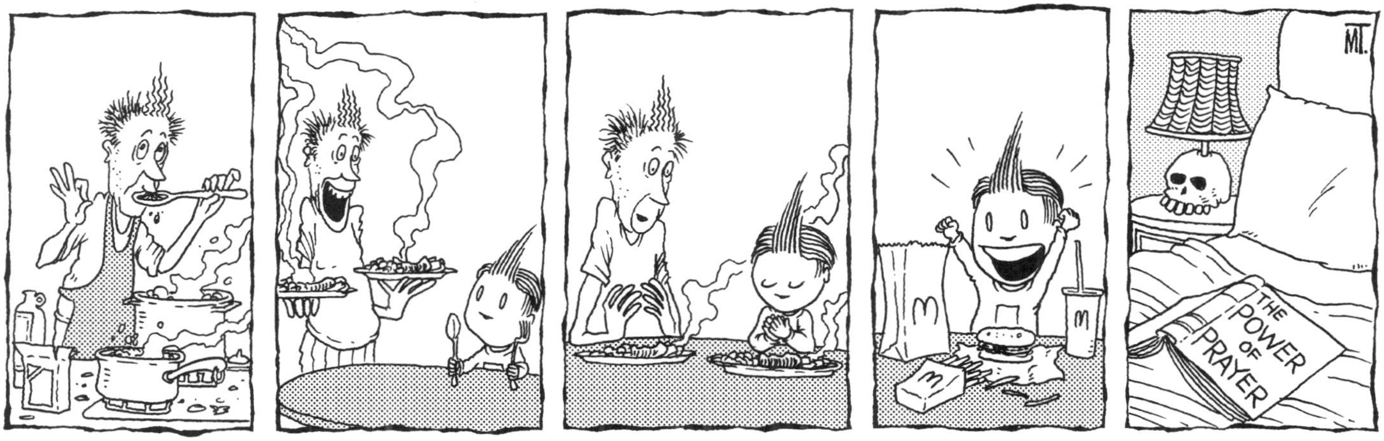
MT.
THE
POWER
OF
PRAYER

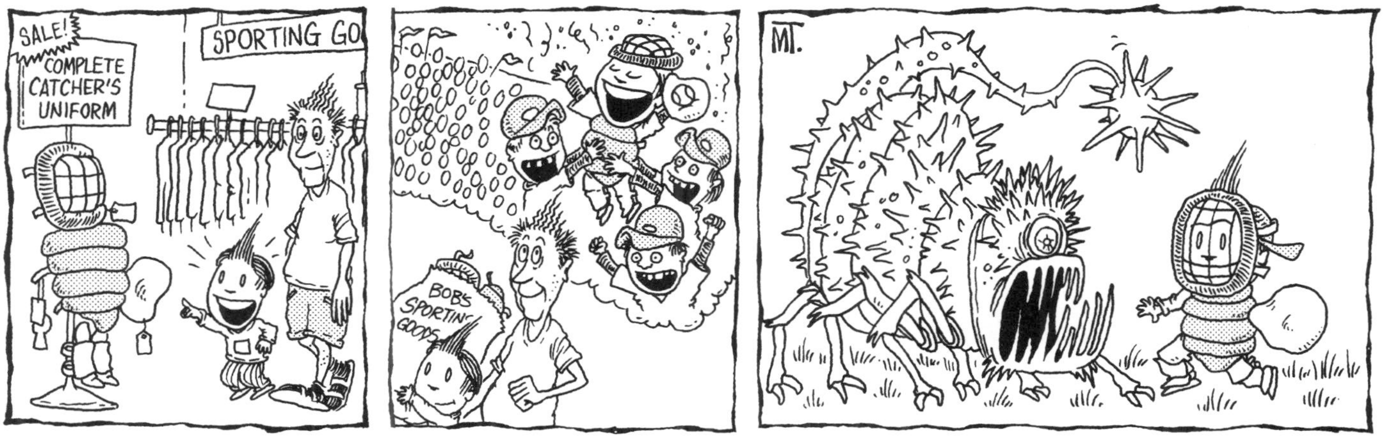
SALE!
COMPLETE
CATCHER'S
UNIFORM
SPORTING GO
BOB'S
SPORTIN
GOODS
MT.

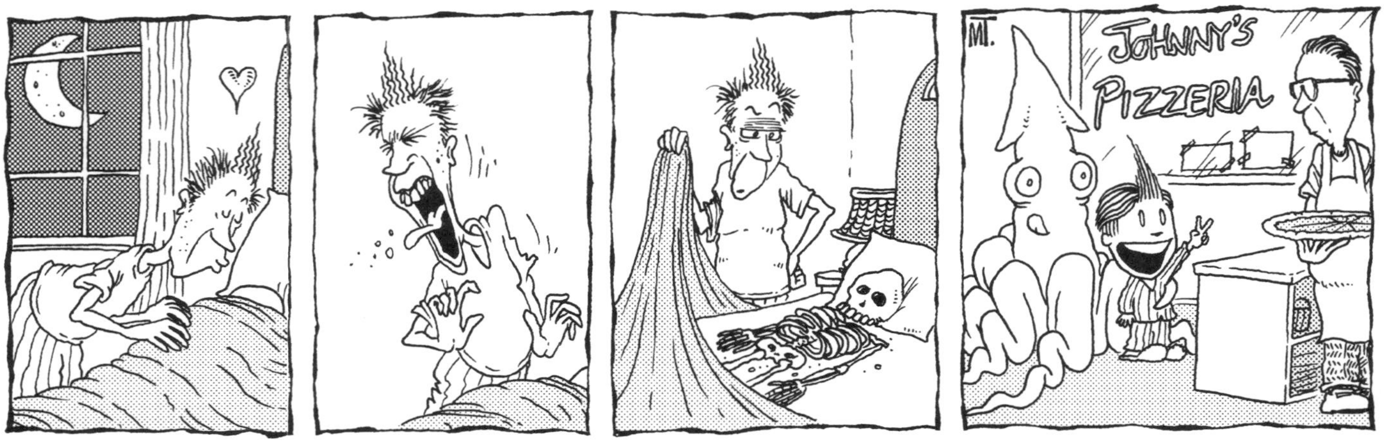
MT.
JOHNNY'S
PIZZERIA

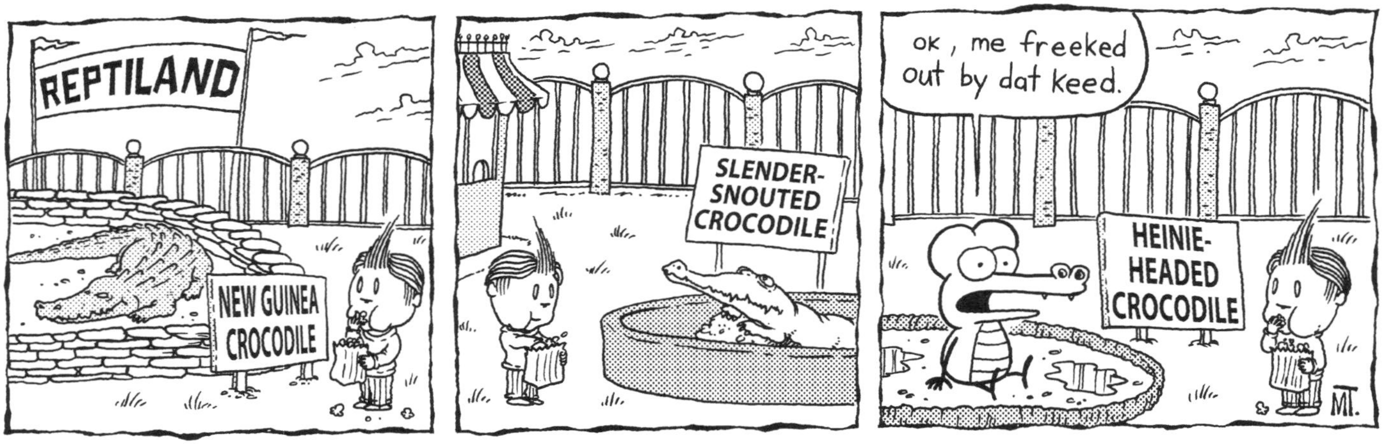
REPTILAND
NEW GUINEA CROCODILE
SLENDER-SNOUTED CROCODILE
ok, me freeked out by dat keed.
HEINIE-HEADED CROCODILE
MT.

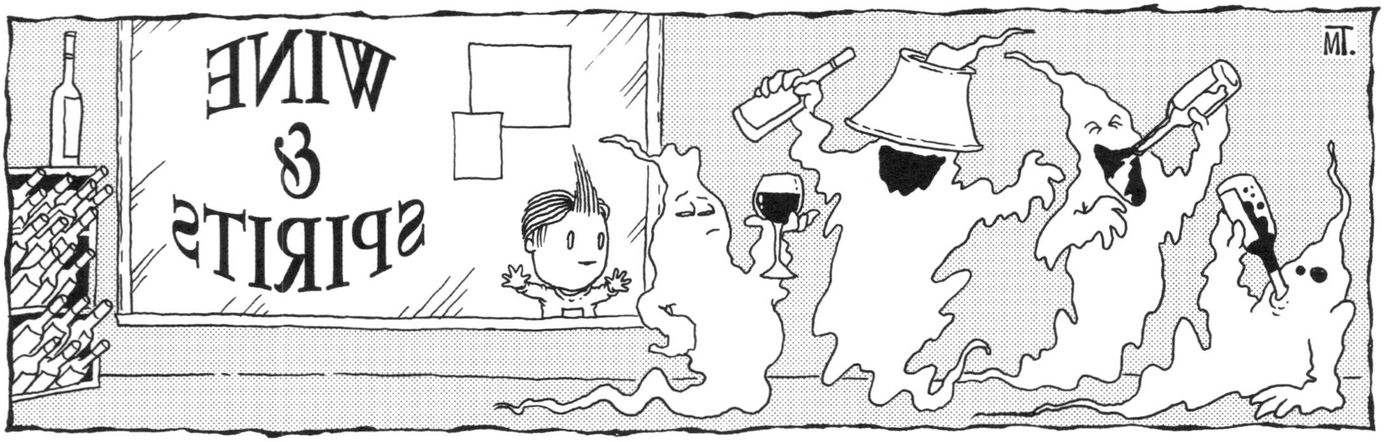
WINE & SPIRITS
MT.

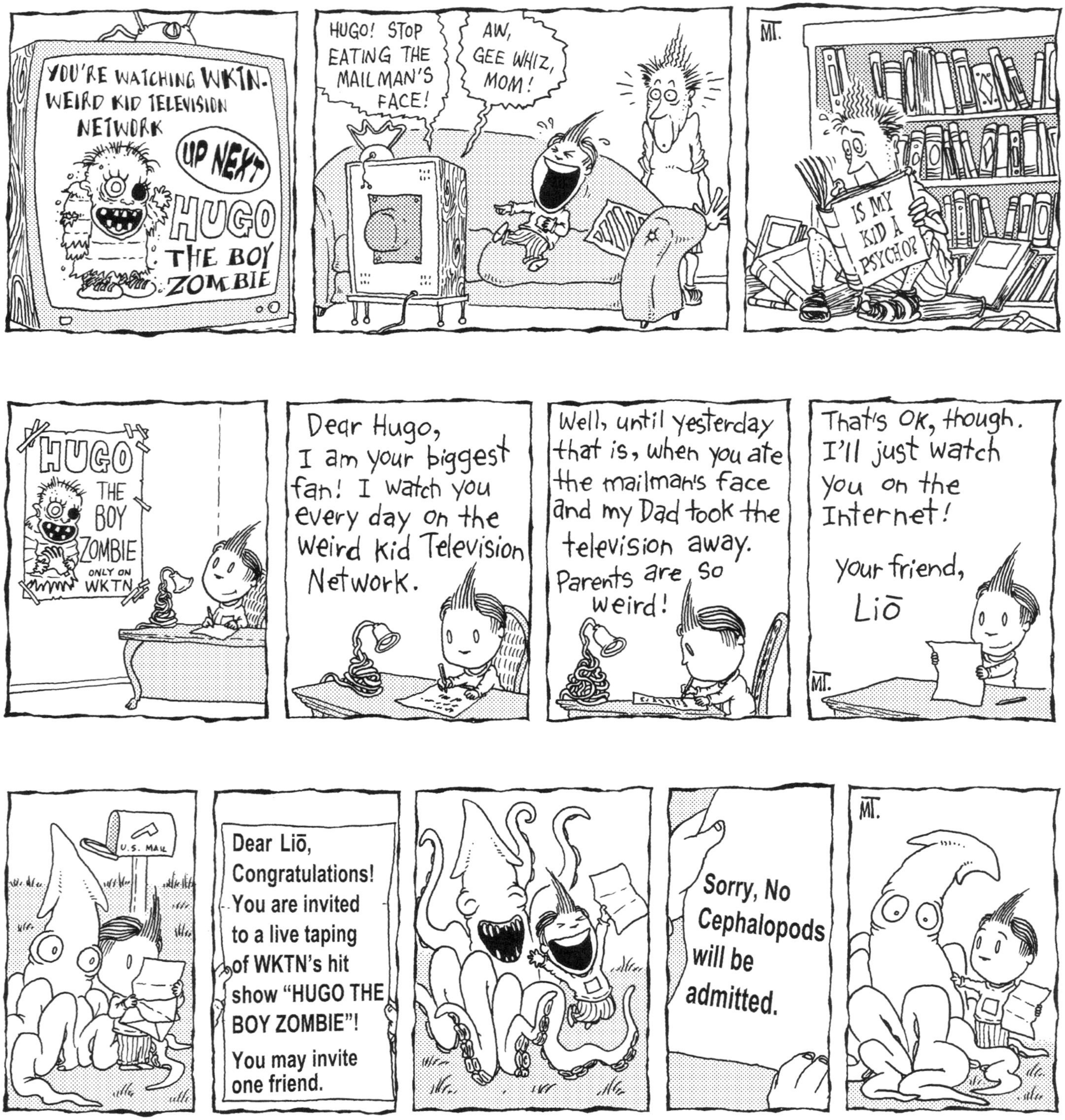
YOU'RE WATCHING WKTN-
WEIRD KID TELEVISION NETWORK
UP NEXT
HUGO THE BOY ZOMBIE
HUGO! STOP EATING THE MAILMAN'S FACE!
AW, GEE WHIZ, MOM!
MT.
IS MY KID A PSYCHO?
HUGO THE BOY ZOMBIE ONLY ON WKTN
Dear Hugo,
I am your biggest fan! I watch you every day on the Weird Kid Television Network.
Well, until yesterday that is, when you ate the mailman's face and my Dad took the television away.
Parents are so weird!
That's OK, though. I'll just watch you on the Internet!
Your friend,
Liō
MT.
U.S. MAIL
Dear Liō,
Congratulations!
You are invited to a live taping of WKTN's hit show "HUGO THE BOY ZOMBIE"!
You may invite one friend.
Sorry, No Cephalopods will be admitted.
MT.

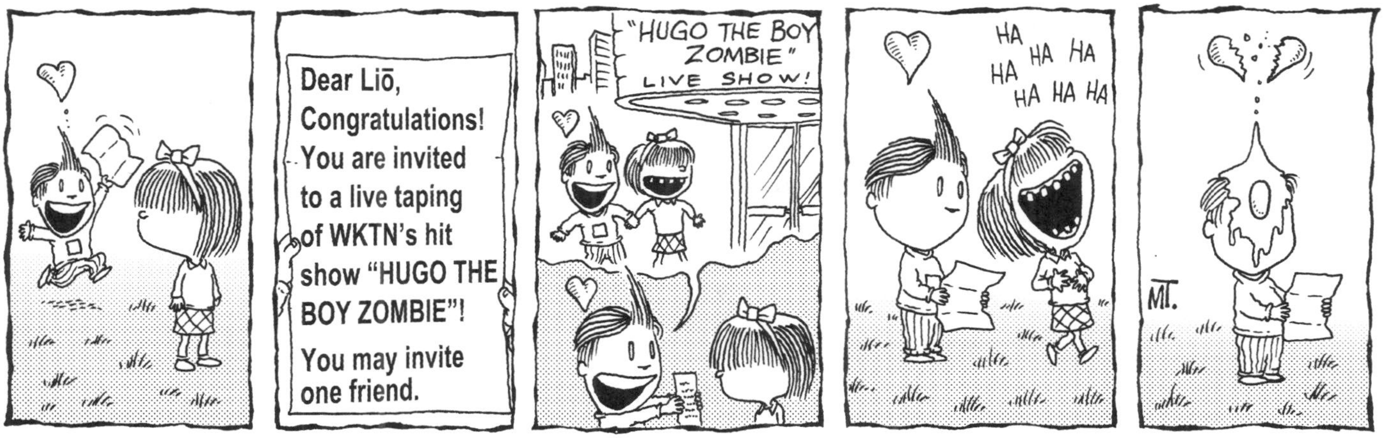
Dear Liō,
Congratulations!
You are invited to a live taping of WKTN's hit show "HUGO THE BOY ZOMBIE"!
You may invite one friend.
"HUGO THE BOY ZOMBIE" LIVE SHOW!
HA HA HA HA HA HA HA HA

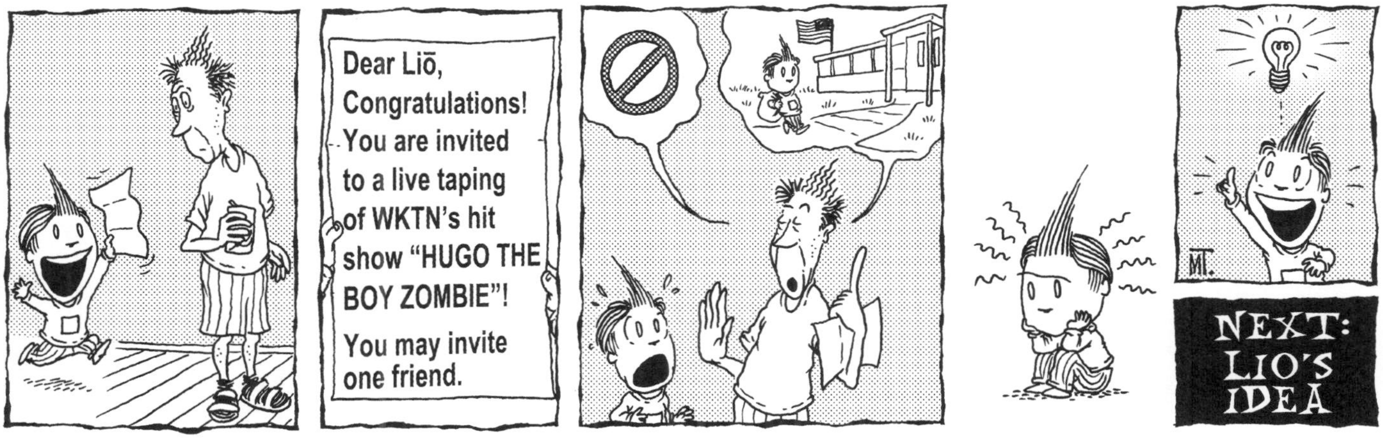
Dear Liō,
Congratulations!
You are invited to a live taping of WKTN's hit show "HUGO THE BOY ZOMBIE"!
You may invite one friend.
NEXT: LIO'S IDEA

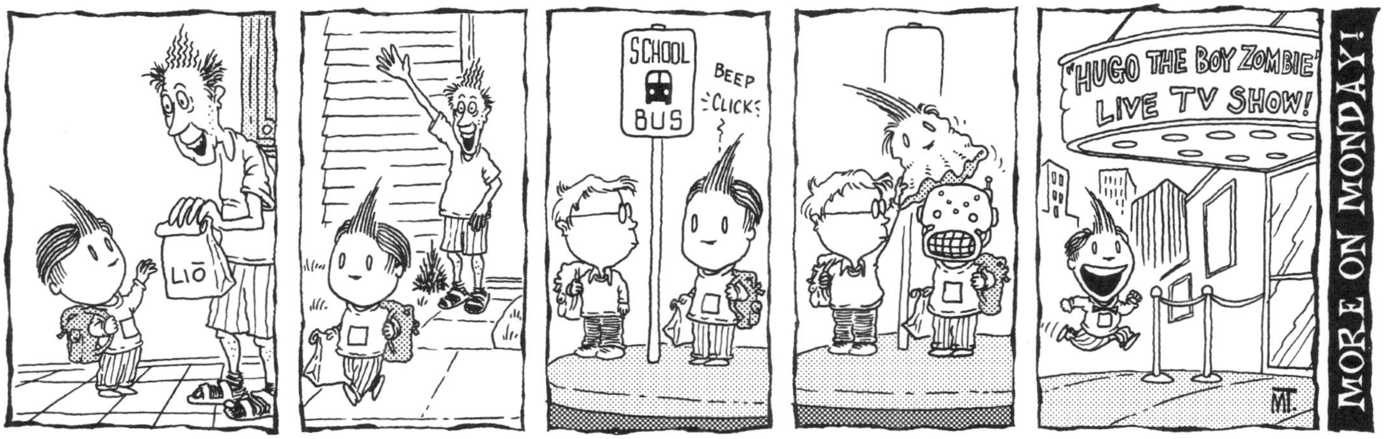
LIŌ
SCHOOL BUS
BEEP CLICK
"HUGO THE BOY ZOMBIE" LIVE TV SHOW!
MORE ON MONDAY!

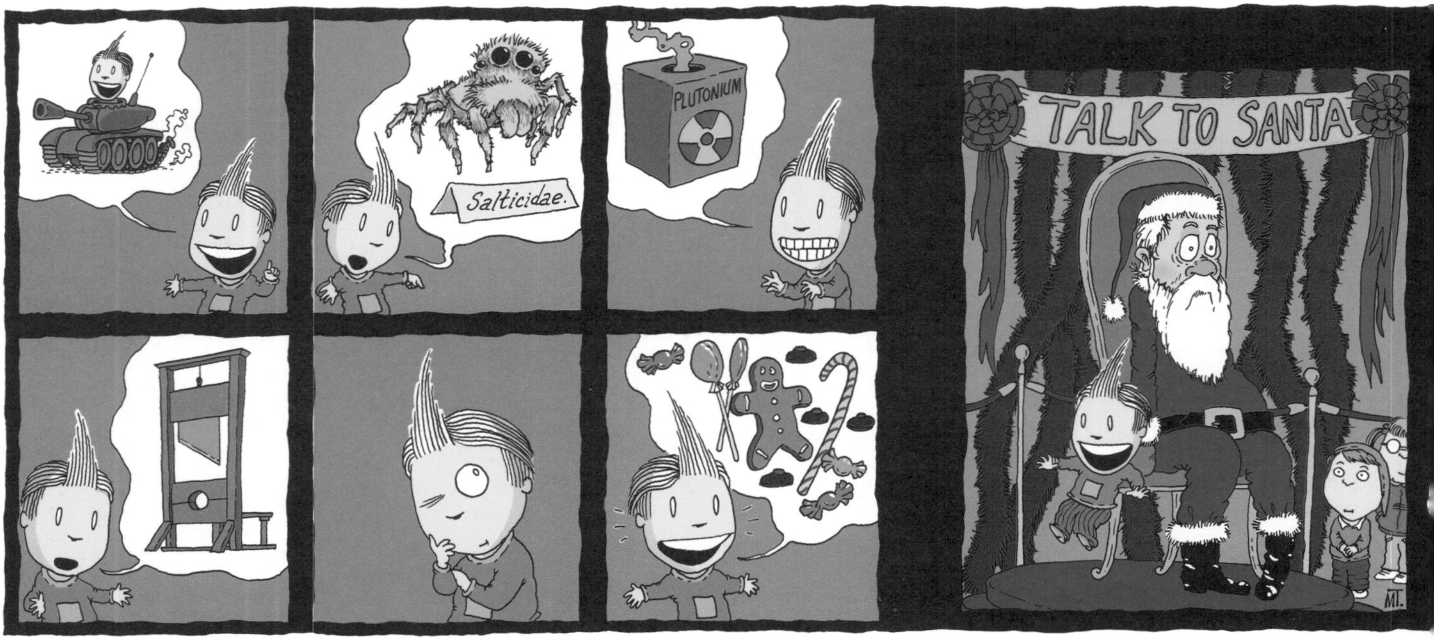

Salticidae.
PLUTONIUM
TALK TO SANTA
MT.

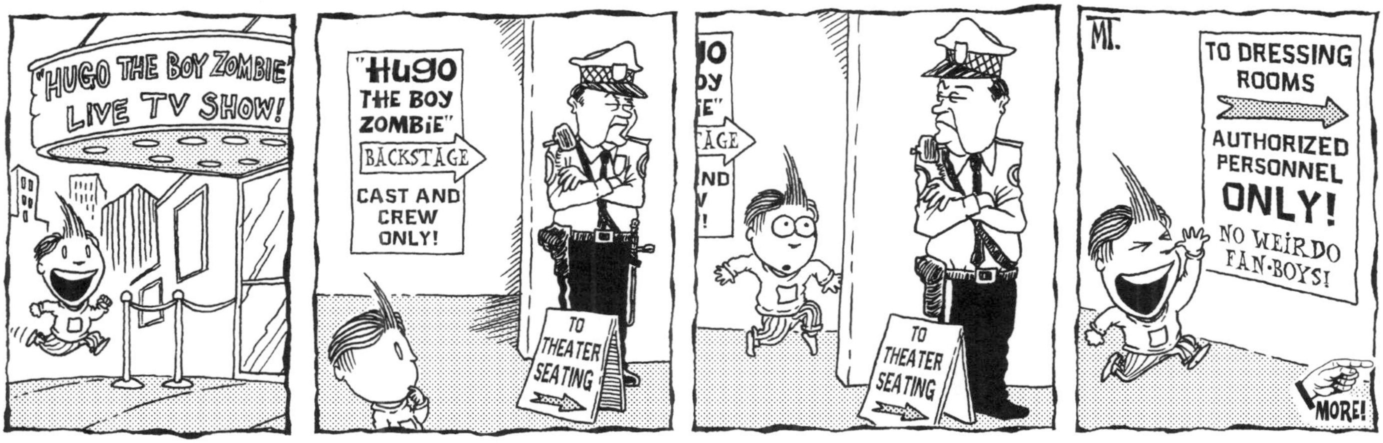
"HUGO THE BOY ZOMBIE"
LIVE TV SHOW!
"Hugo THE BOY ZOMBiE"
BACKSTAGE
CAST AND CREW ONLY!
TO THEATER SEATING
TO THEATER SEATING
MT.
TO DRESSING ROOMS
AUTHORIZED PERSONNEL ONLY!
NO WEIRDO FAN-BOYS!
MORE!

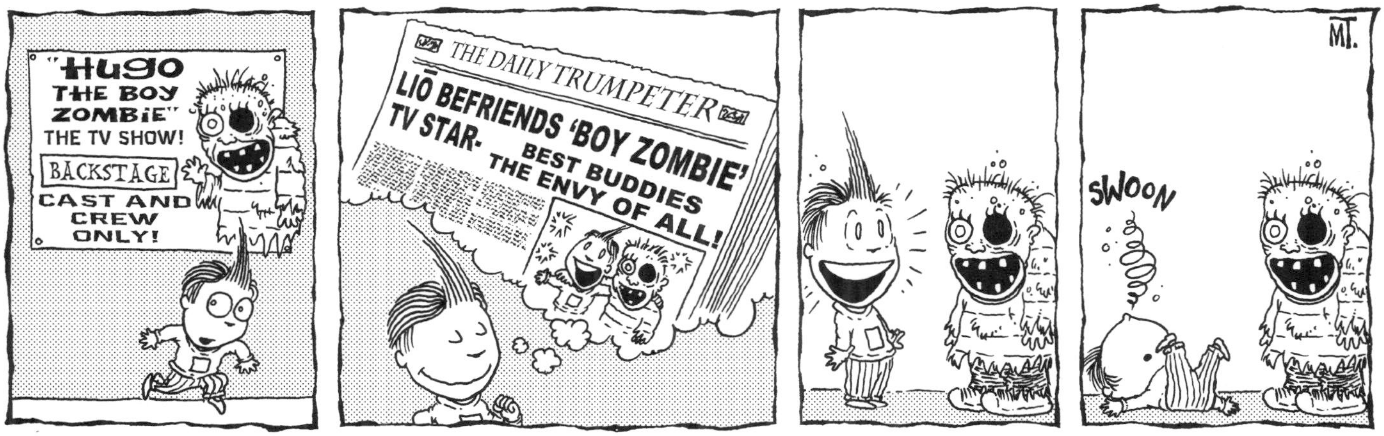
"Hugo THE BOY ZOMBiE" THE TV SHOW!
BACKSTAGE
CAST AND CREW ONLY!
THE DAILY TRUMPETER
LIŌ BEFRIENDS 'BOY ZOMBIE' TV STAR-
BEST BUDDIES THE ENVY OF ALL!
MT.
SWOON

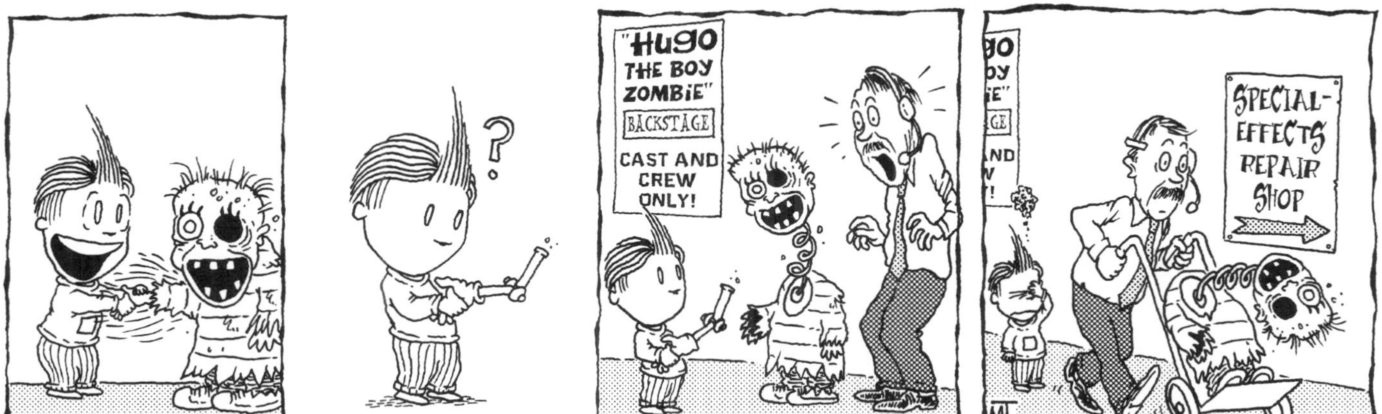
?
"Hugo THE BOY ZOMBiE"
BACKSTAGE
CAST AND CREW ONLY!
SPECIAL-EFFECTS REPAIR SHOP
MT.

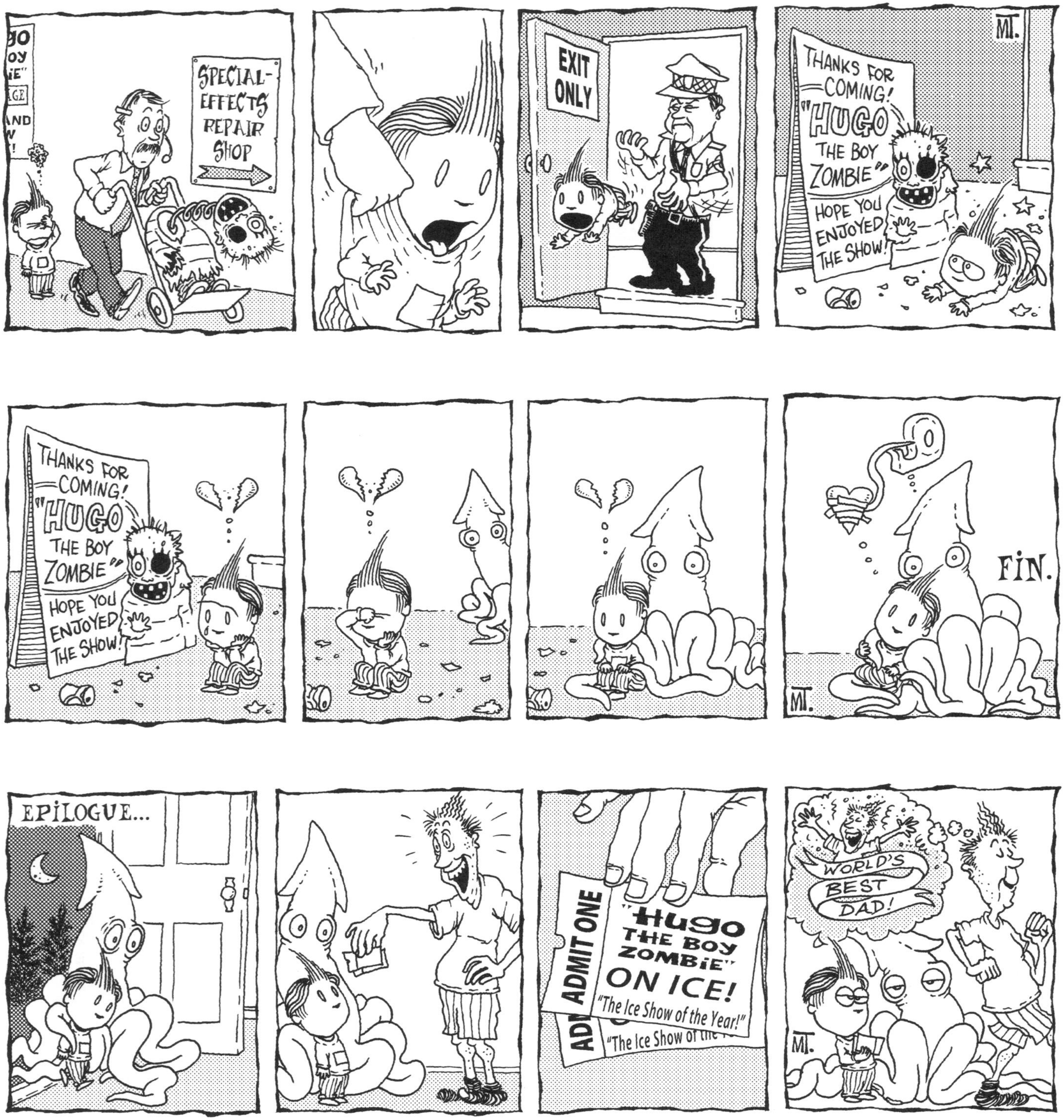
SPECIAL-EFFECTS REPAIR SHOP
EXIT ONLY
THANKS FOR COMING! "HUGO THE BOY ZOMBIE" HOPE YOU ENJOYED THE SHOW!
THANKS FOR COMING! "HUGO THE BOY ZOMBIE" HOPE YOU ENJOYED THE SHOW!
FIN.
EPILOGUE...
ADMIT ONE
"HUGO THE BOY ZOMBIE" ON ICE!
"The Ice Show of the Year!"
WORLD'S BEST DAD!

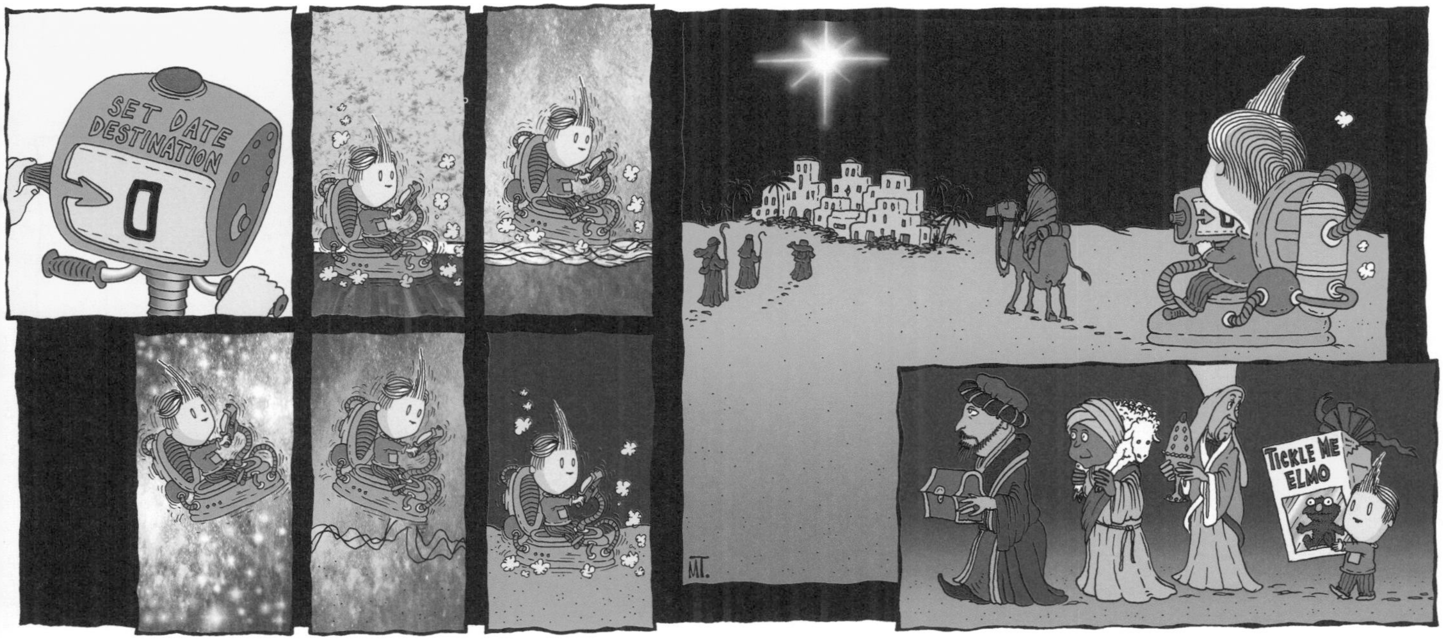
SET DATE
DESTINATION
D
TICKLE ME
ELMO
MT.

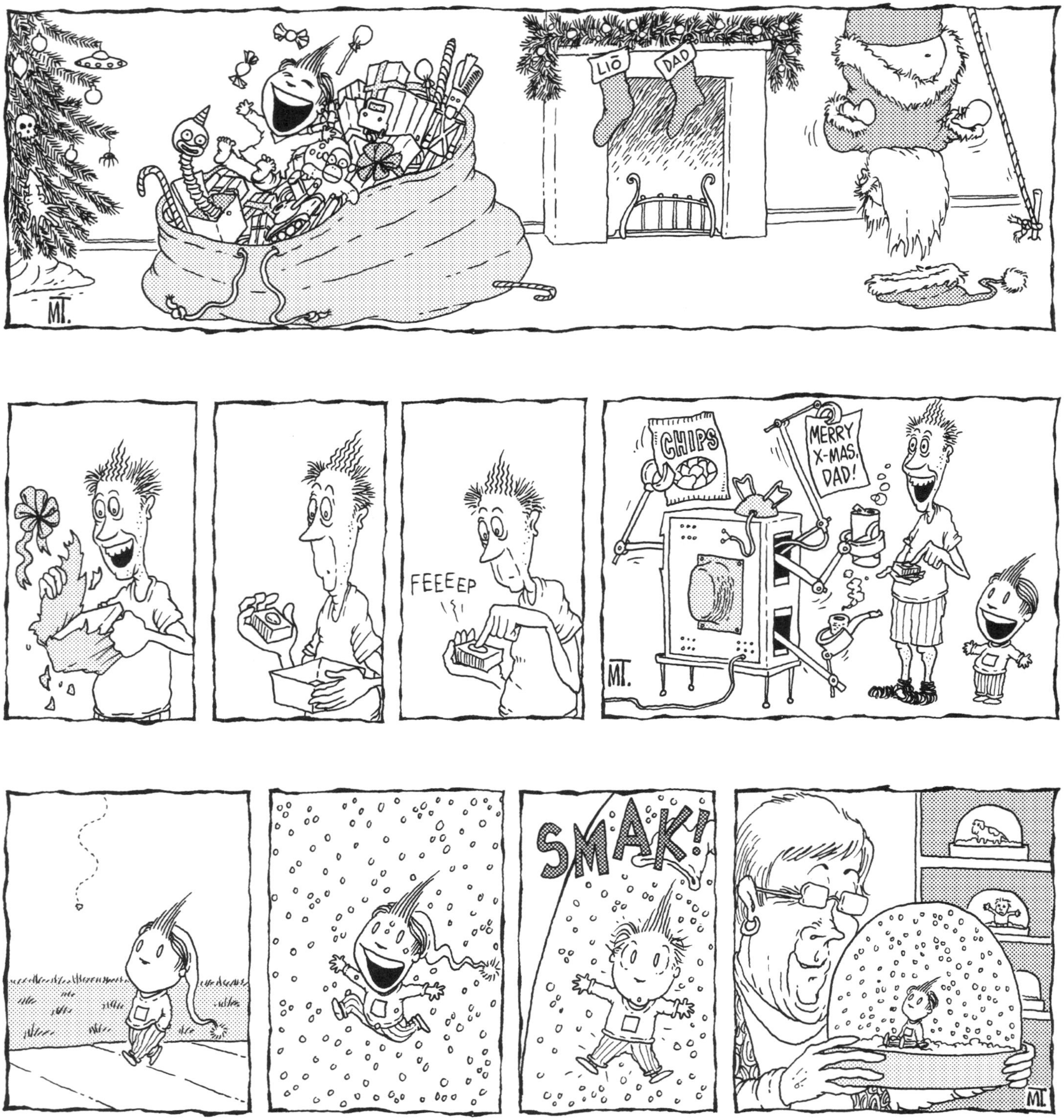
LIŌ
DAD
FEEEEP
CHIPS
MERRY X-MAS, DAD!
SMAK!

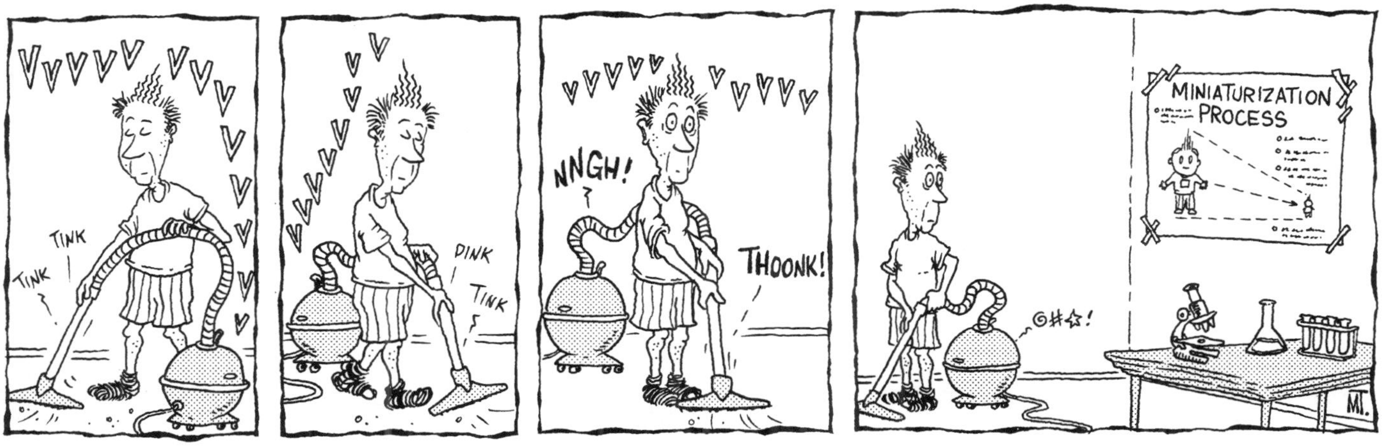
VVVVV VVVVVVVVV
TINK
TINK
DINK
TINK
NNGH!
THOONK!
MINIATURIZATION PROCESS
@#☆!

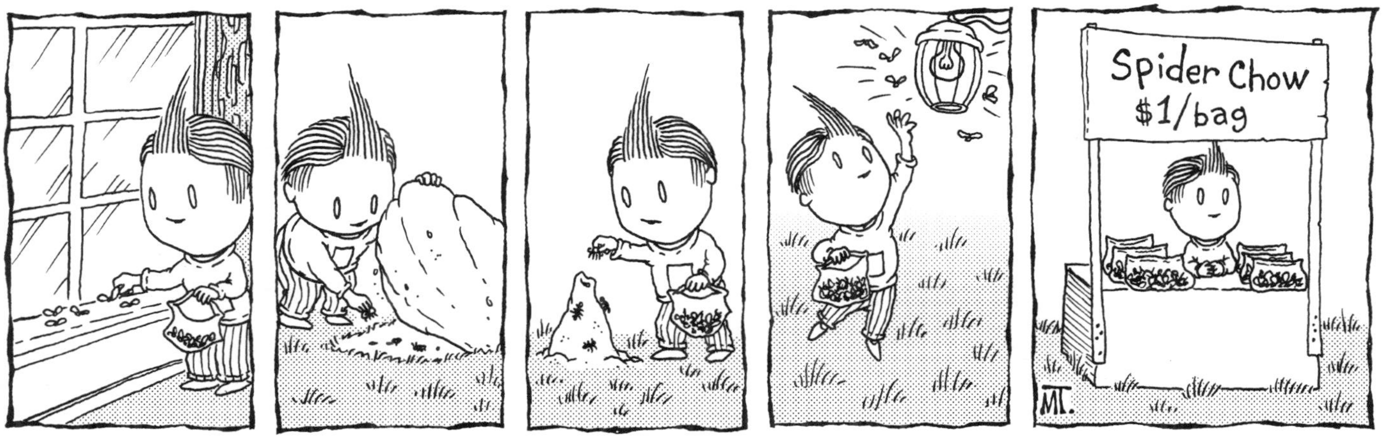
Spider Chow
$1/bag

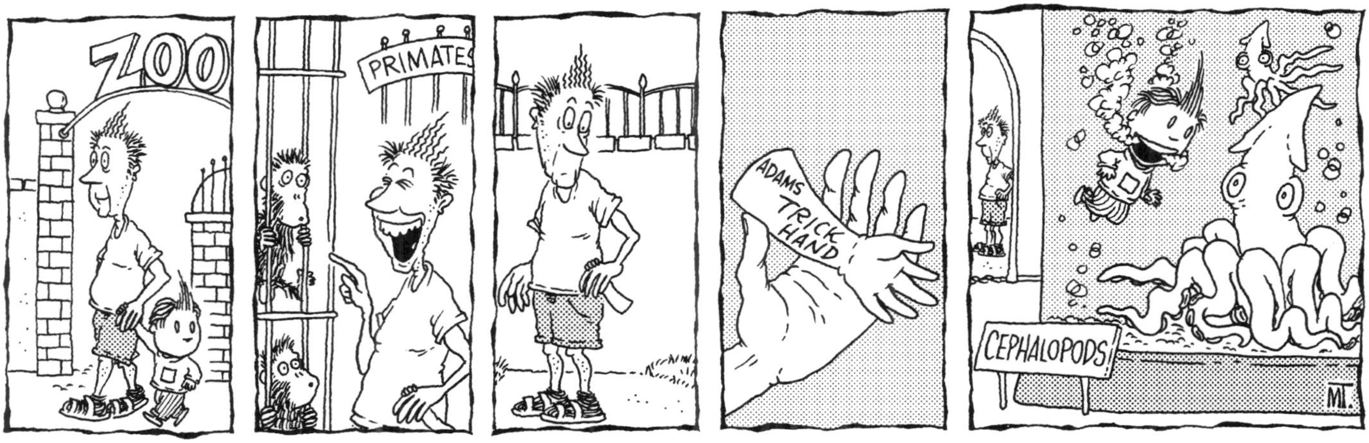
ZOO
PRIMATES
ADAMS TRICK HAND
CEPHALOPODS

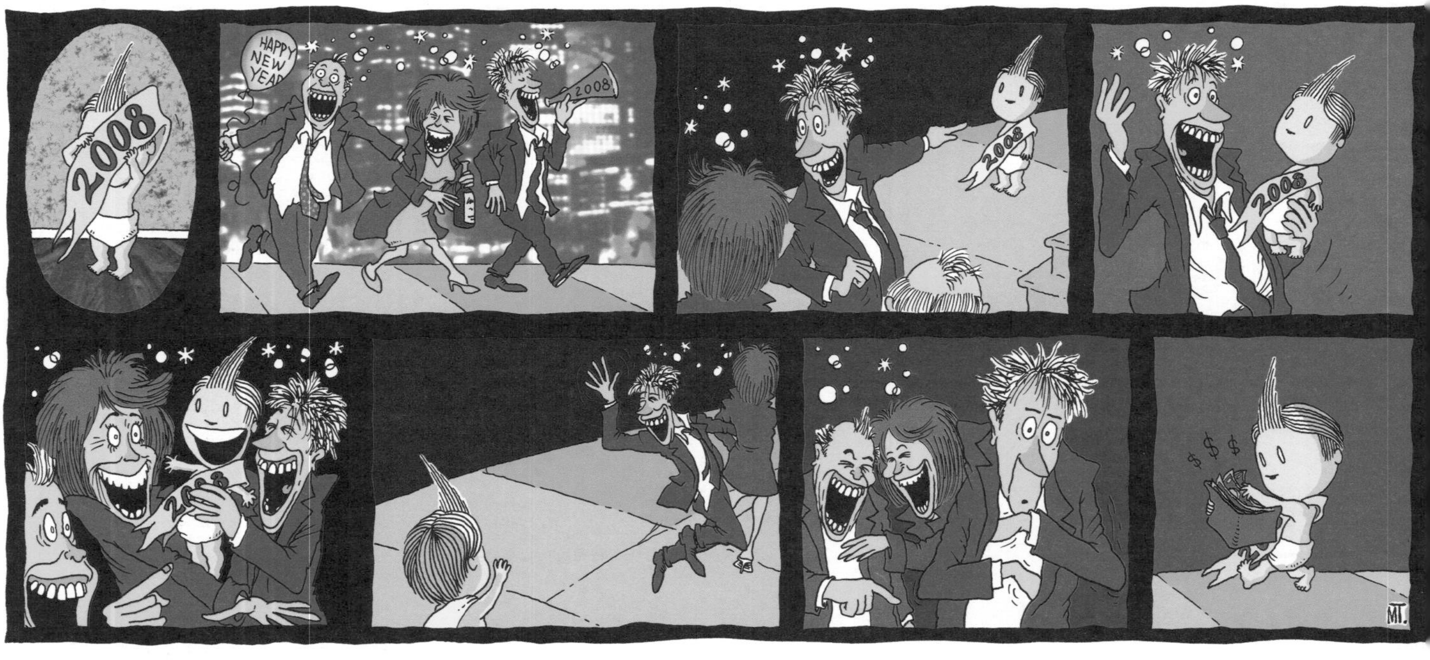
2008
HAPPY NEW YEAR
2008
2008
2008
MT.

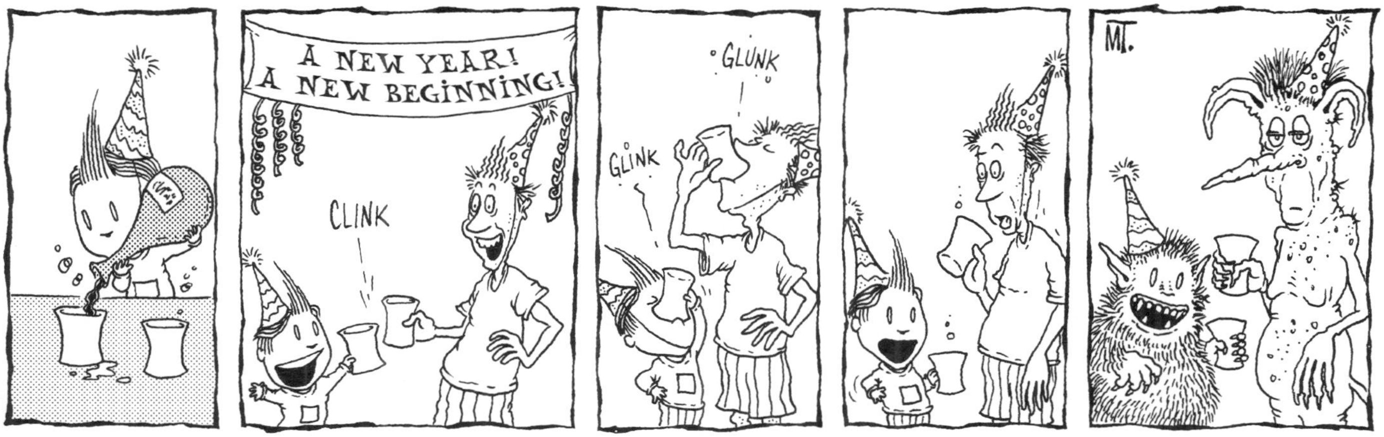
A NEW YEAR!
A NEW BEGINNING!
CLINK
GLINK
GLUNK
MT.

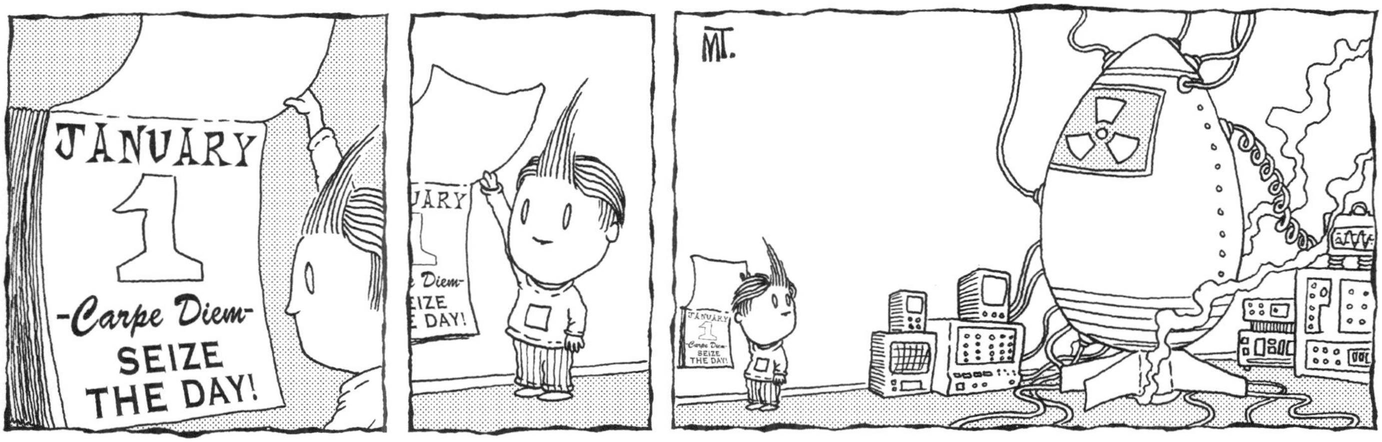
JANUARY
1
-Carpe Diem-
SEIZE
THE DAY!
MT.

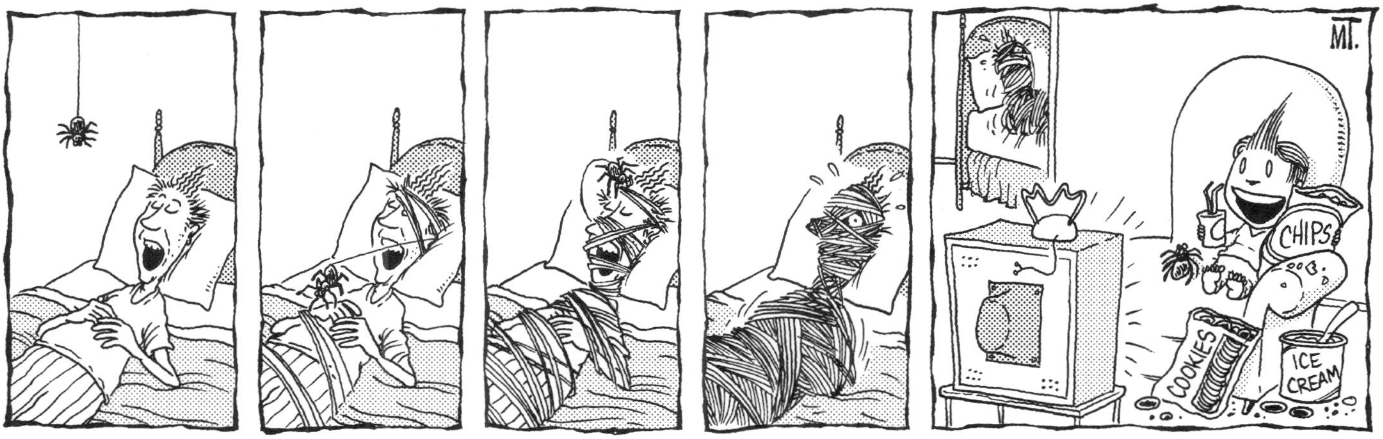
MT.
CHIPS
COOKIES
ICE
CREAM

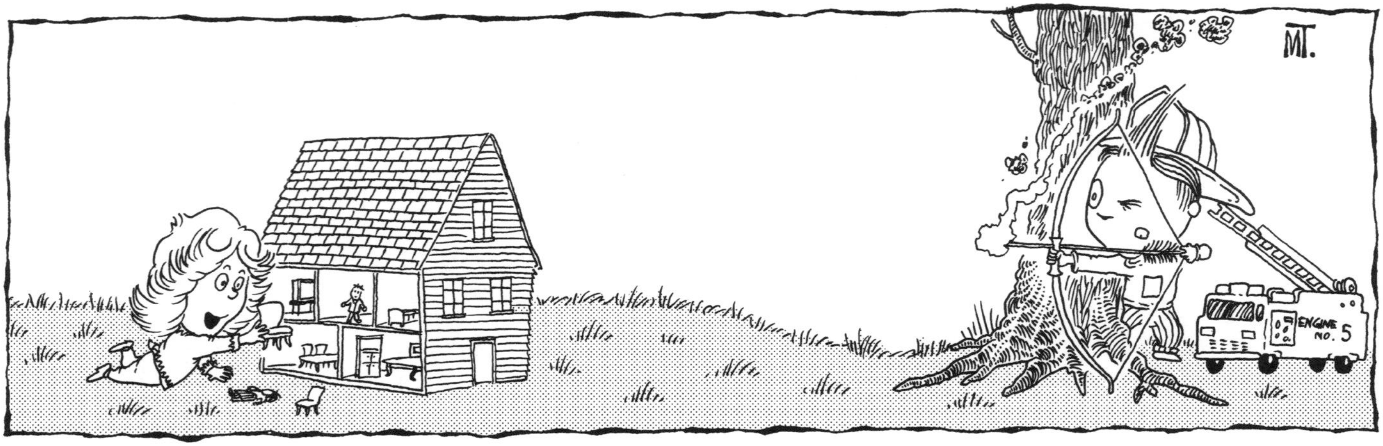
MT.
ENGINE NO. 5

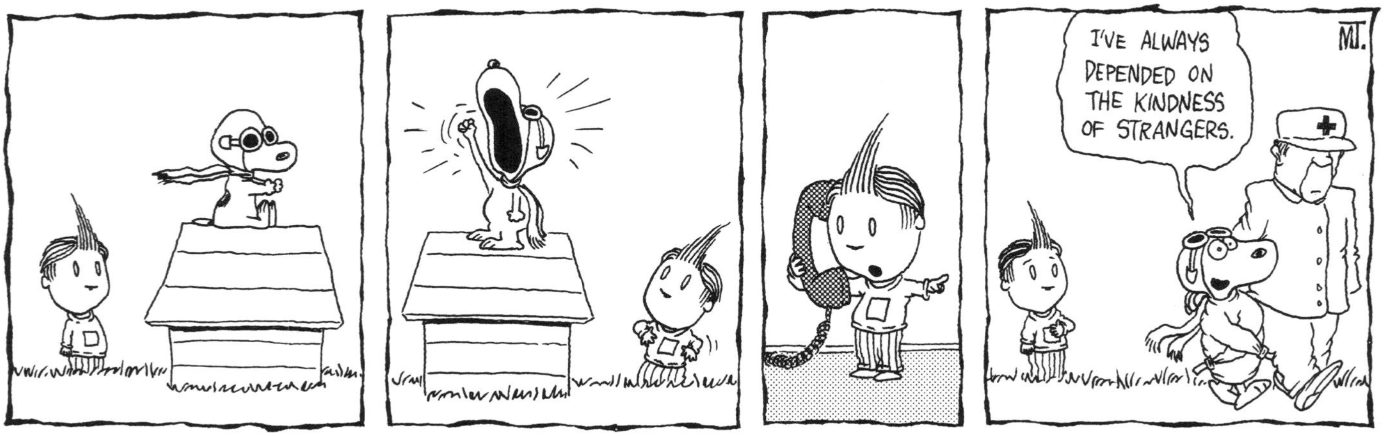
MT.
I'VE ALWAYS DEPENDED ON THE KINDNESS OF STRANGERS.

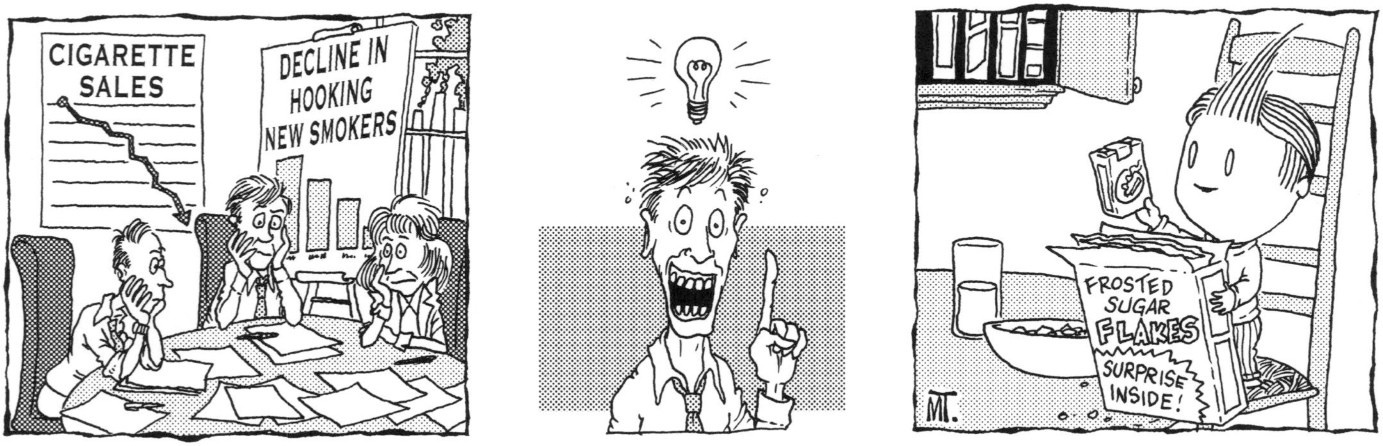
CIGARETTE SALES
DECLINE IN HOOKING NEW SMOKERS
FROSTED SUGAR FLAKES
SURPRISE INSIDE!
MT.

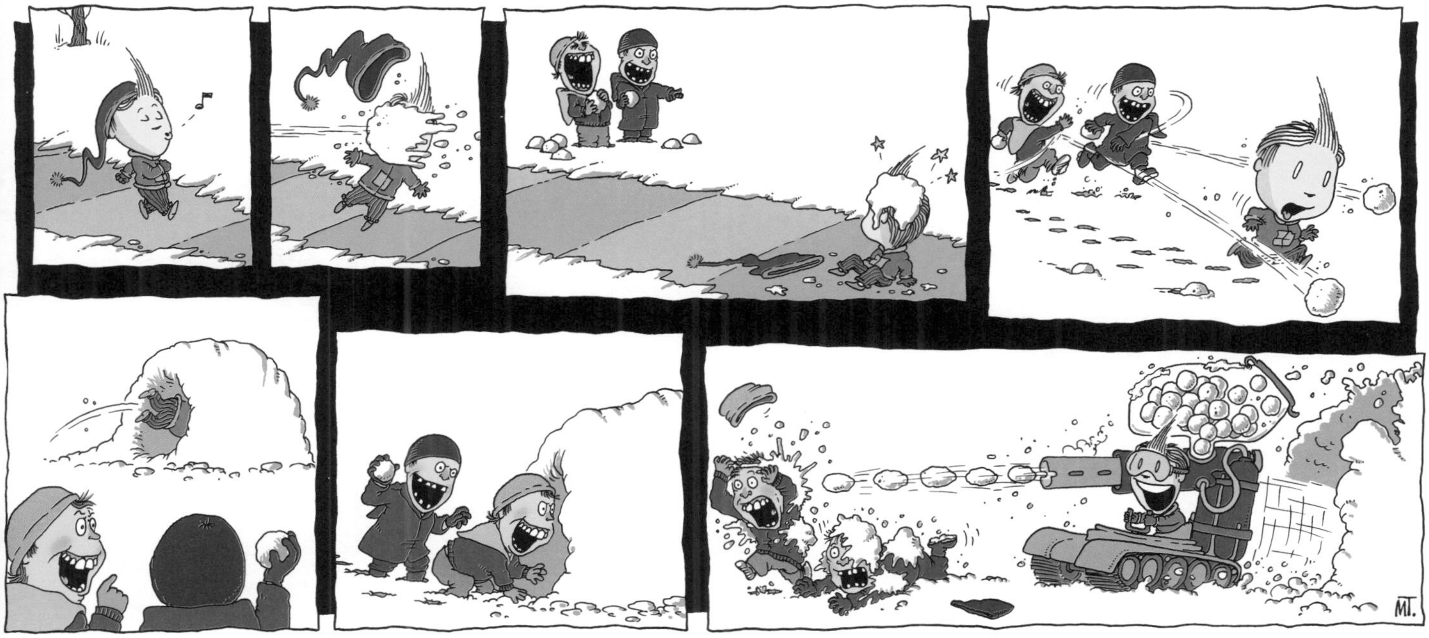
MT.

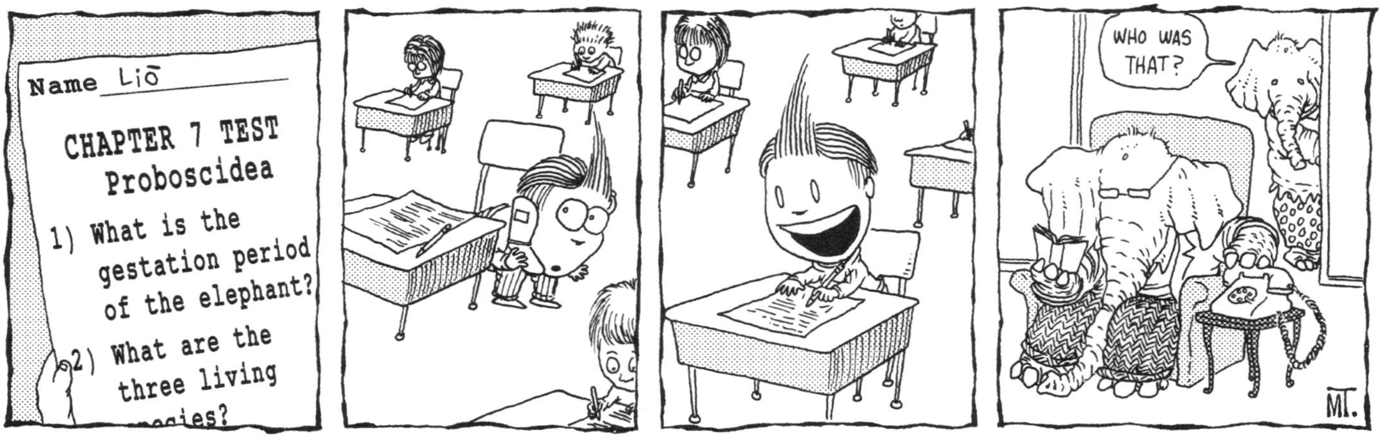
Name Liō
CHAPTER 7 TEST
Proboscidea
1) What is the gestation period of the elephant?
2) What are the three living
WHO WAS THAT?
MT.

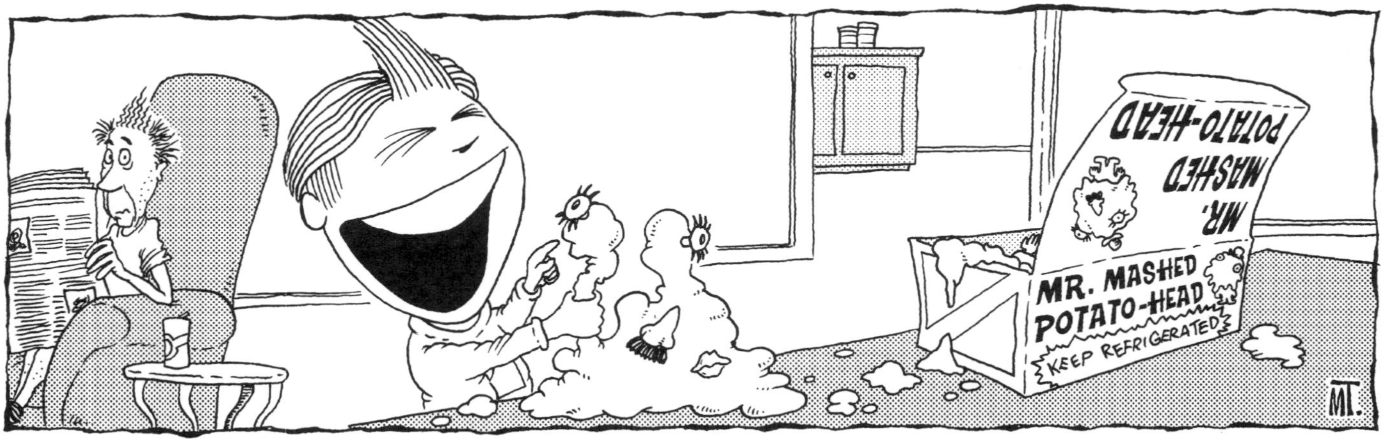
MR. MASHED POTATO-HEAD
KEEP REFRIGERATED
MT.

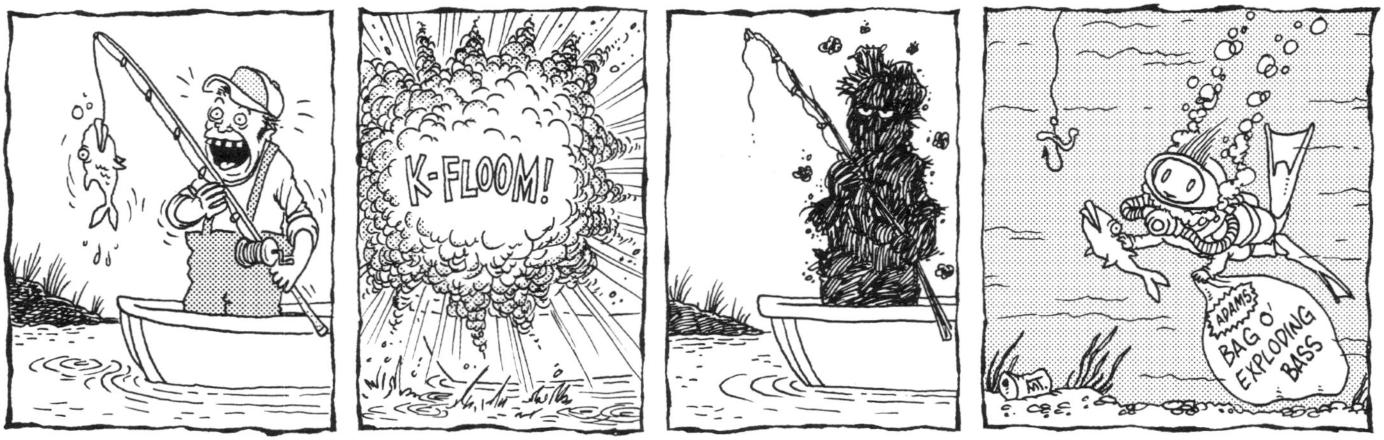
K-FLOOM!
ADAMS
BAG O' EXPLODING BASS
MT.

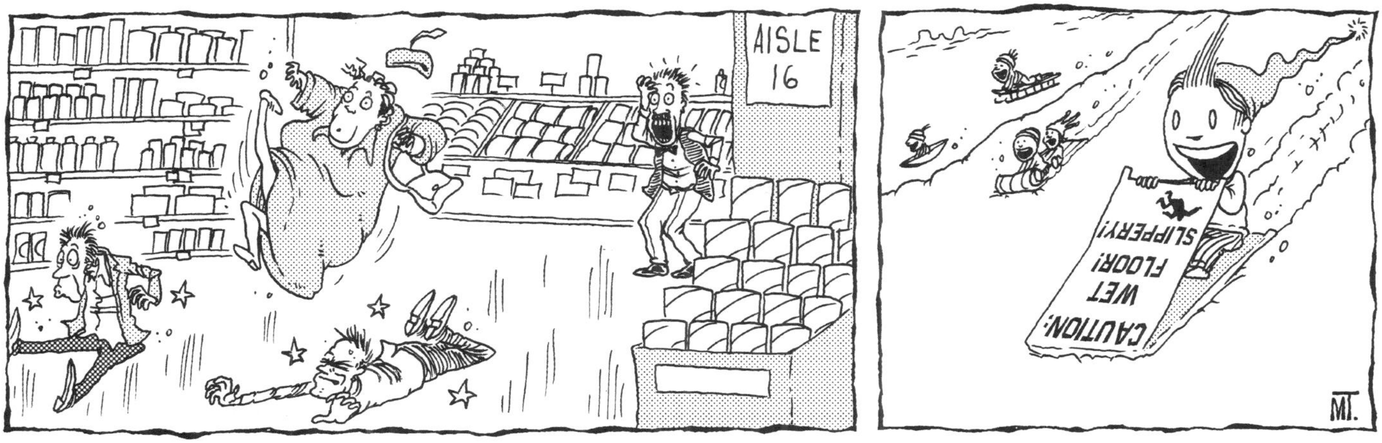
AISLE 16
CAUTION: WET FLOOR! SLIPPERY!
MT.

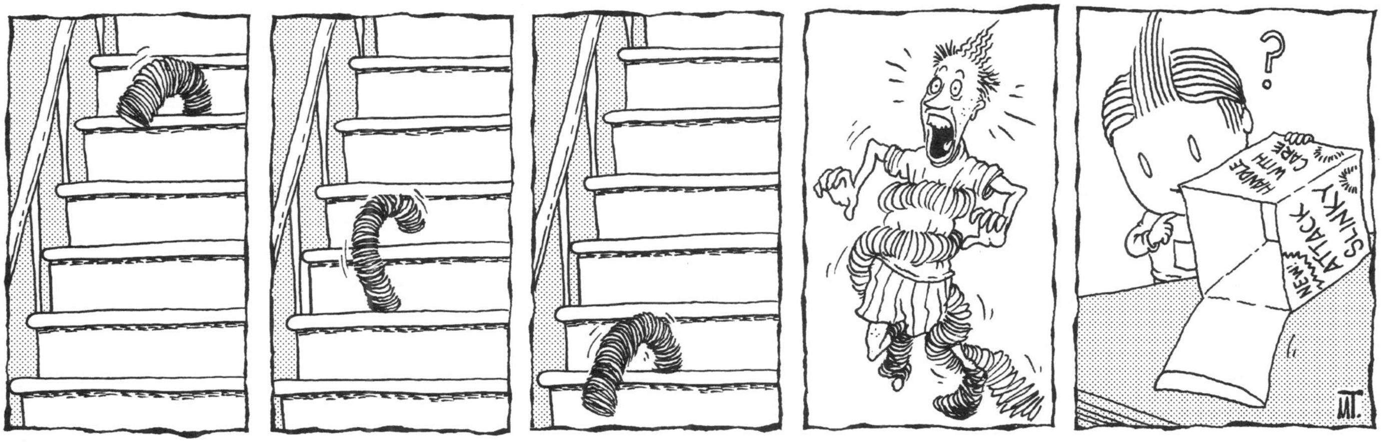
?
HANDLE WITH CARE
NEW! ATTACK SLINKY
MT.

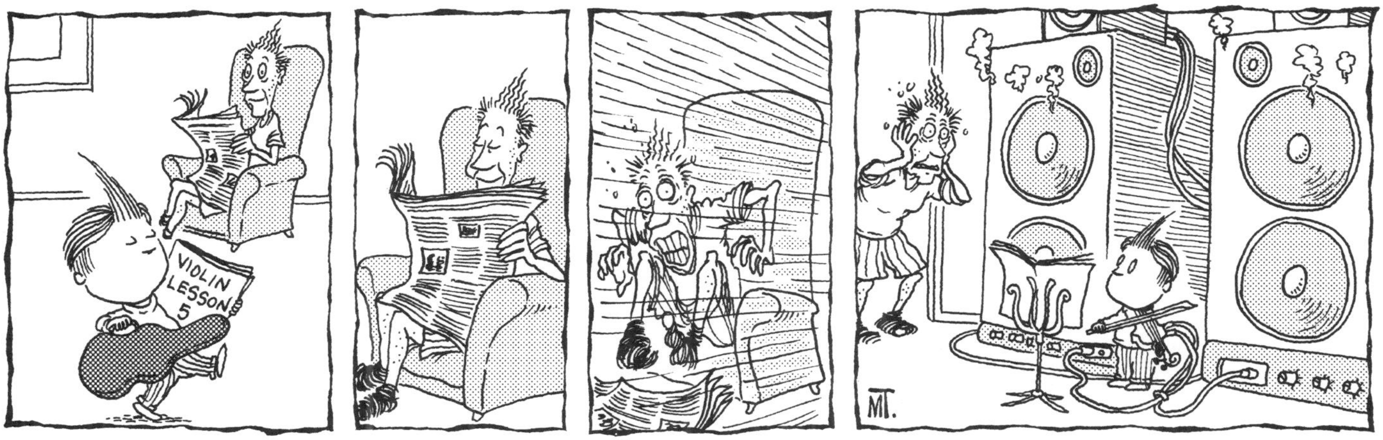
VIOLIN LESSON 5
MT.

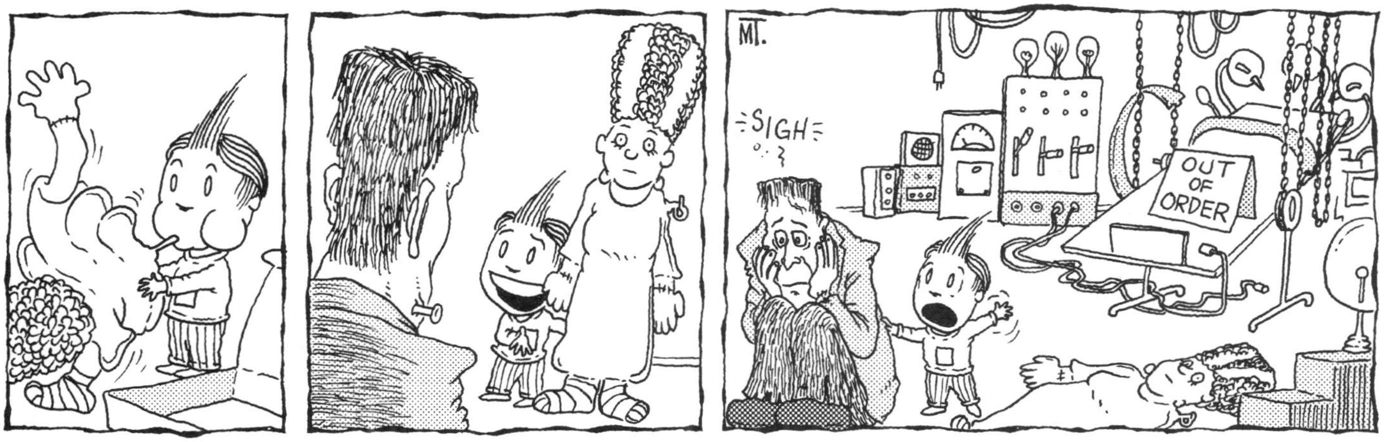
MT.
SIGH
OUT OF ORDER

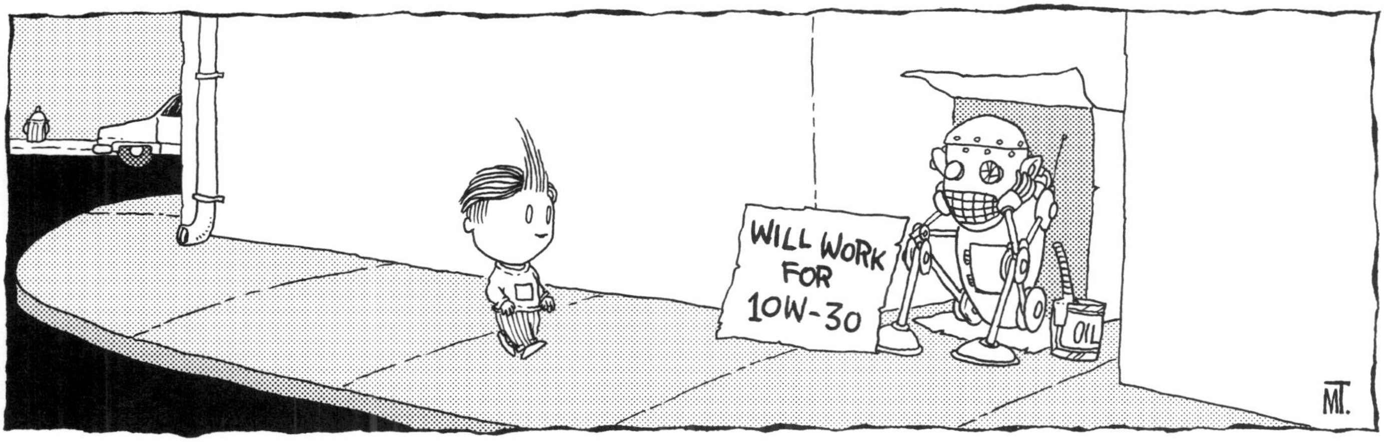
WILL WORK FOR 10W-30
OIL
MT.

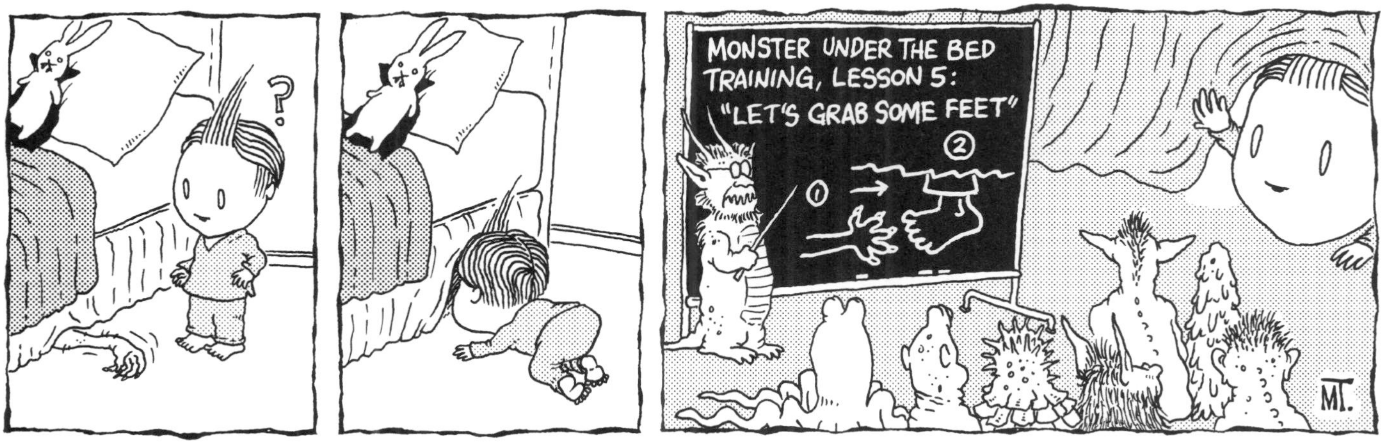
?
MONSTER UNDER THE BED TRAINING, LESSON 5:
"LET'S GRAB SOME FEET"
①
②
MT.

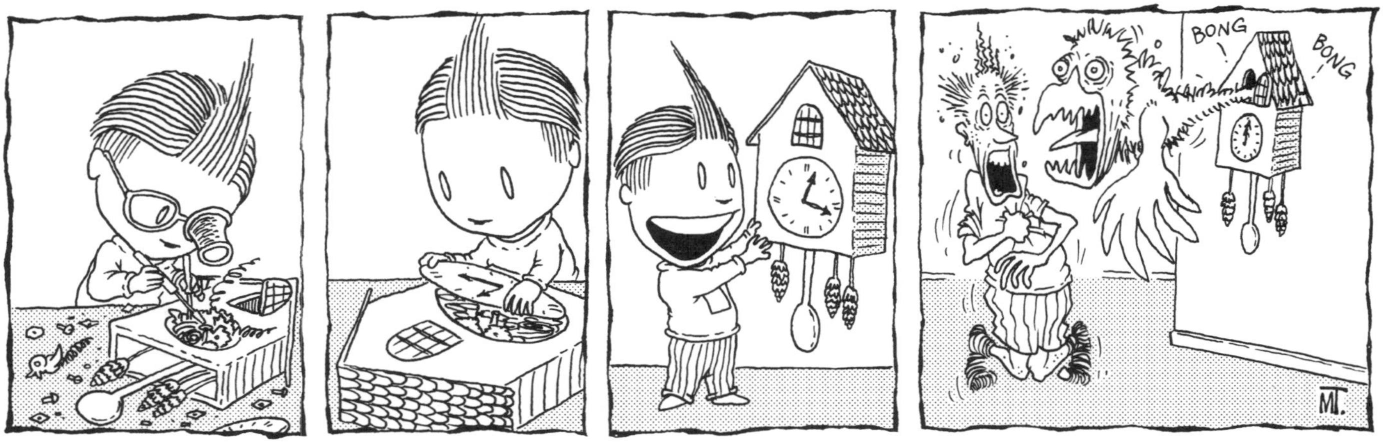
BONG
BONG

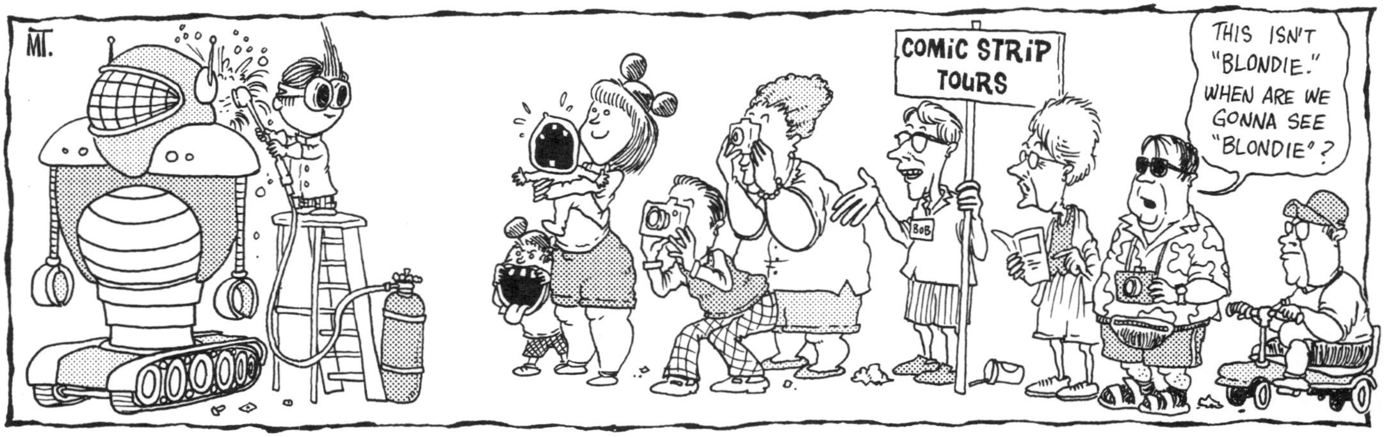
COMIC STRIP TOURS
BOB
THIS ISN'T "BLONDIE." WHEN ARE WE GONNA SEE "BLONDIE"?

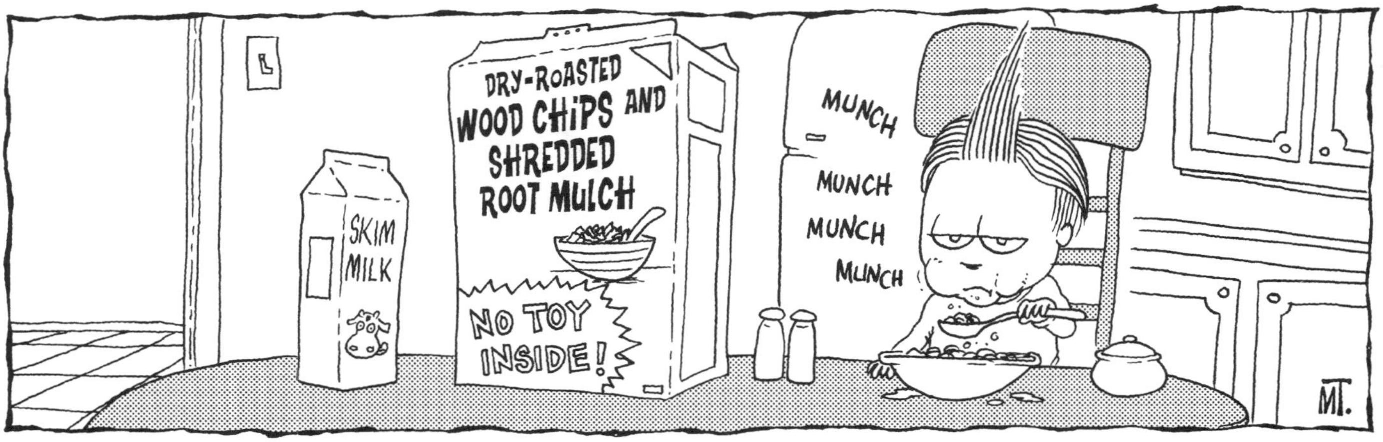
SKIM MILK
DRY-ROASTED WOOD CHIPS AND SHREDDED ROOT MULCH
NO TOY INSIDE!
MUNCH
MUNCH
MUNCH
MUNCH

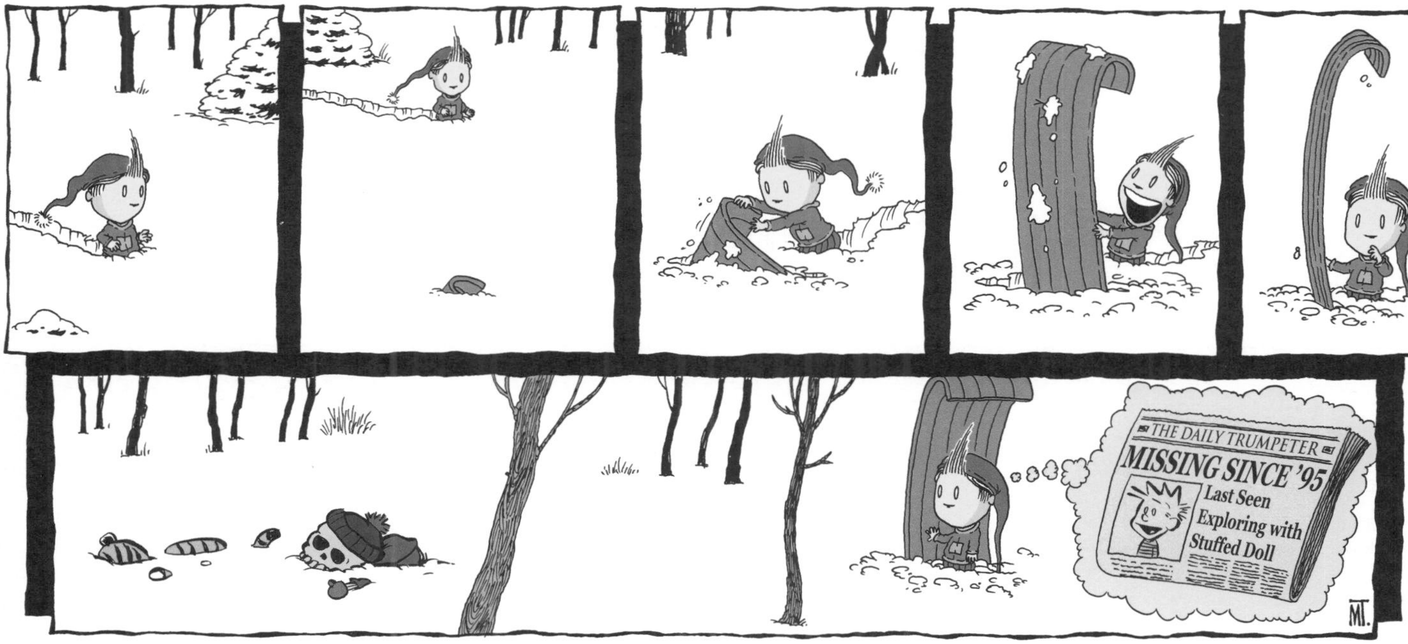
THE DAILY TRUMPETER
MISSING SINCE '95
Last Seen Exploring with Stuffed Doll
MT.

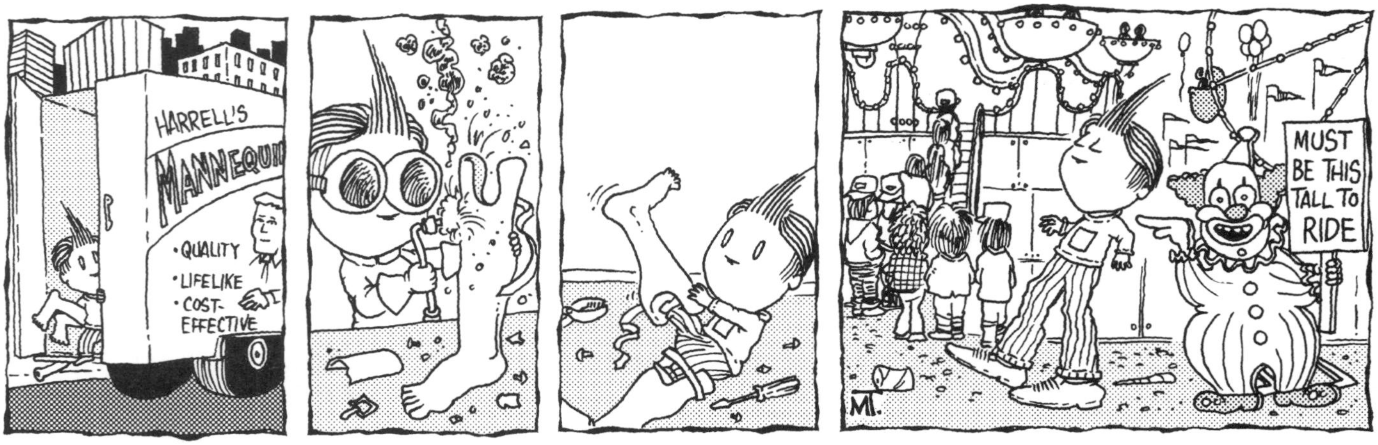
HARRELL'S
MANNEQUI
•QUALITY
•LIFELIKE
•COST-EFFECTIVE
MUST BE THIS TALL TO RIDE
MT.

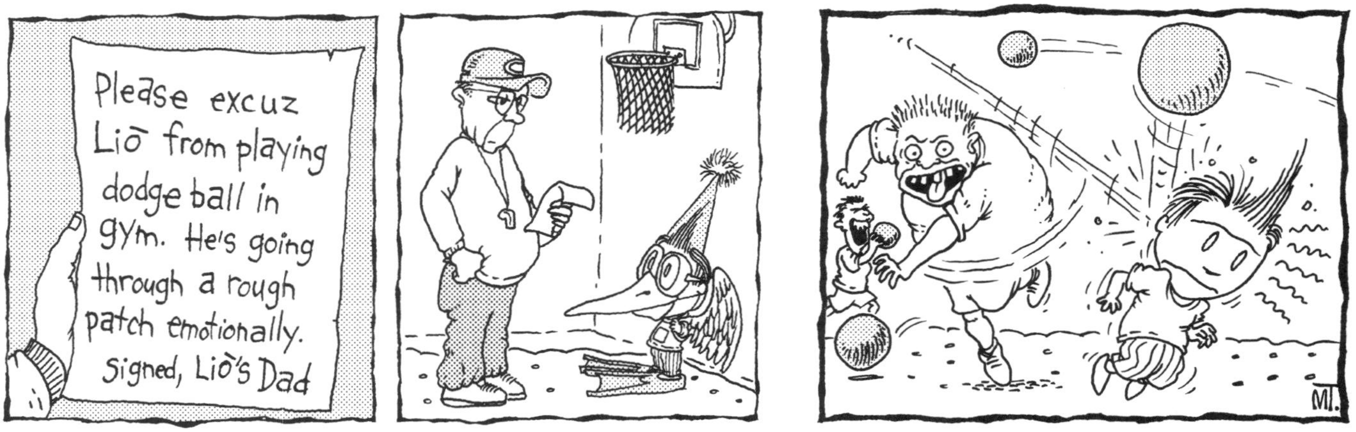
Please excuz Liō from playing dodge ball in gym. He's going through a rough patch emotionally.
Signed, Liō's Dad
MT.

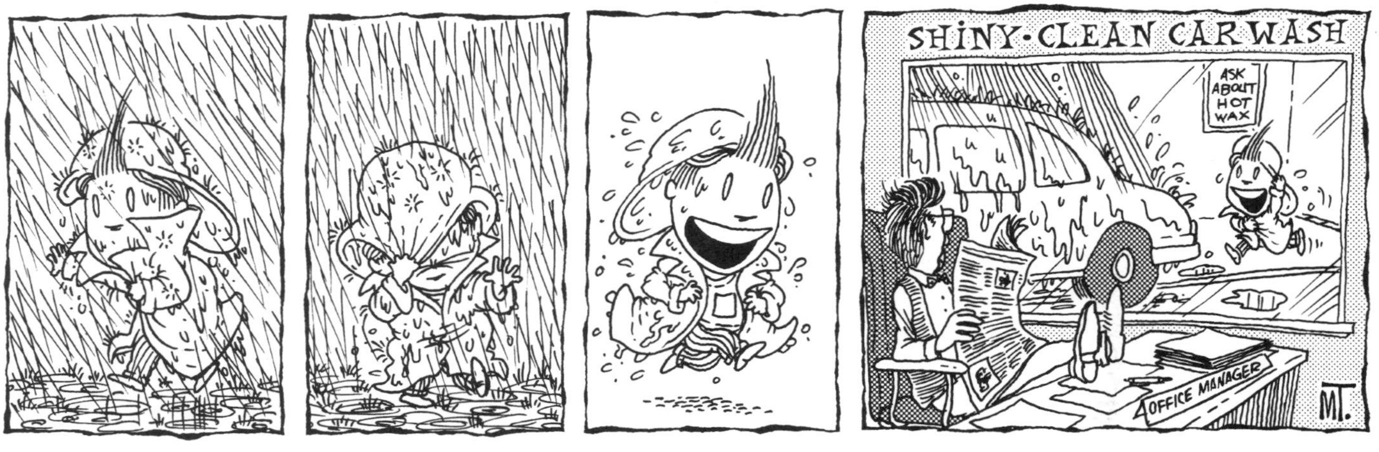
SHINY-CLEAN CAR WASH
ASK ABOUT HOT WAX
OFFICE MANAGER
MT.

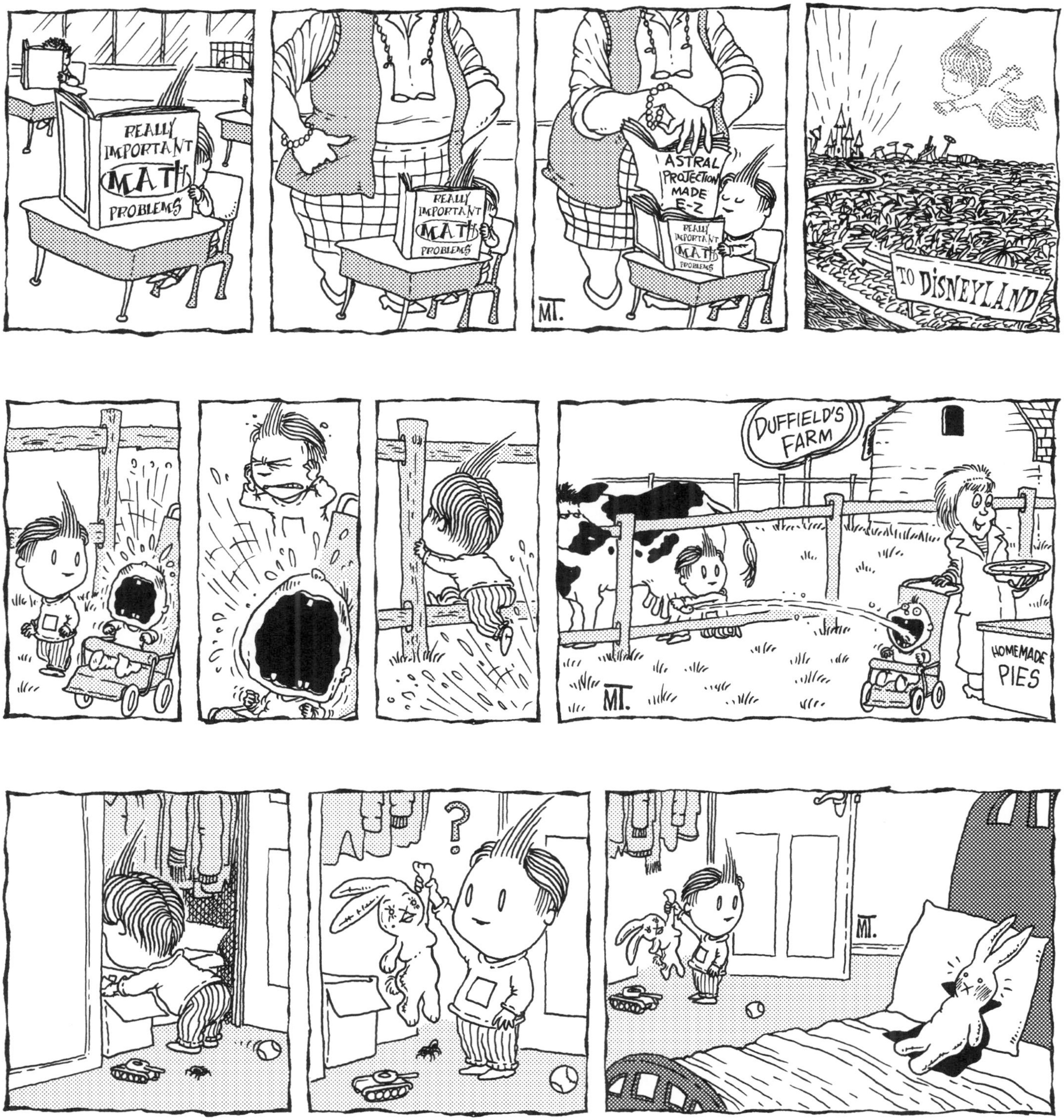
REALLY IMPORTANT MATH PROBLEMS
REALLY IMPORTANT MATH PROBLEMS
ASTRAL PROJECTION MADE E-Z
REALLY IMPORTANT MATH PROBLEMS
MT.
TO DISNEYLAND
MT.
DUFFIELD'S FARM
HOMEMADE PIES
?
MT.

ELEMENTARY
SCHOOL

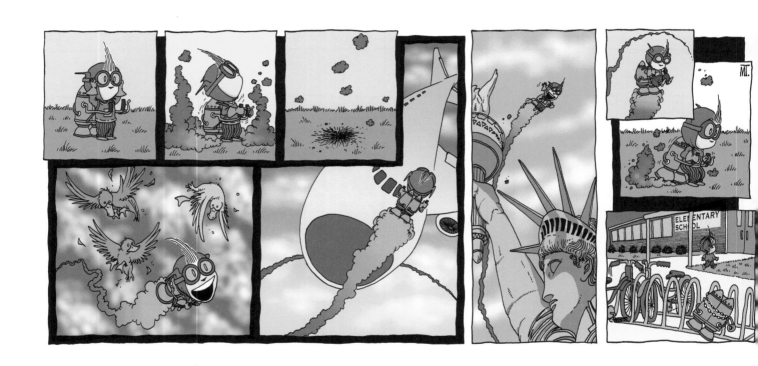

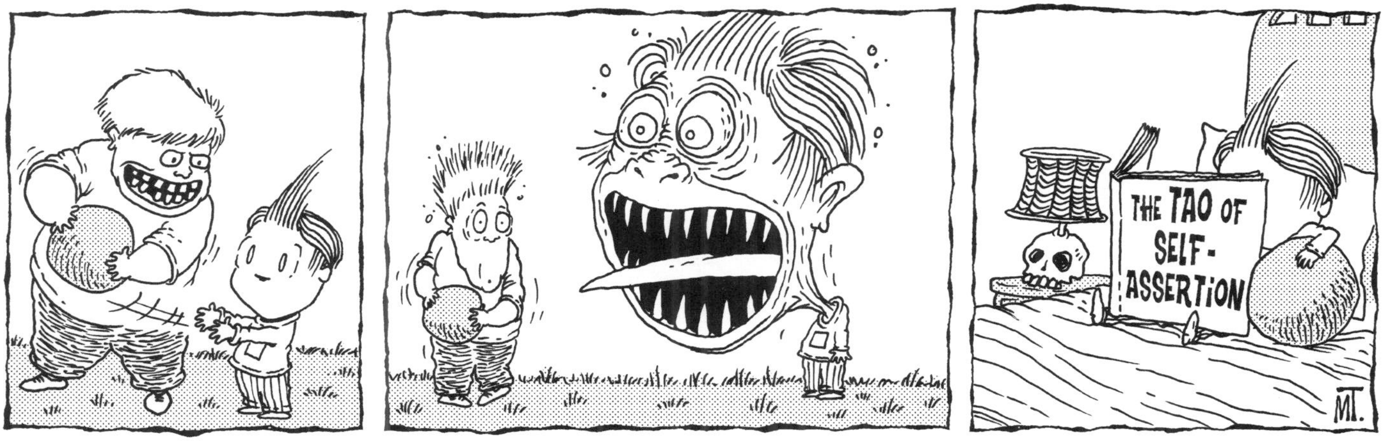
THE TAO OF SELF-ASSERTION

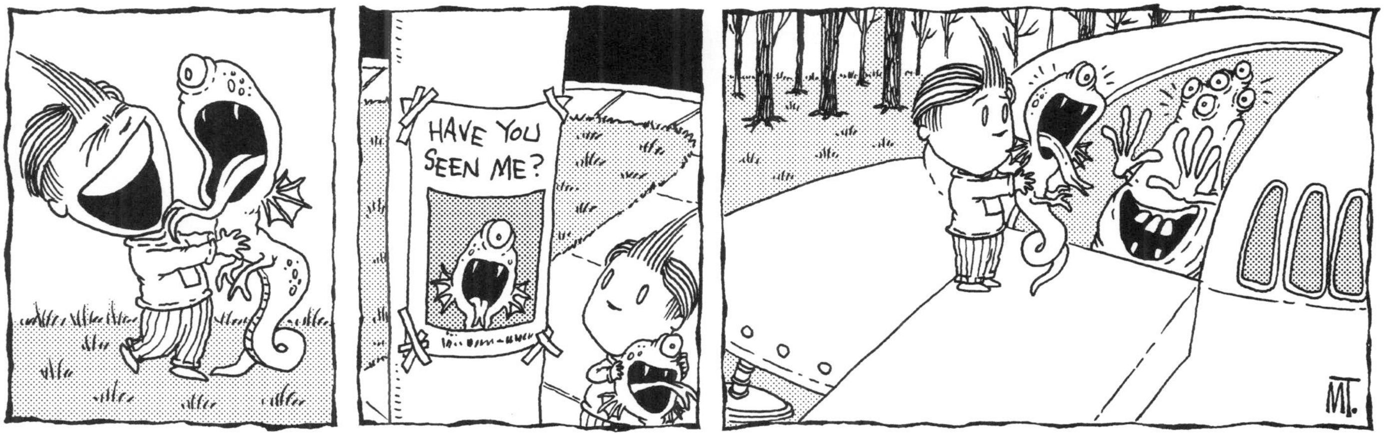
HAVE YOU SEEN ME?

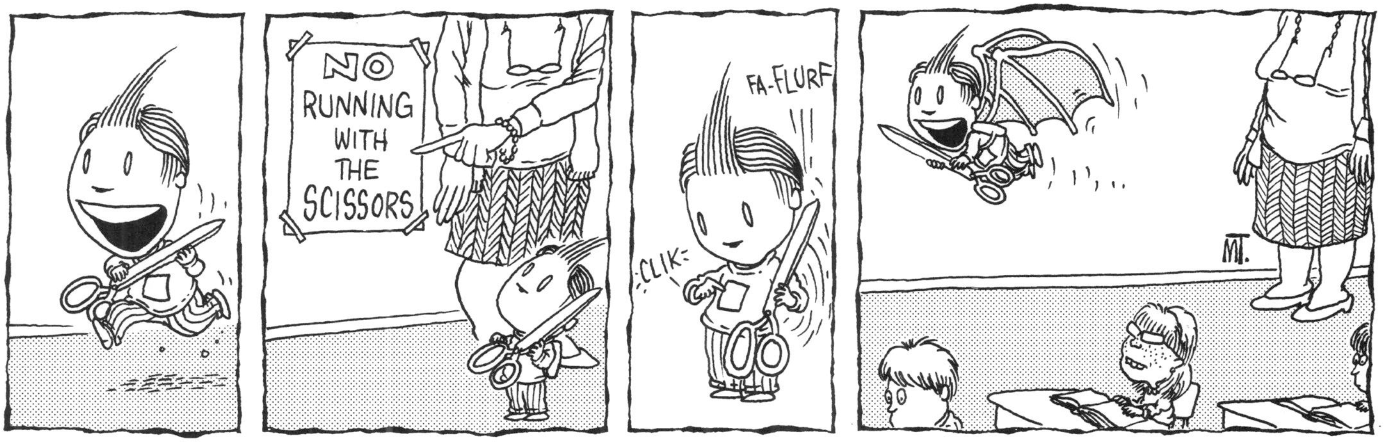
NO RUNNING WITH THE SCISSORS
FA-FLURF
CLIK

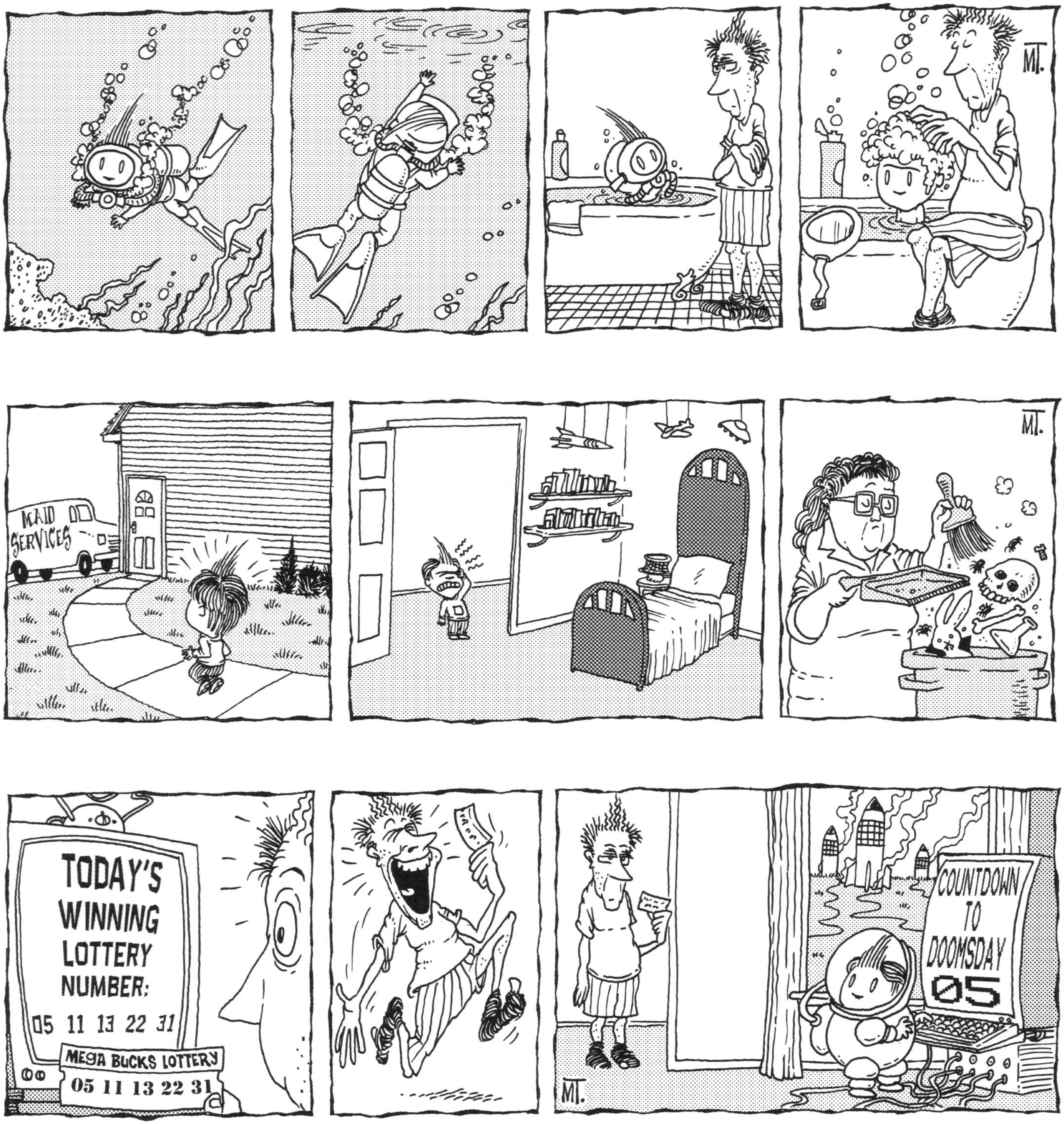
MT.
MAID SERVICES
MT.
TODAY'S WINNING LOTTERY NUMBER:
05 11 13 22 31
MEGA BUCKS LOTTERY
05 11 13 22 31
COUNTDOWN TO DOOMSDAY
05
MT.

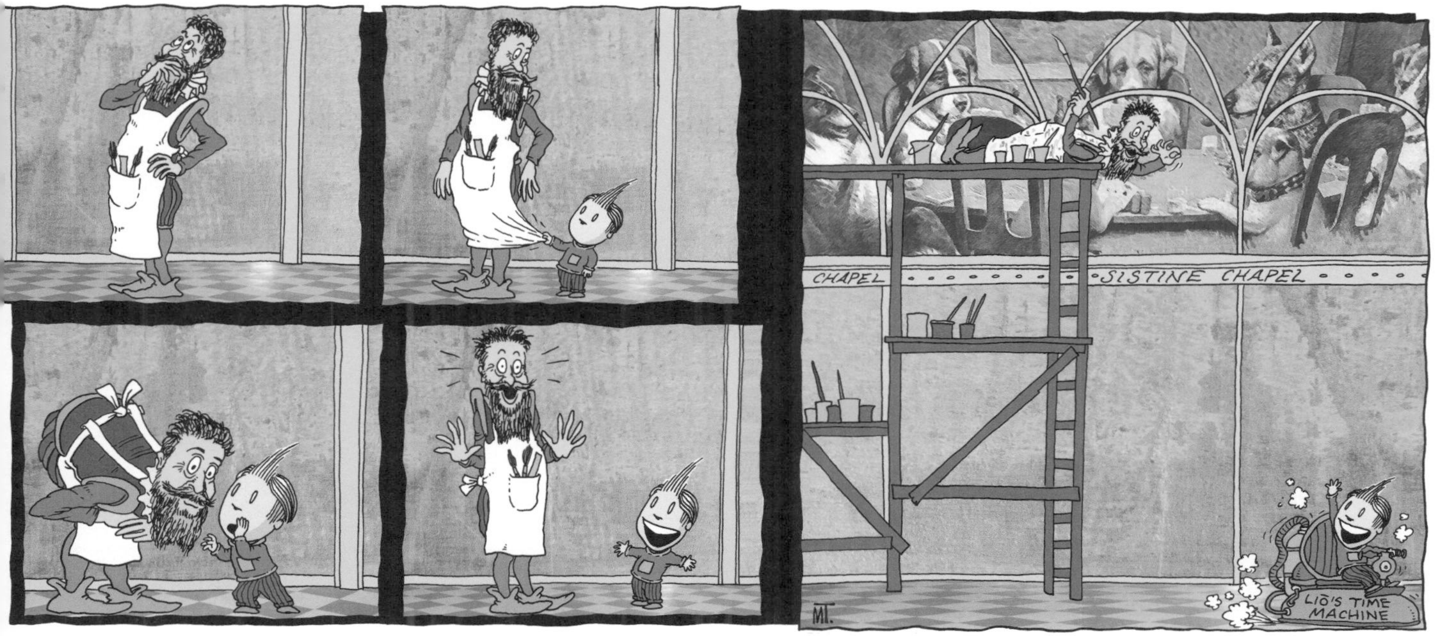
CHAPEL
SISTINE CHAPEL
LIO'S TIME MACHINE

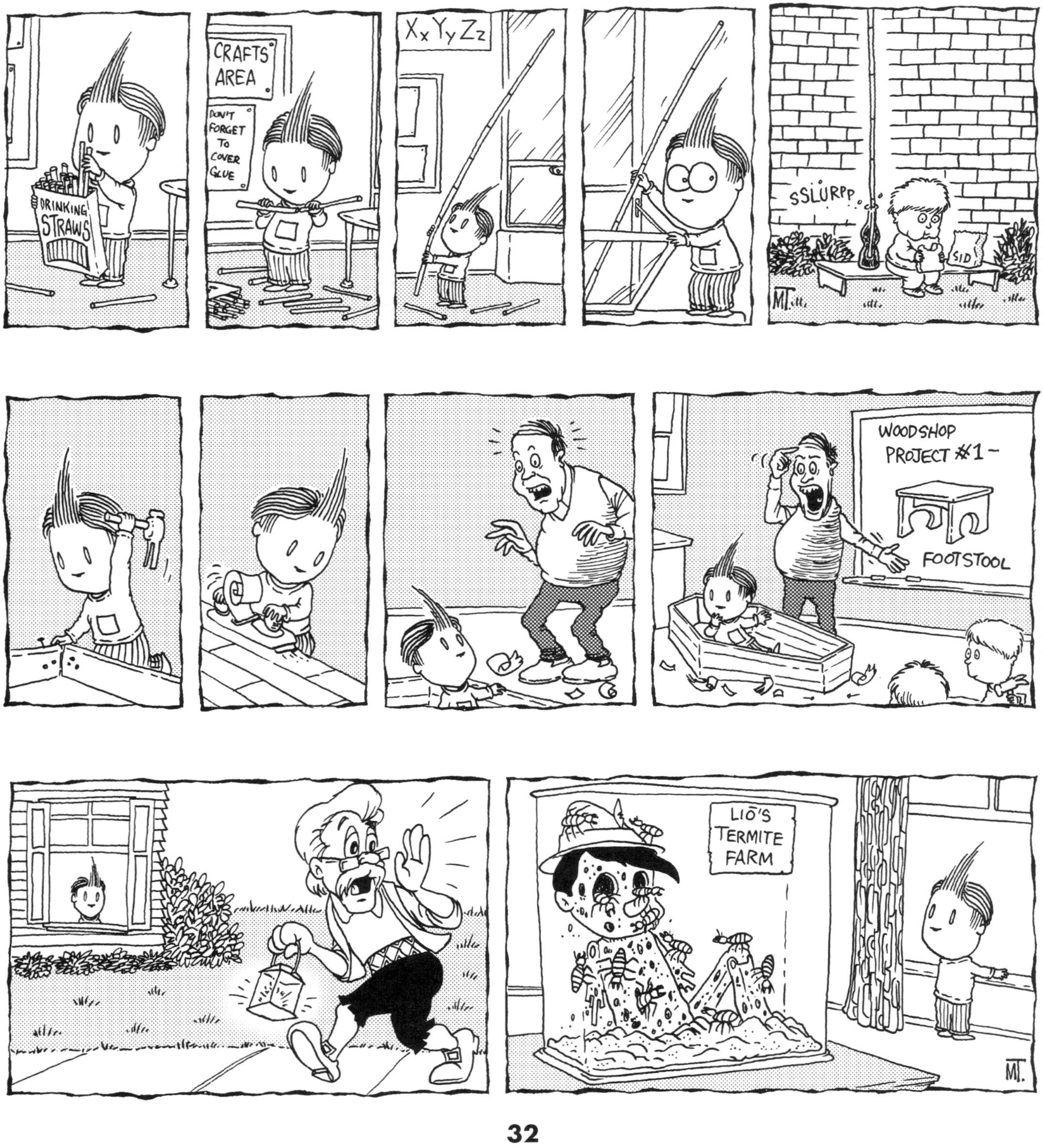
DRINKING STRAWS
CRAFTS AREA
DON'T FORGET TO COVER GLUE
XxYyZz
SSLURPP
SID
MT.
WOODSHOP PROJECT #1 -
FOOTSTOOL
LIŌ'S TERMITE FARM
MT.

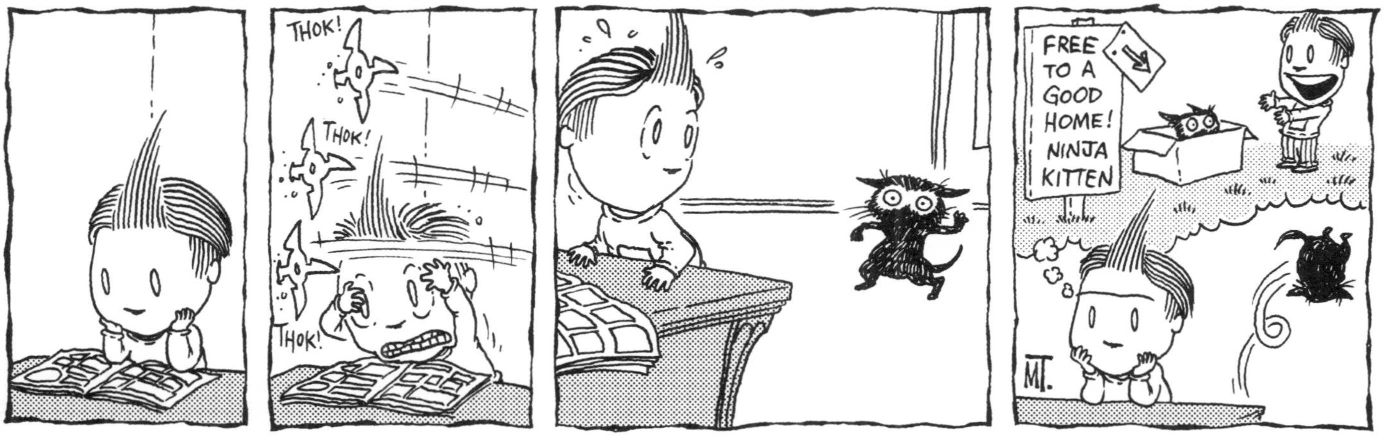
THOK!
THOK!
THOK!
FREE TO A GOOD HOME! NINJA KITTEN

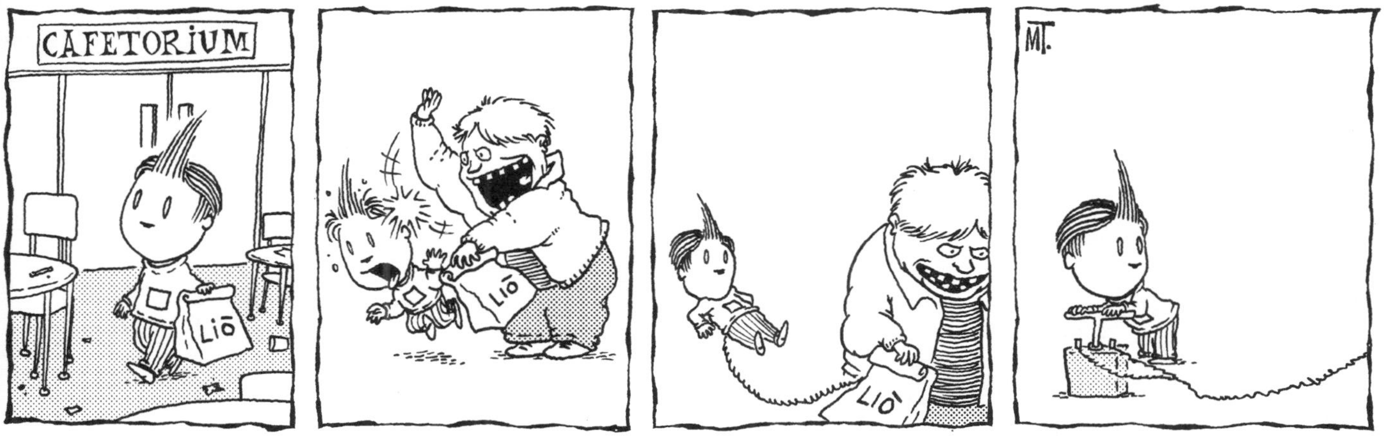
CAFETORIUM
LIŌ

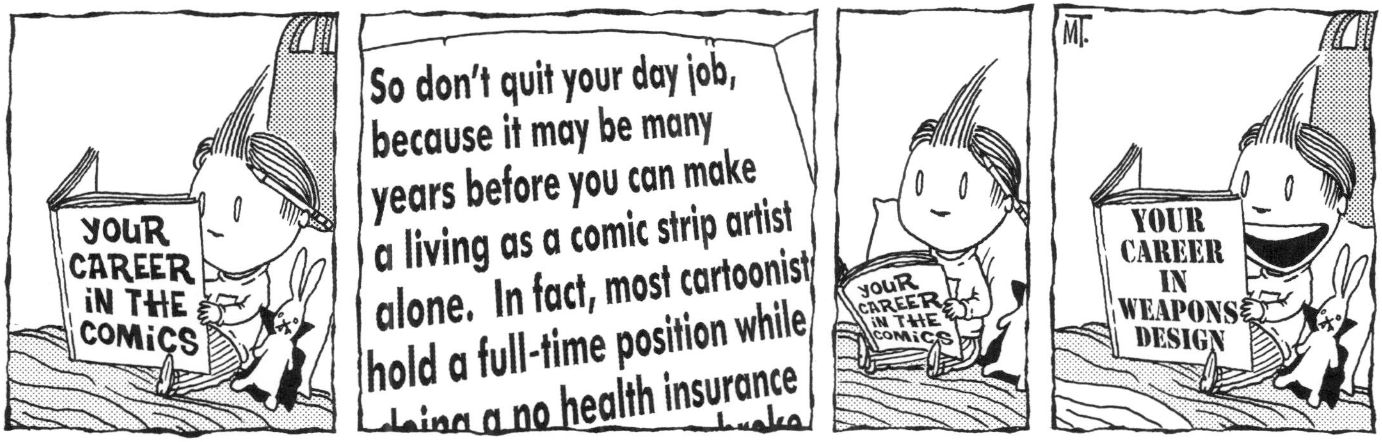
YOUR CAREER IN THE COMICS
So don't quit your day job, because it may be many years before you can make a living as a comic strip artist alone. In fact, most cartoonist hold a full-time position while
a no health insurance
YOUR CAREER IN THE COMICS
YOUR CAREER IN WEAPONS DESIGN

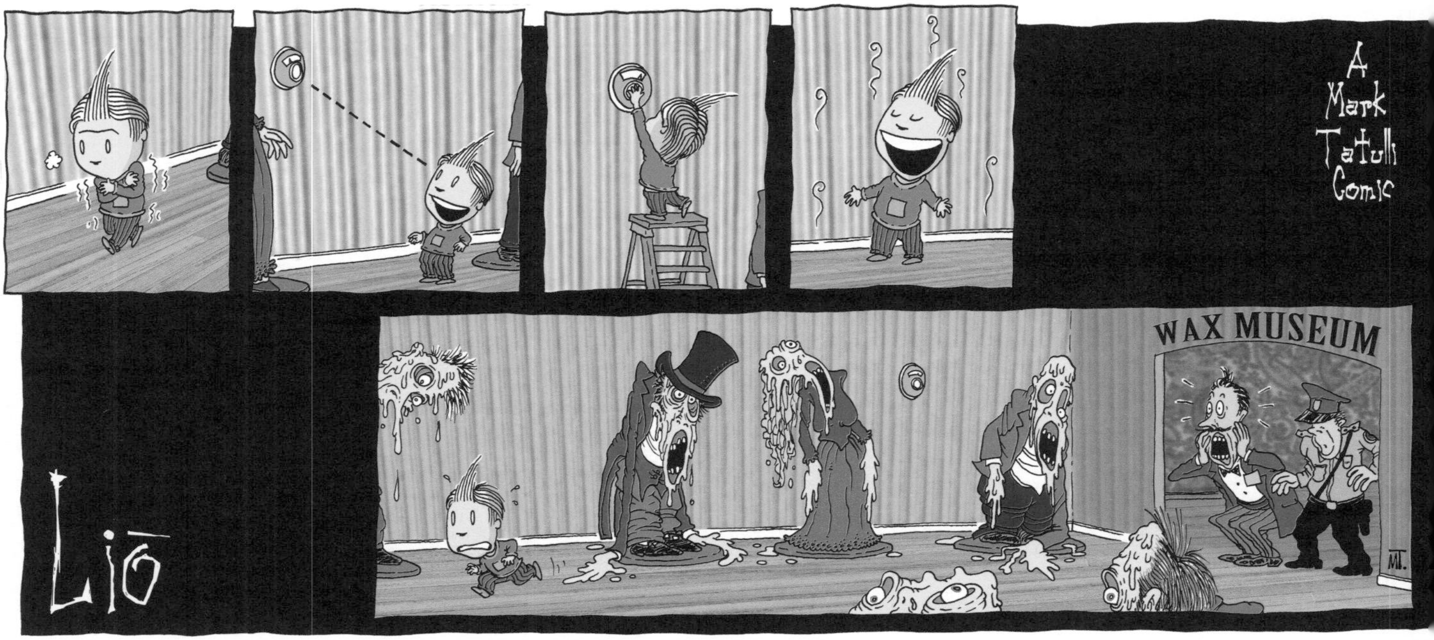
A Mark Tatulli Comic
Liō
WAX MUSEUM
MT.

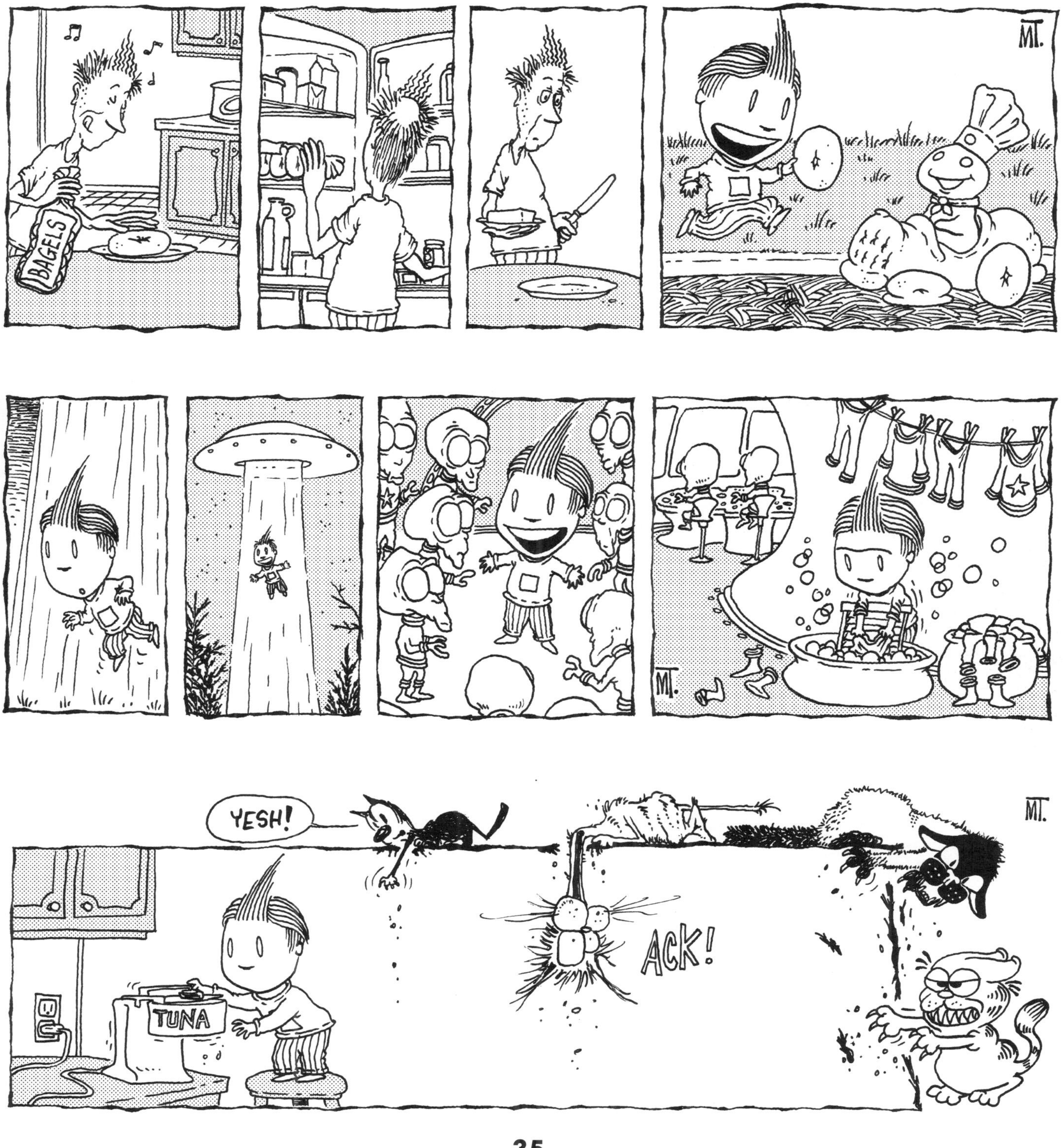
BAGELS
MT.
MT.
YESH!
MT.
TUNA
ACK!

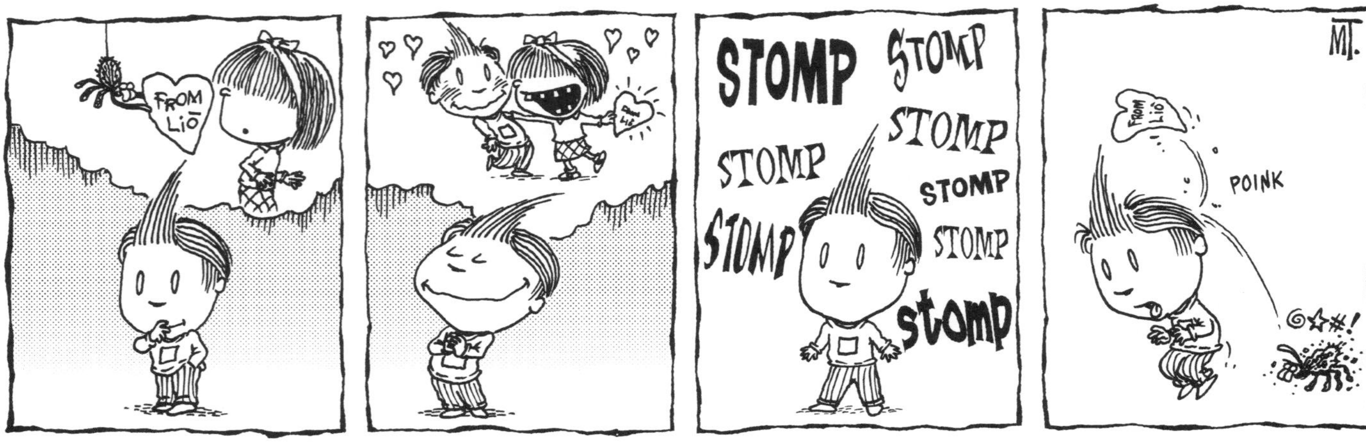
FROM LIO
STOMP
STOMP
STOMP
STOMP
STOMP
STOMP
STOMP
stomp
FROM LIO
POINK

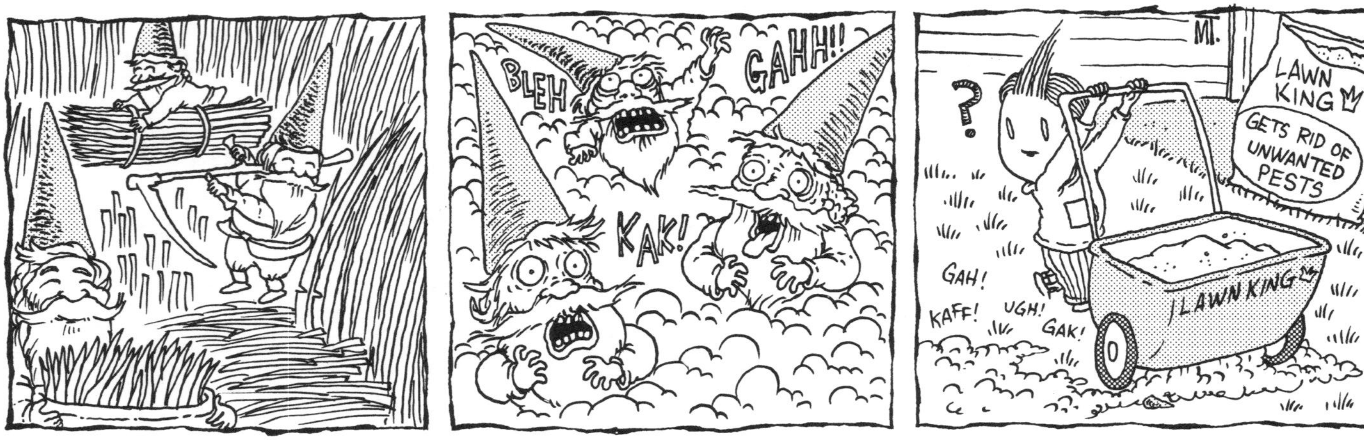
BLEH
GAHH!!
KAK!
?
LAWN KING
GETS RID OF UNWANTED PESTS
GAH!
KAFF!
UGH!
GAK!
LAWN KING

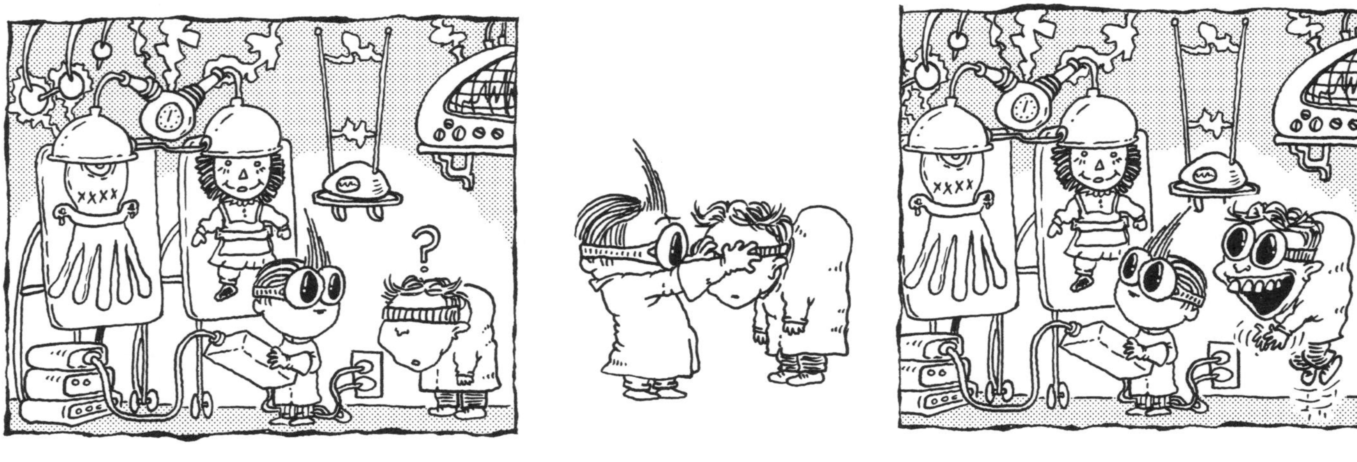
?

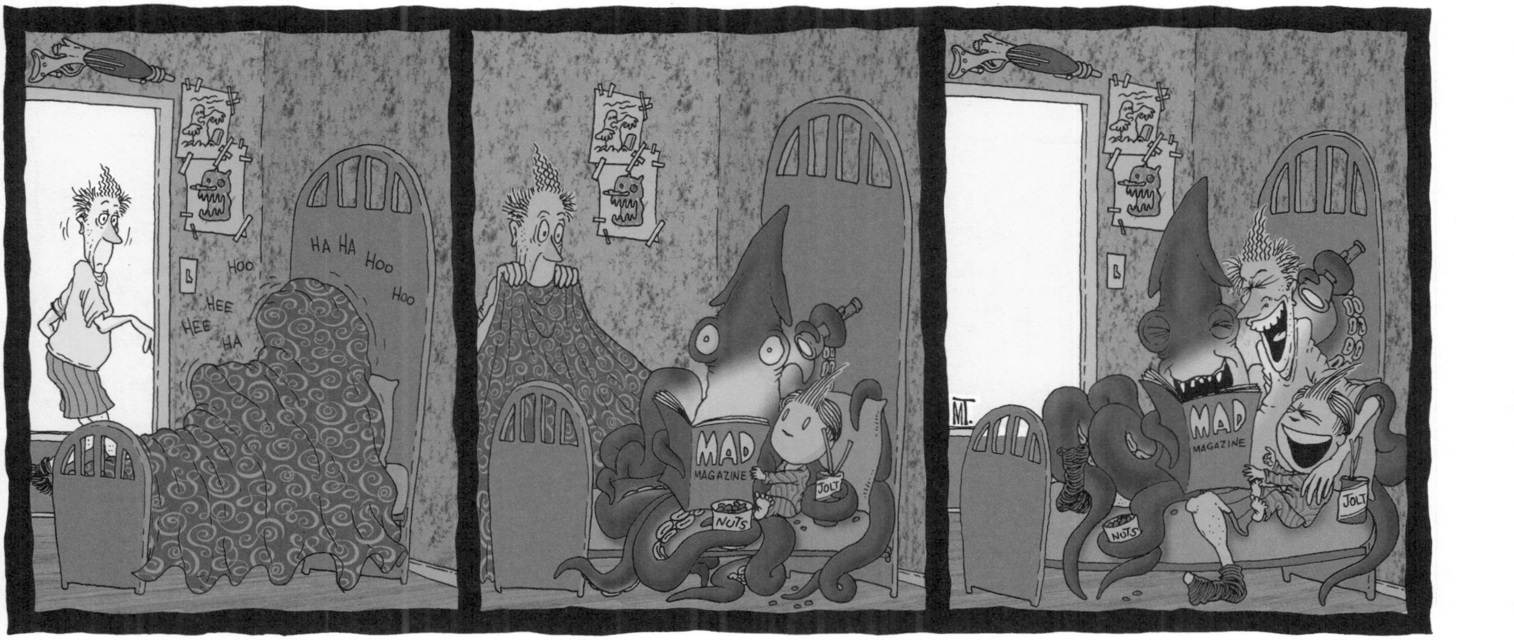
B
HA HA HOO
HOO
HOO
HEE
HEE
HA
MAD
MAGAZINE
NUTS
JOLT
MT.
MAD
MAGAZINE
NUTS
JOLT

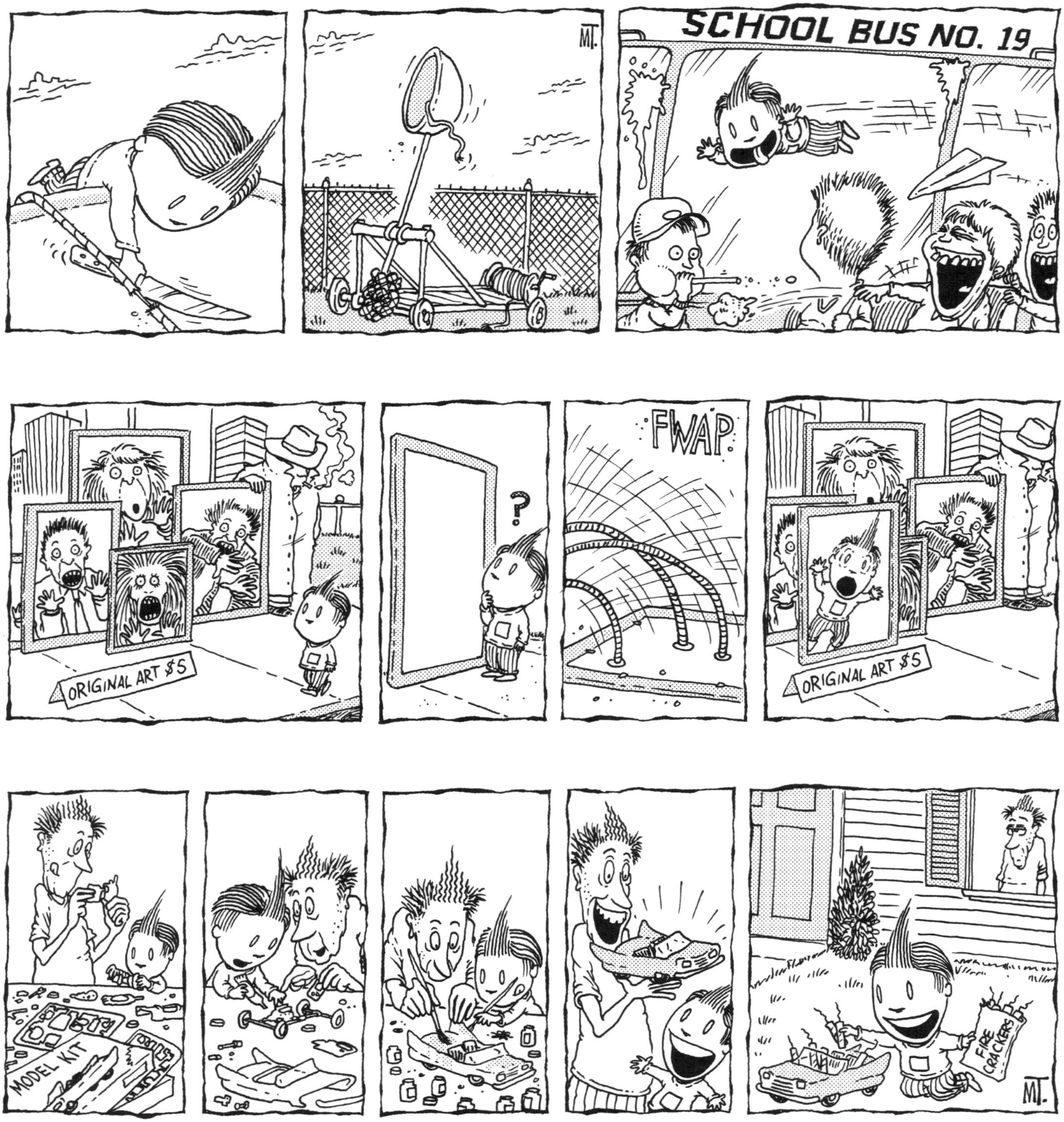
MT.
SCHOOL BUS NO. 19
ORIGINAL ART $5
?
FWAP
ORIGINAL ART $5
MODEL KIT
FIRE CRACKERS
MT.

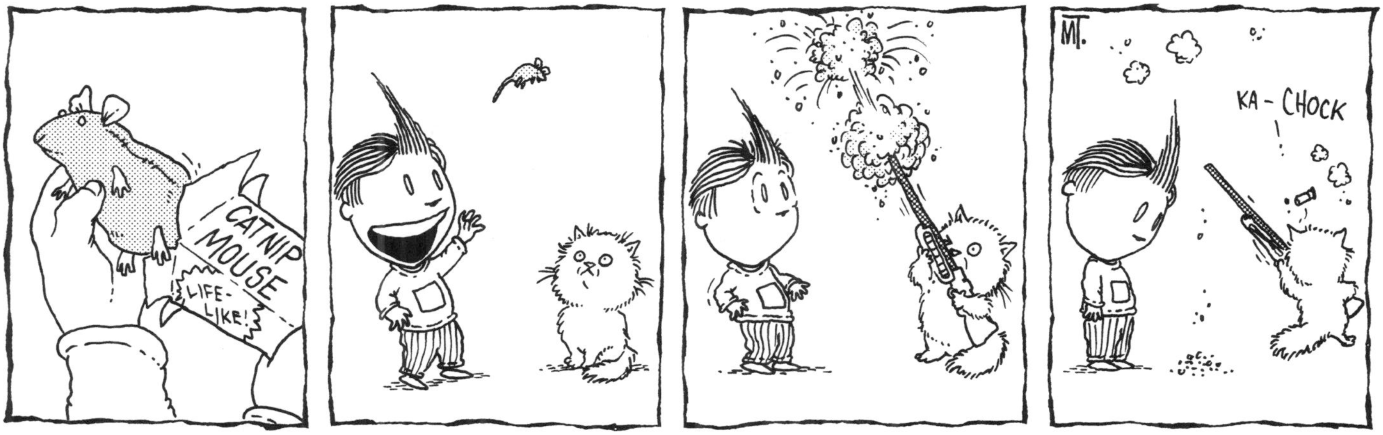
CATNIP MOUSE
LIFE-LIKE!
MT.
KA-CHOCK

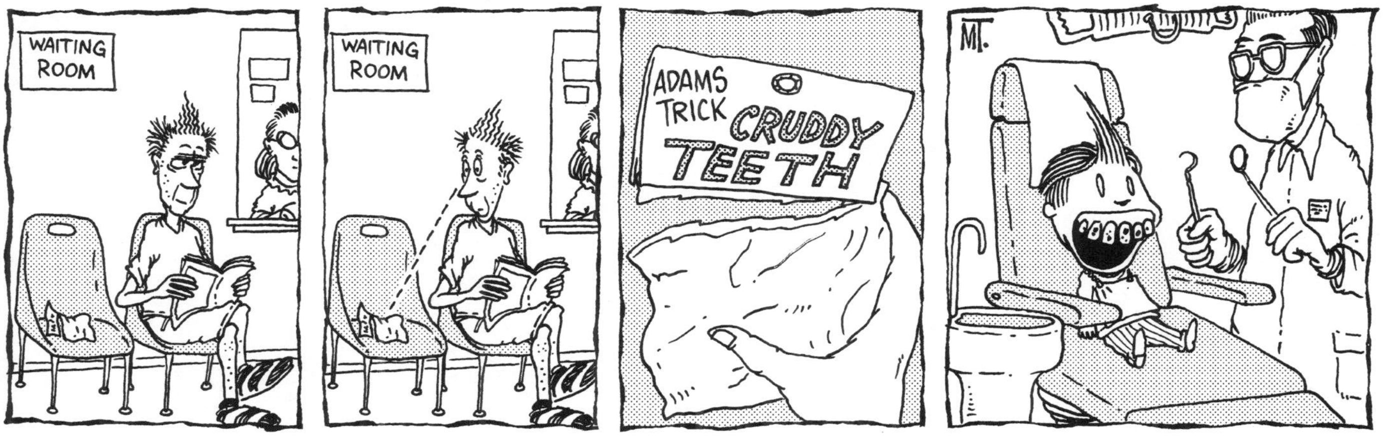
WAITING ROOM
WAITING ROOM
ADAMS TRICK
CRUDDY TEETH
MT.

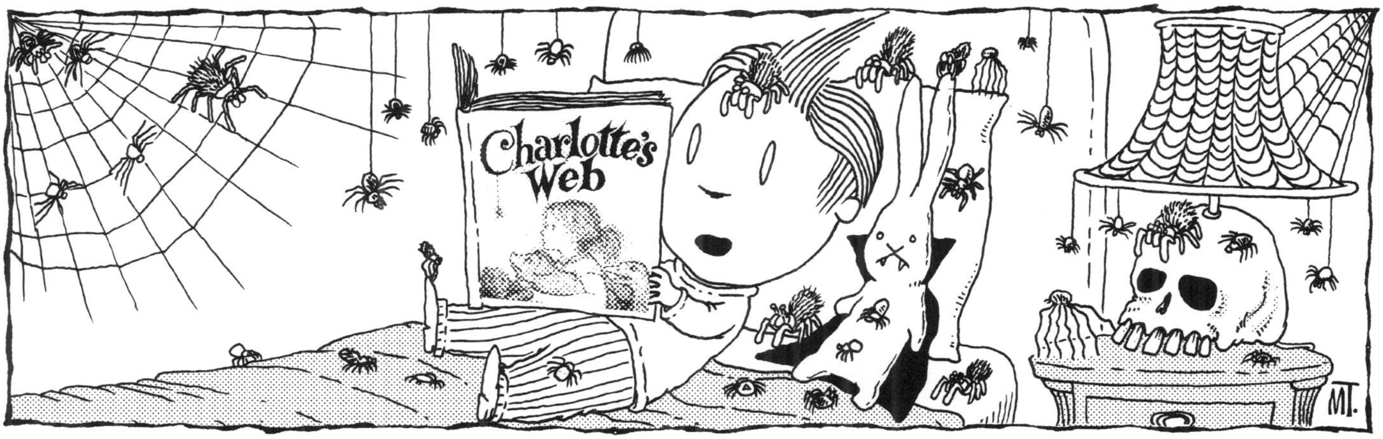
Charlotte's Web
MT.

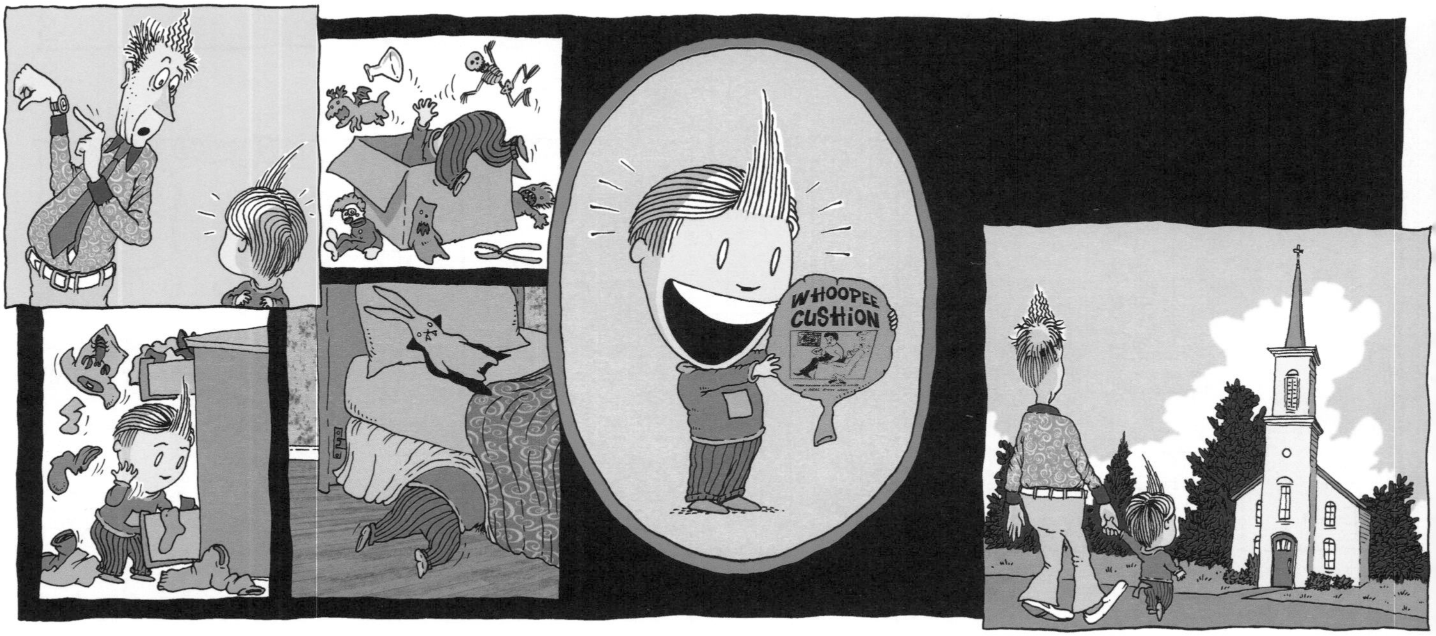
WHOOPEE CUSHION

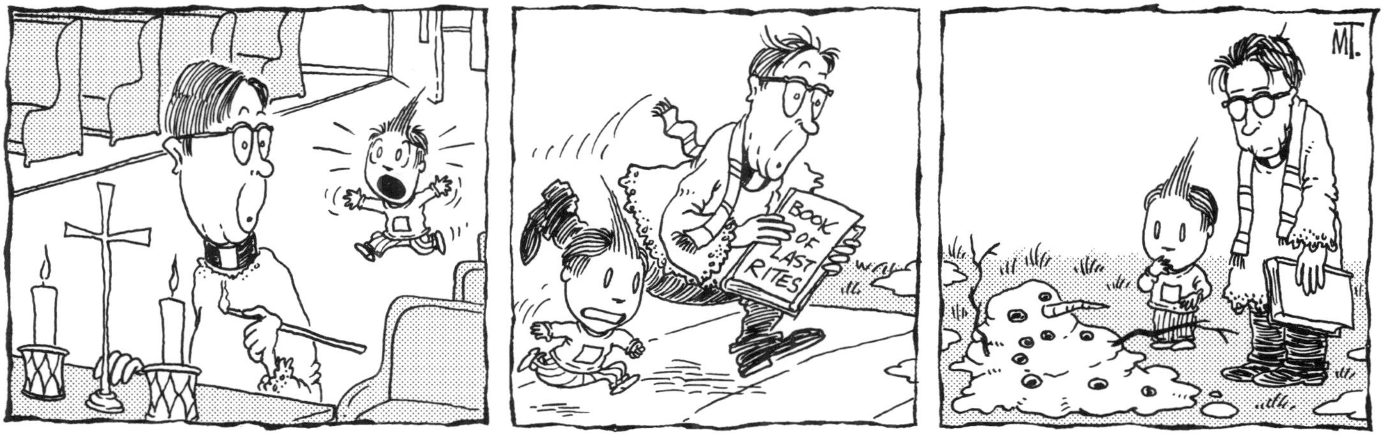
BOOK OF LAST RITES
MT.

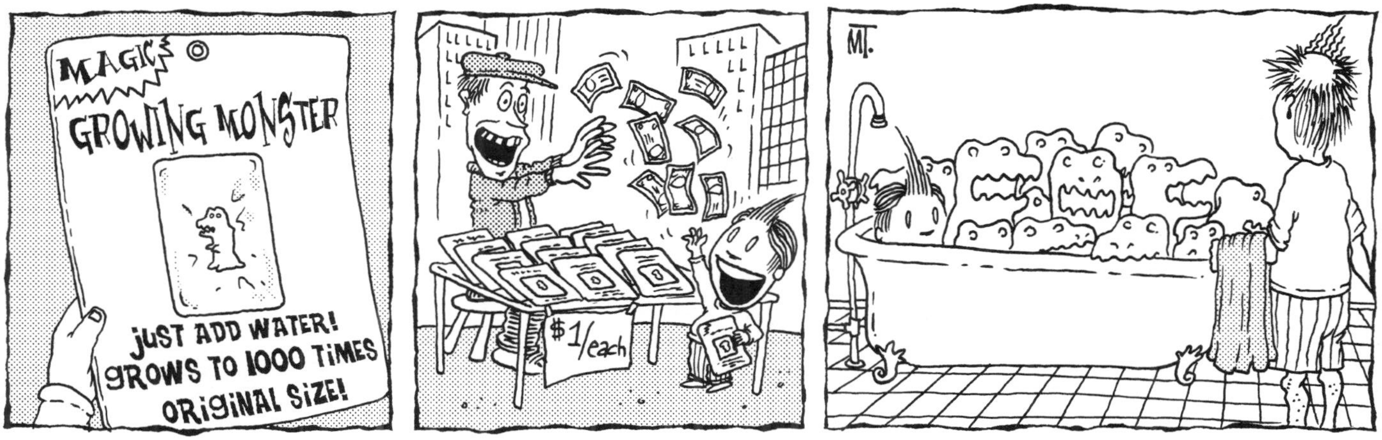
MAGIC ©
GROWING MONSTER
JUST ADD WATER!
GROWS TO 1000 TIMES
ORIGINAL SIZE!
$1/each
MT.

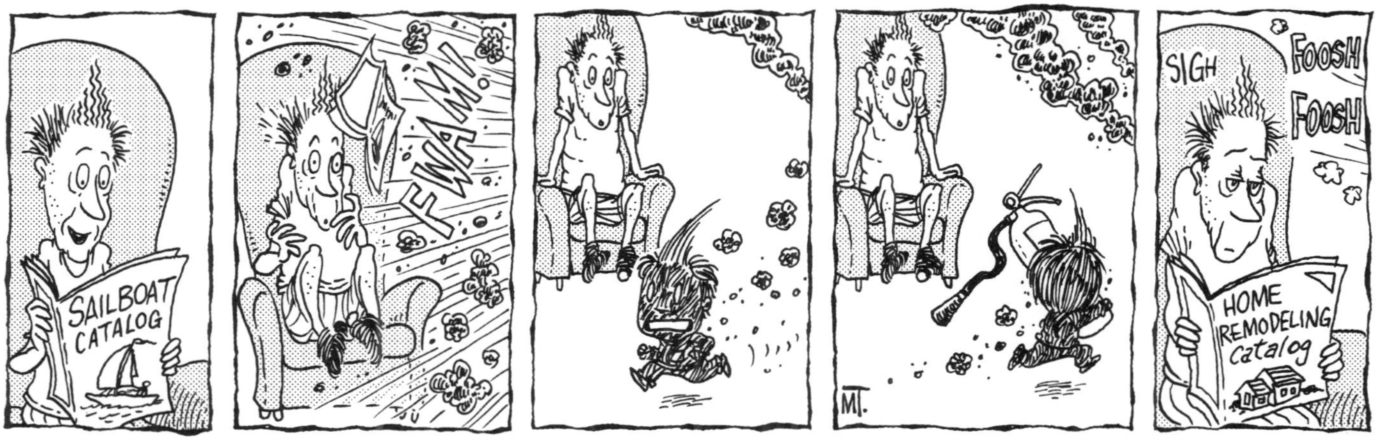
SAILBOAT
CATALOG
FWAM!
MT.
SIGH
FOOSH
FOOSH
HOME
REMODELING
Catalog

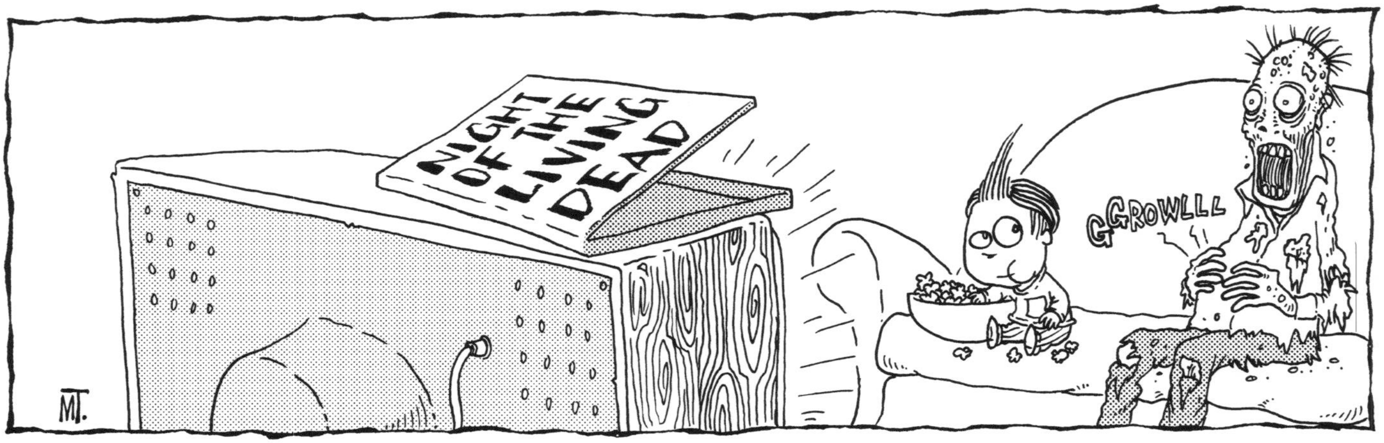
NIGHT OF THE LIVING DEAD
GGROWLLL

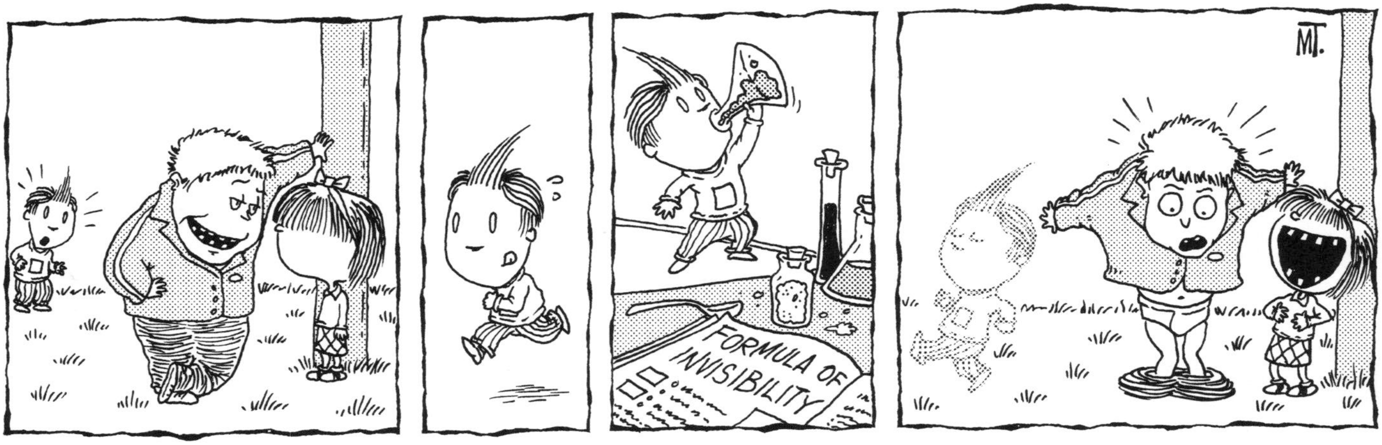
FORMULA OF INVISIBILITY

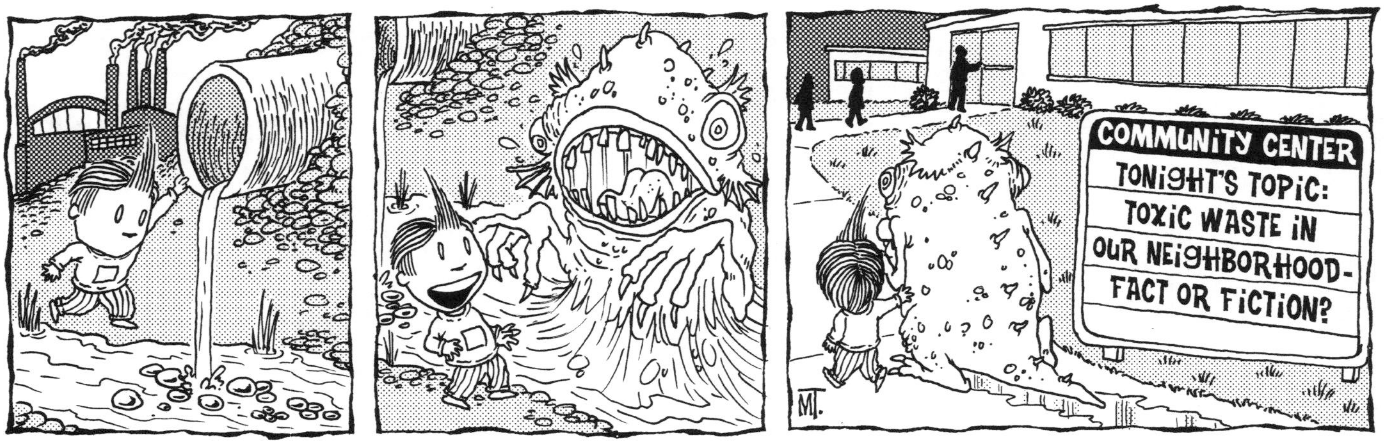
COMMUNITY CENTER
TONIGHT'S TOPIC:
TOXIC WASTE IN
OUR NEIGHBORHOOD-
FACT OR FICTION?

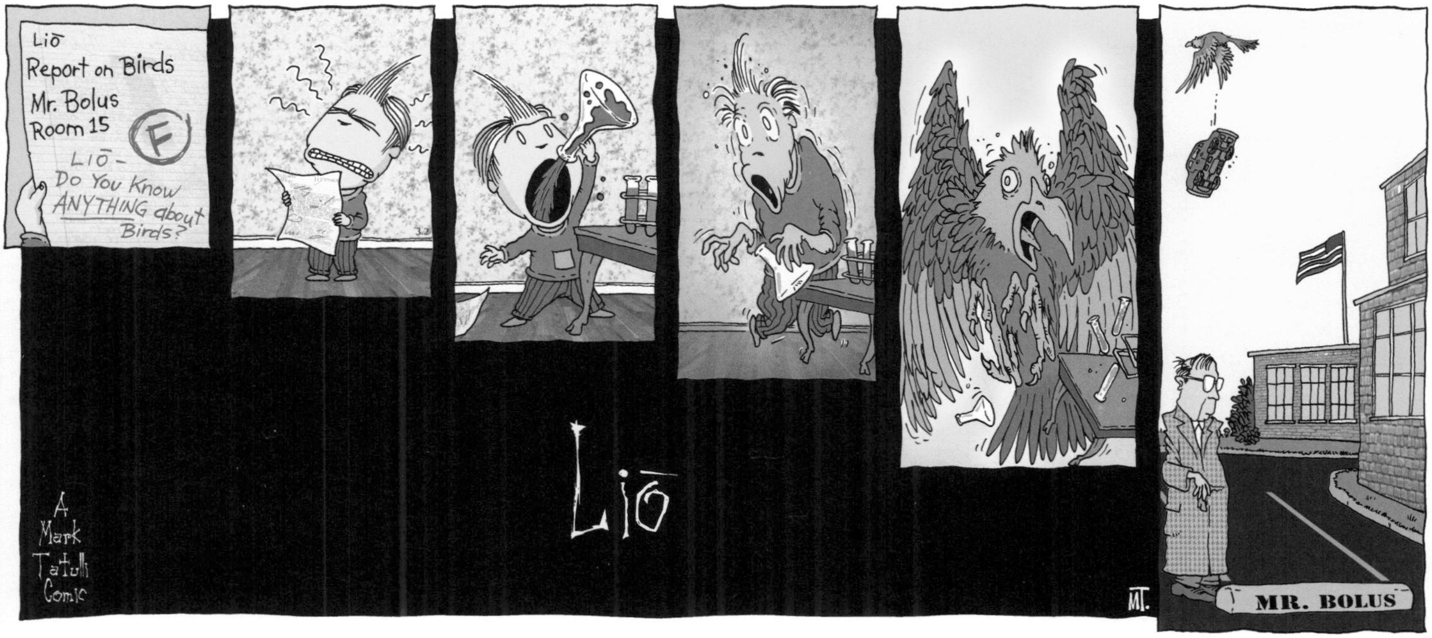

Liō
Report on Birds
Mr. Bolus
Room 15
F
LIŌ-
Do You Know
ANYTHING about
Birds?
Liō
A
Mark
Tatulli
Comic
MT.
MR. BOLUS

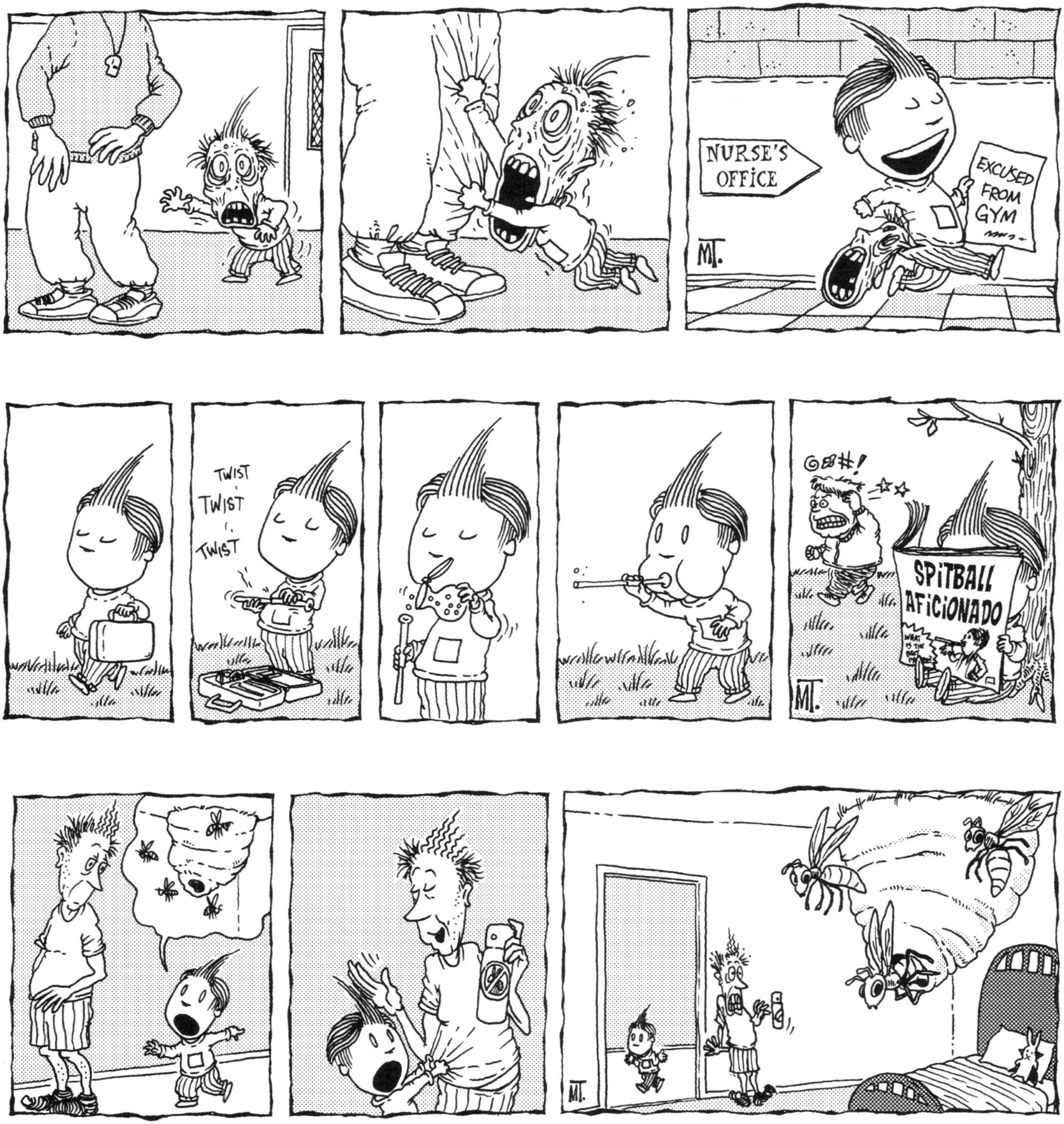
NURSE'S OFFICE
EXCUSED FROM GYM
MT.
TWIST
TWIST
TWIST
SPITBALL AFICIONADO
MT.
MT.

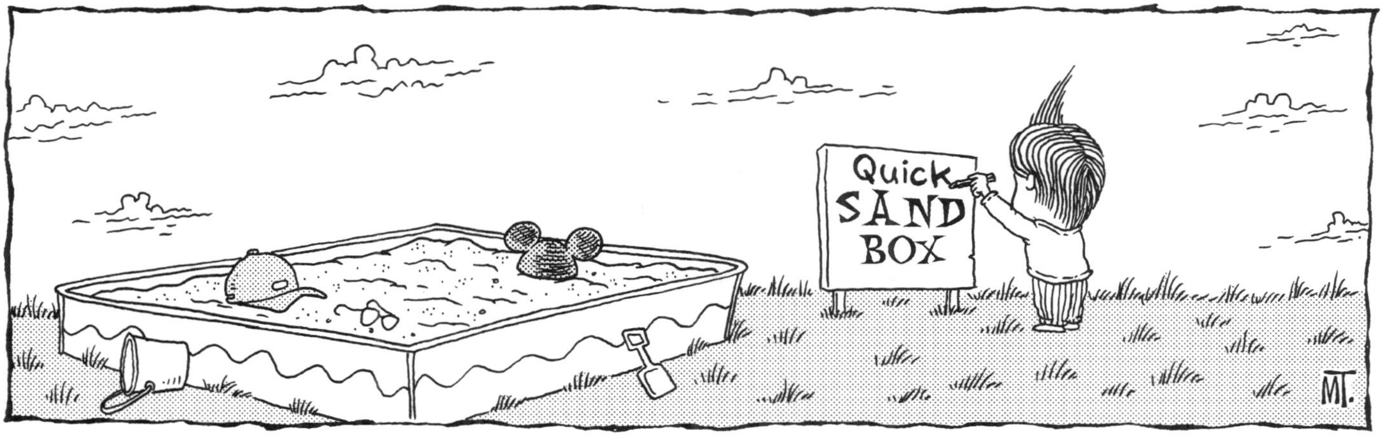
Quick
SAND
BOX

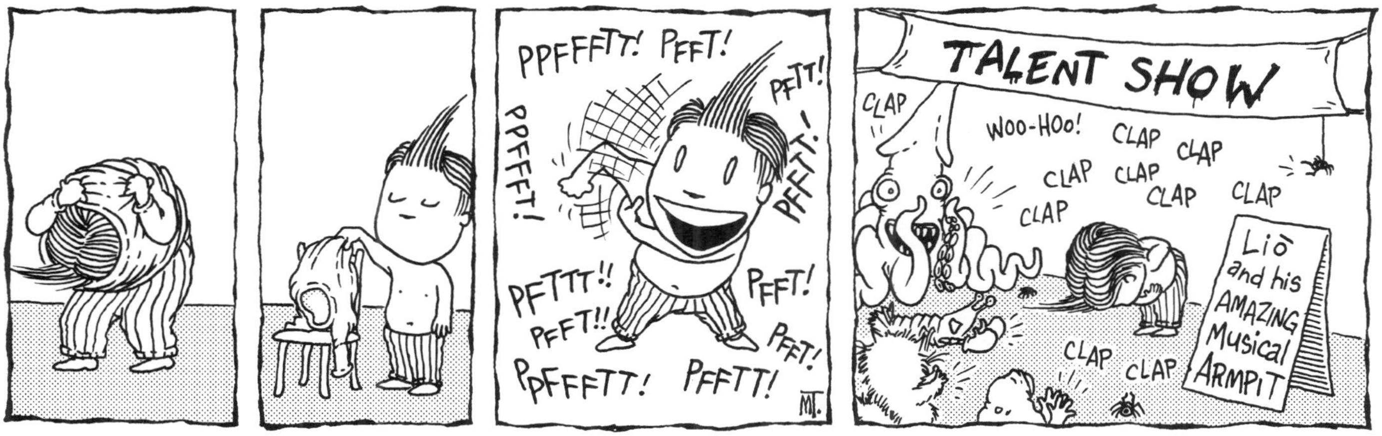
PPFFFTT! PFFT!
PPFFFT!
PFTT!
PFFTT!
PFTTT!!
PFFT!!
PPFFFTT! PFFTT!
PFFT!
PFFT!
TALENT SHOW
CLAP
WOO-HOO!
CLAP CLAP
CLAP CLAP
CLAP CLAP
CLAP
CLAP CLAP
Liō and his AMAZING Musical ARMPIT

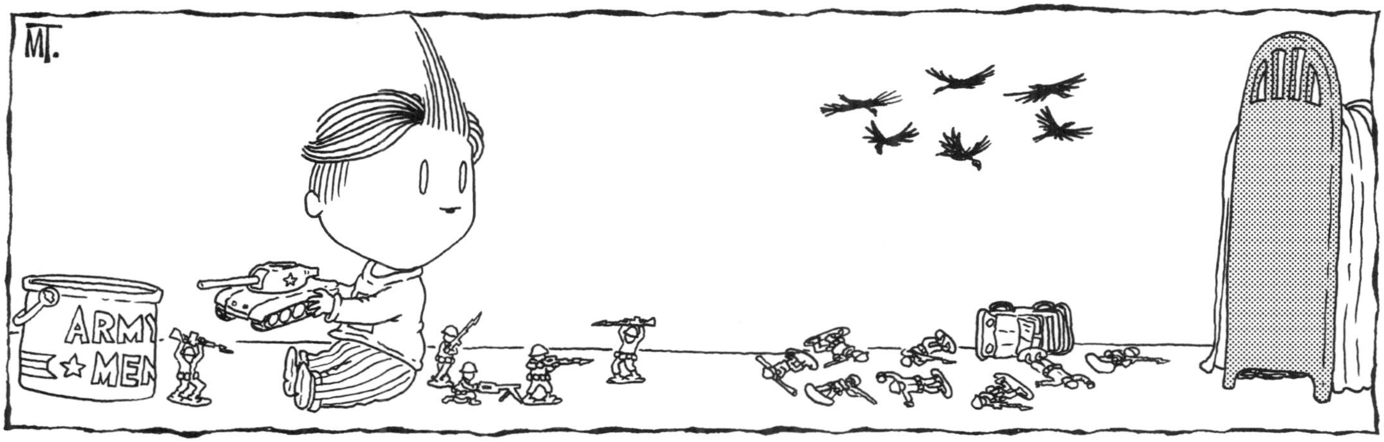
ARMY MEN

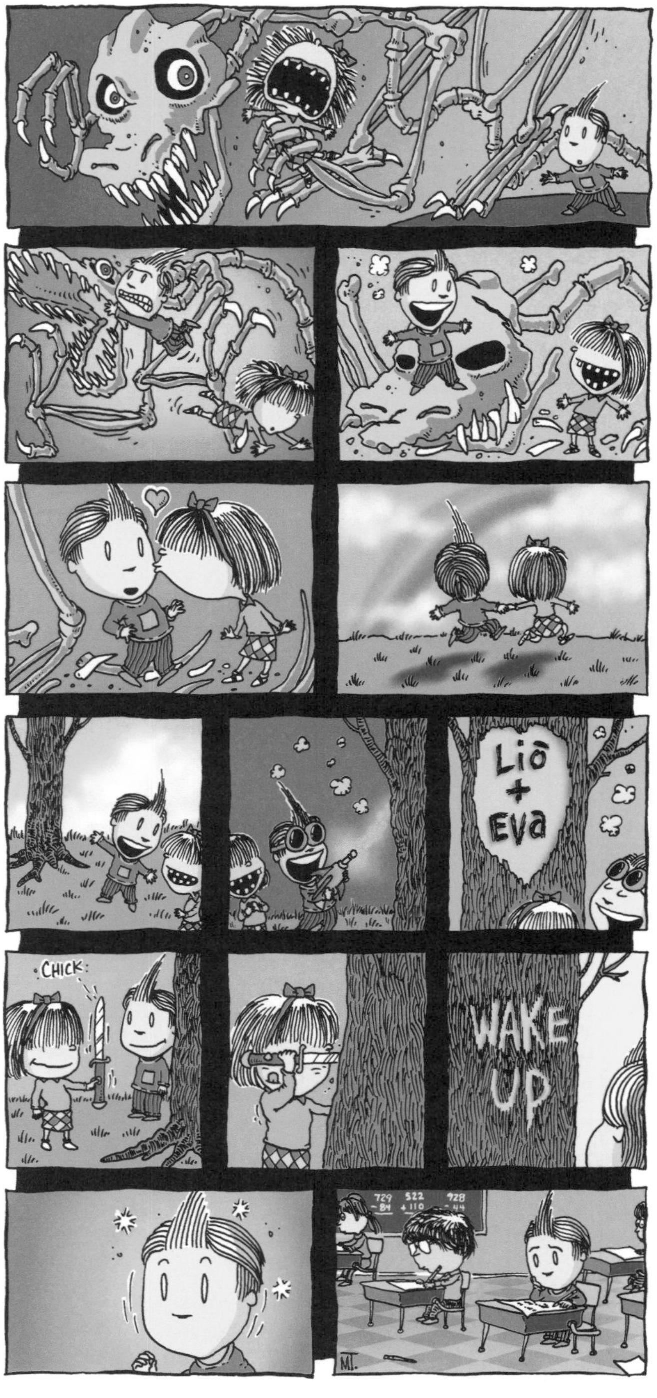
Liō
+
Eva
CHICK
WAKE
UP
MT.

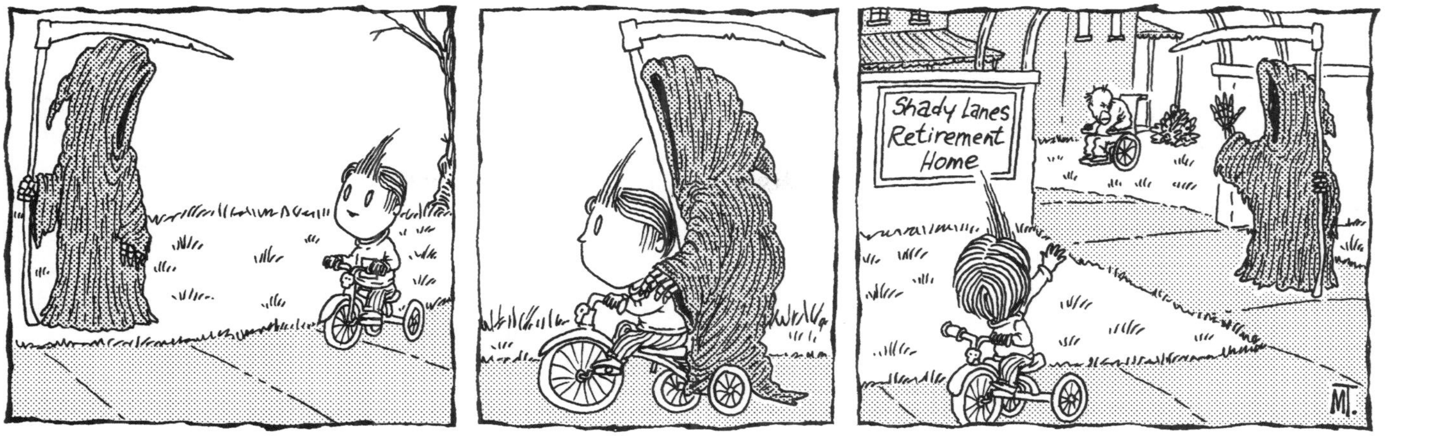
Shady Lanes
Retirement
Home

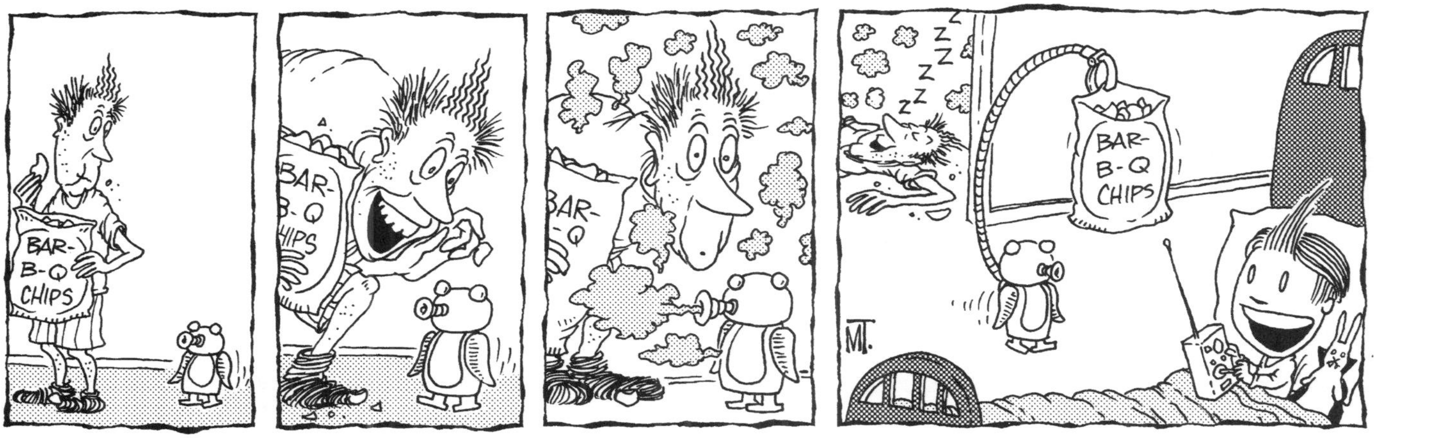
BAR-
B-Q
CHIPS
BAR-
B-Q
CHIPS

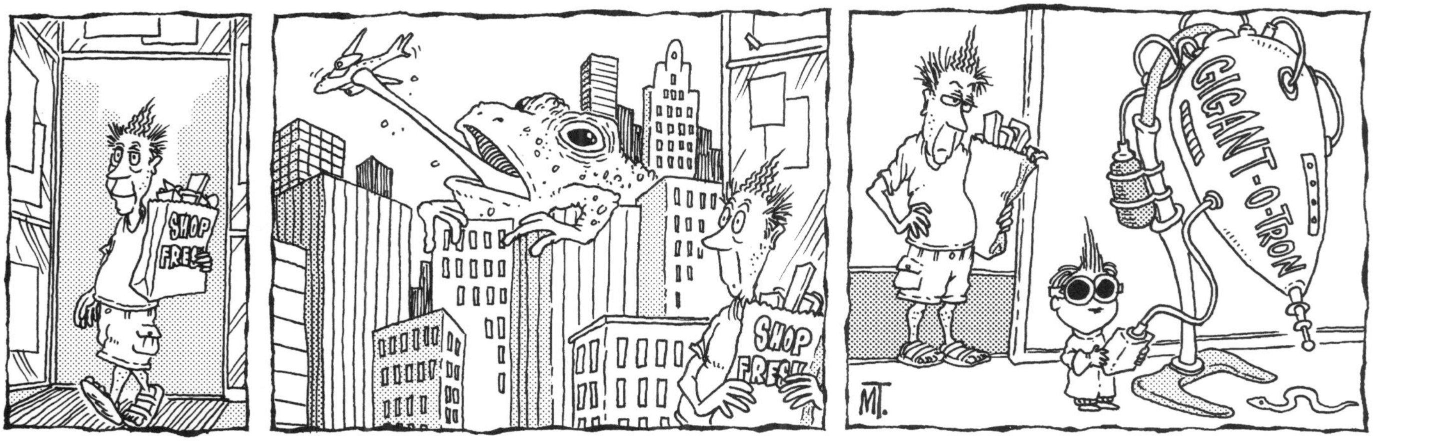
SHOP
SHOP
GIGANT-O-TRON

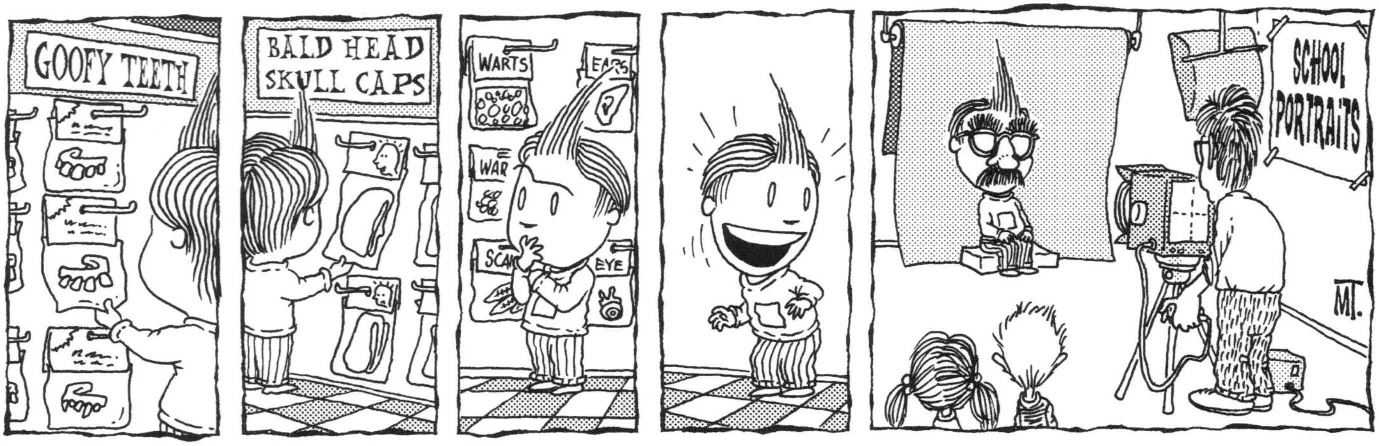
GOOFY TEETH
BALD HEAD SKULL CAPS
WARTS
EYE
SCHOOL PORTRAITS
MT.

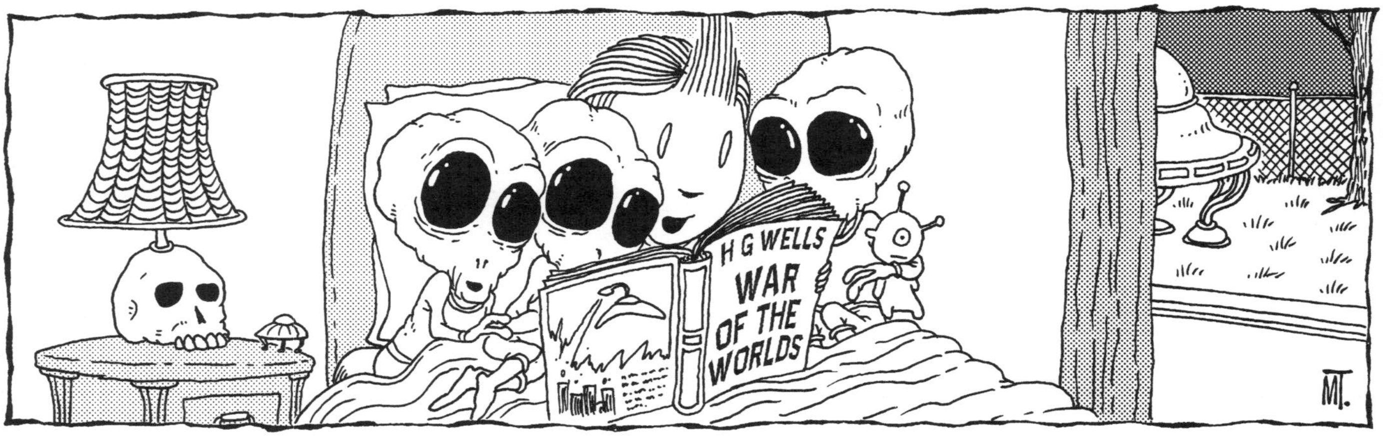
H G WELLS
WAR OF THE WORLDS
MT.

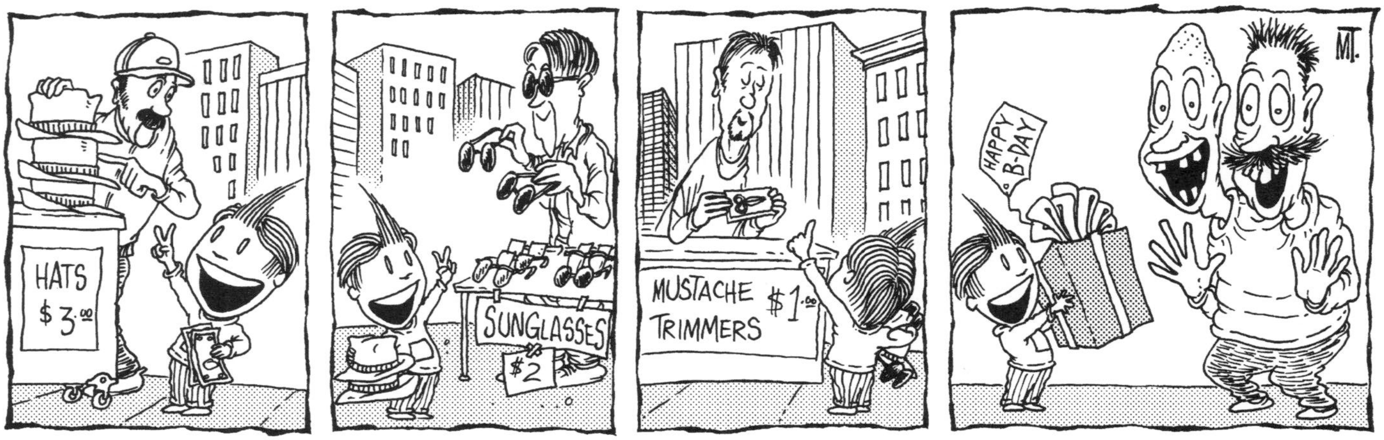
HATS $3.00
SUNGLASSES
$2
MUSTACHE TRIMMERS $1.00
HAPPY B-DAY
MT.

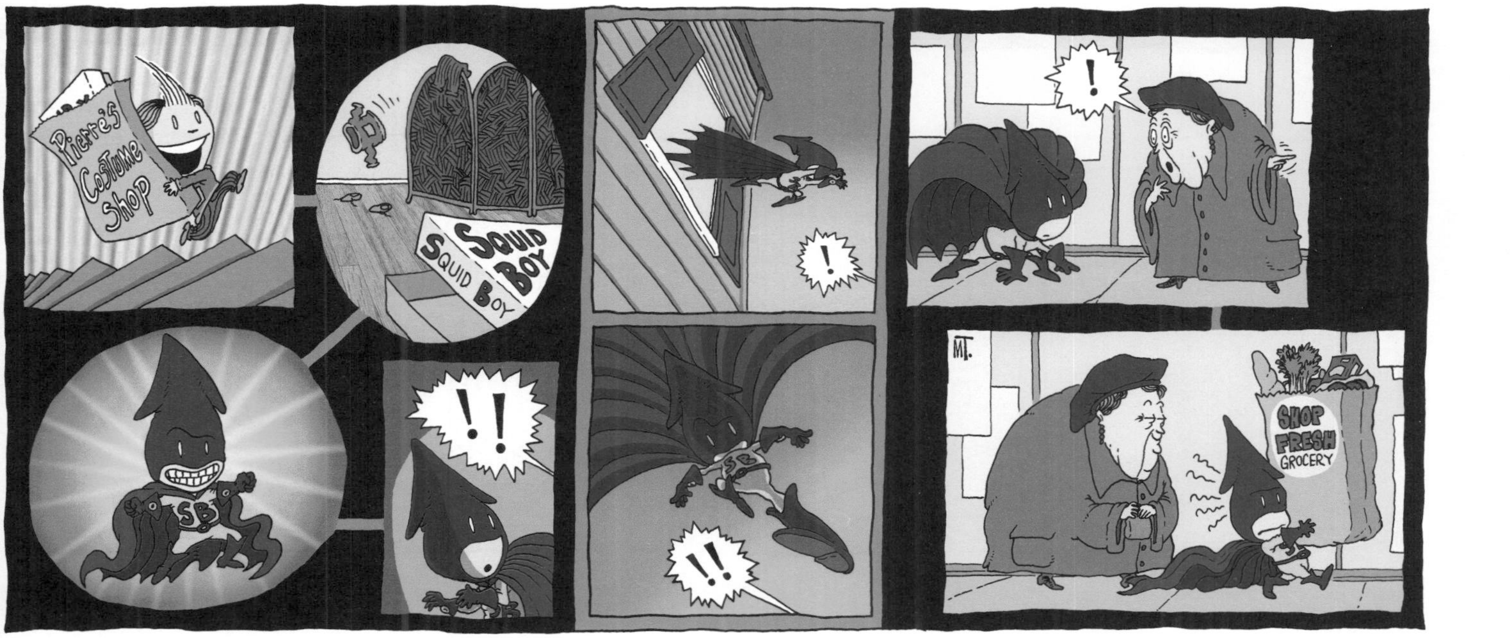
Pierre's Costume Shop
SQUID BOY
SQUID BOY
!!
!
!!
!
SB
SHOP FRESH GROCERY
MT.

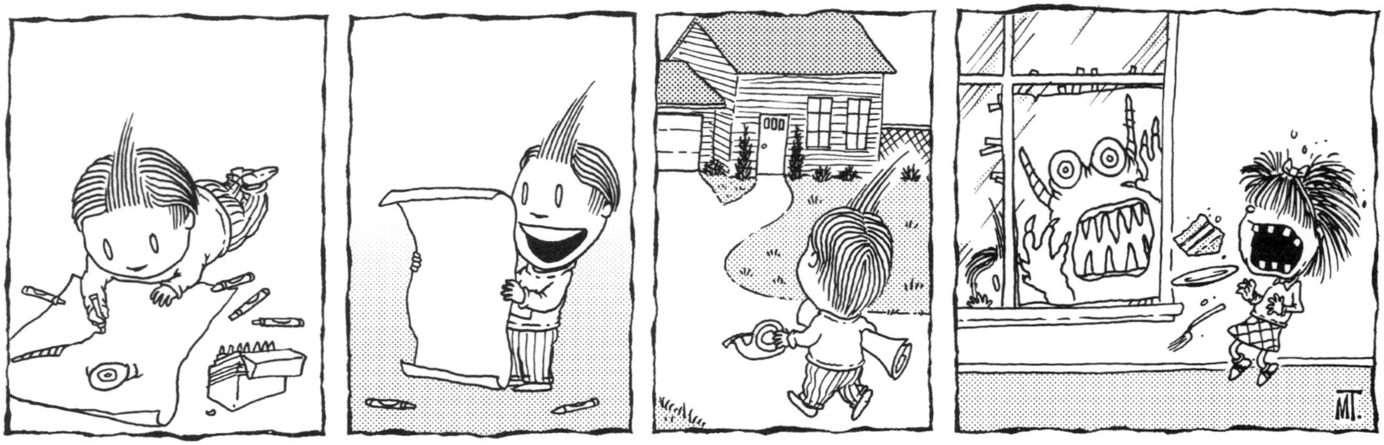

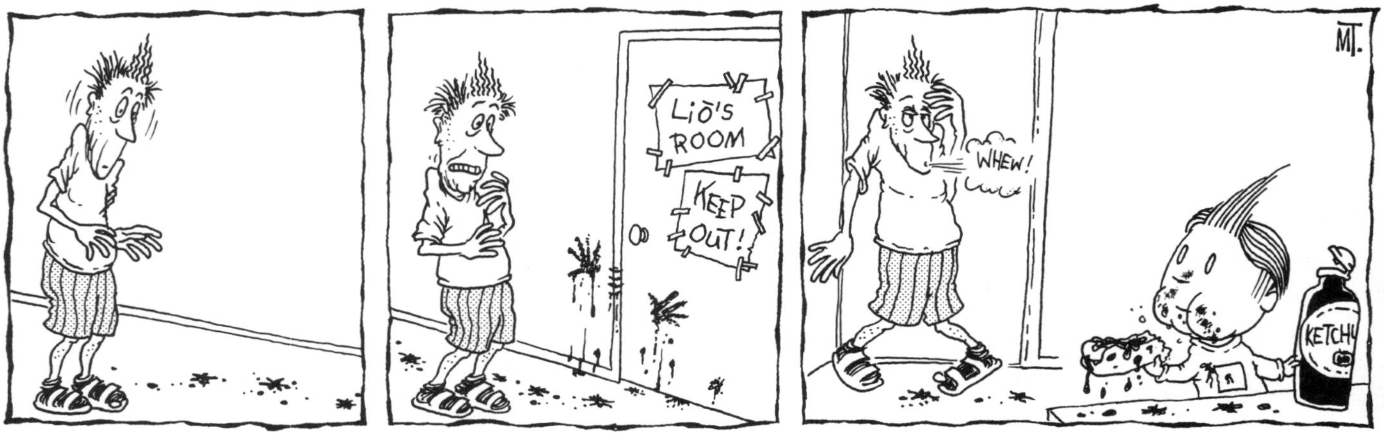
LIO'S ROOM
KEEP OUT!
WHEW!
KETCHU

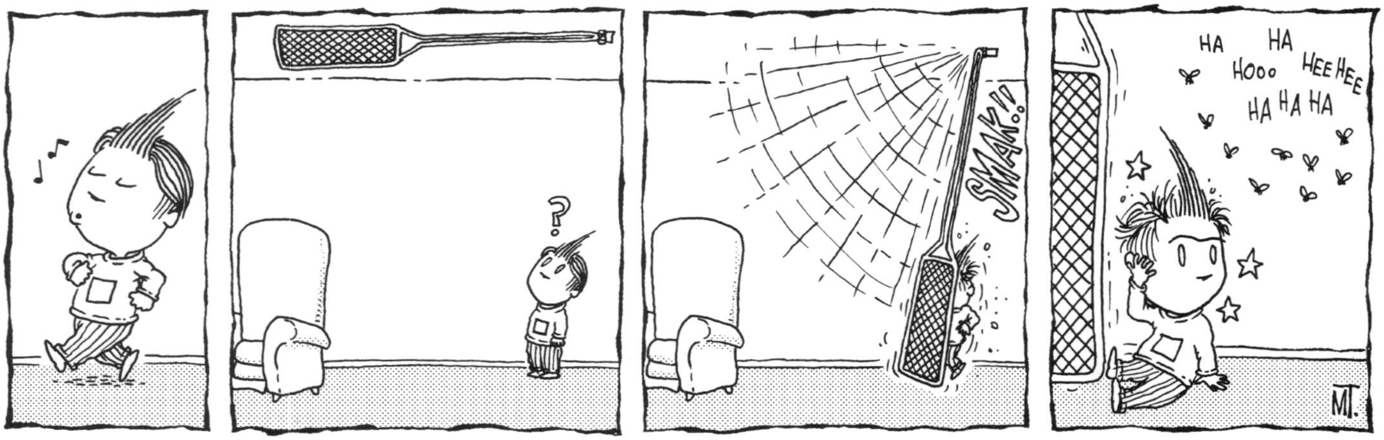
?
SMAK!!
HA HA HOOO HEE HEE HA HA HA

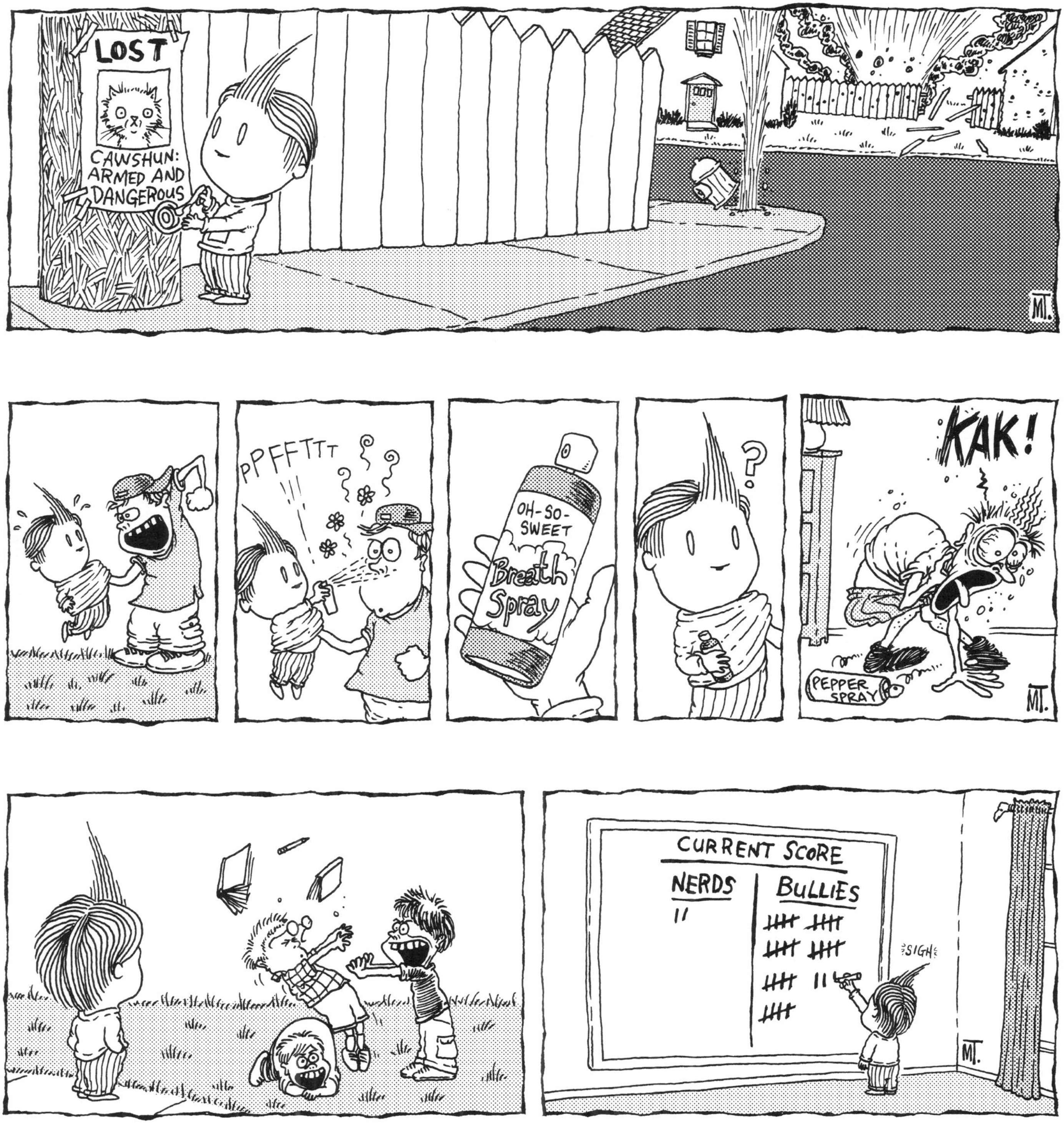
LOST
CAWSHUN: ARMED AND DANGEROUS
MT.
PPFFTTT
?
OH-SO-SWEET
Breath Spray
?
KAK!
PEPPER SPRAY
MT.
CURRENT SCORE
NERDS
BULLIES
SIGH
MT.

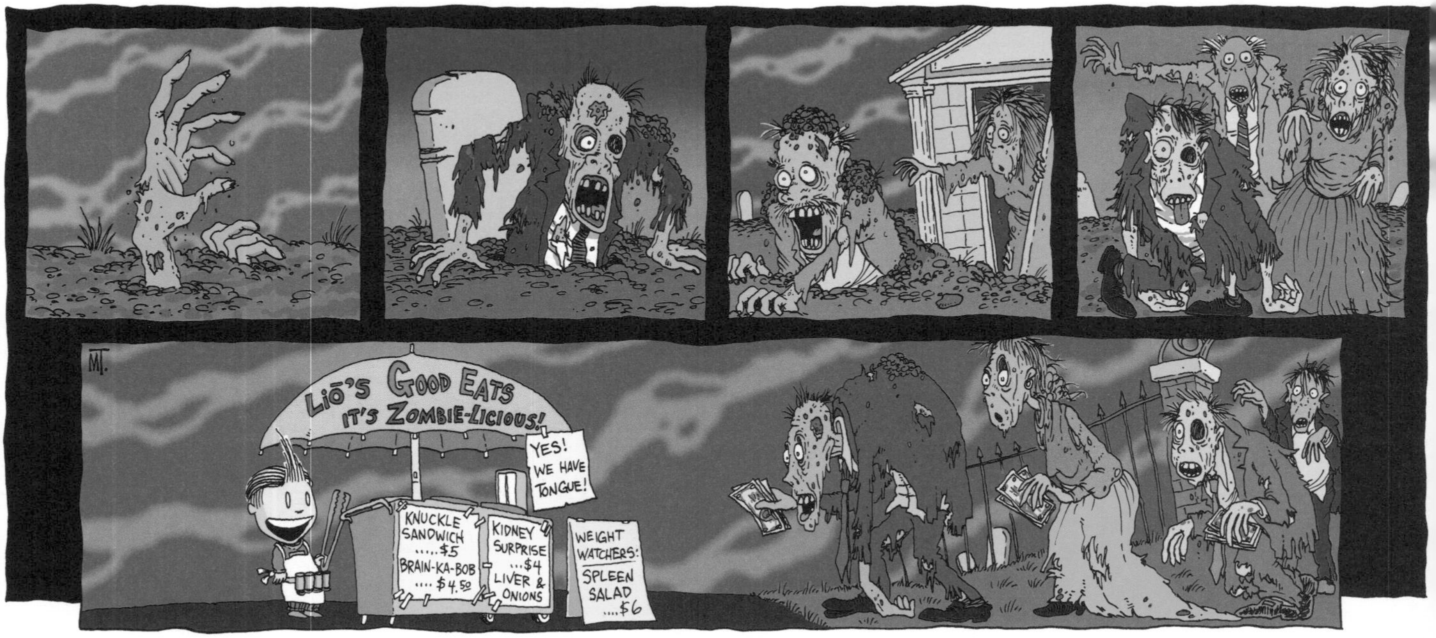
MT.
LIO'S GOOD EATS
IT'S ZOMBIE-LICIOUS!
YES! WE HAVE TONGUE!
KNUCKLE SANDWICH $5
BRAIN-KA-BOB $4.50
KIDNEY SURPRISE ...$4
LIVER & ONIONS
WEIGHT WATCHERS:
SPLEEN SALAD $6

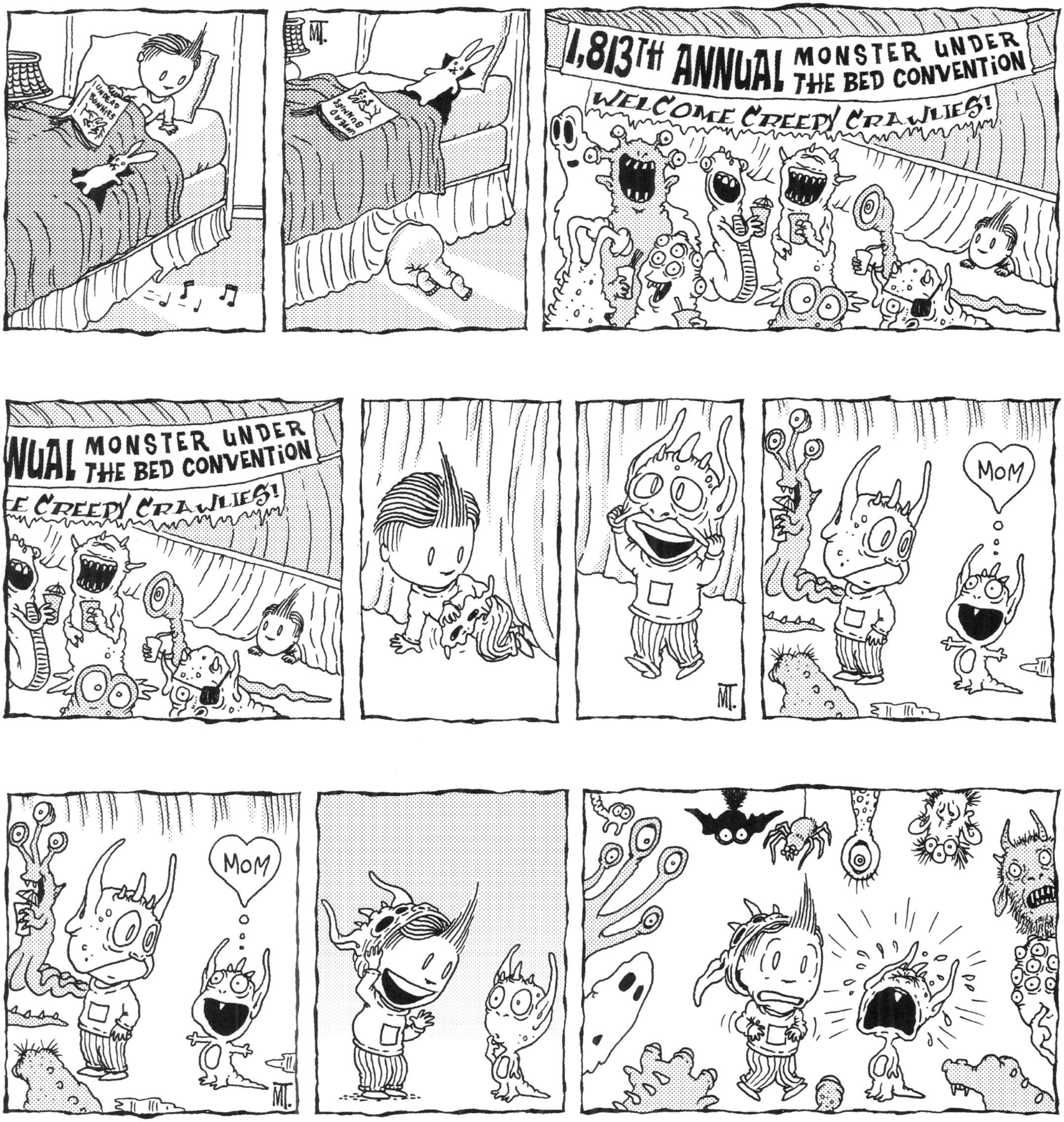
UNDEAD BUNNIES
MT.
UNDEAD BUNNIES
1,813TH ANNUAL MONSTER UNDER THE BED CONVENTION
WELCOME CREEPY CRAWLIES!
NUAL MONSTER UNDER THE BED CONVENTION
E CREEPY CRAWLIES!
MT.
MOM
MOM
MT.

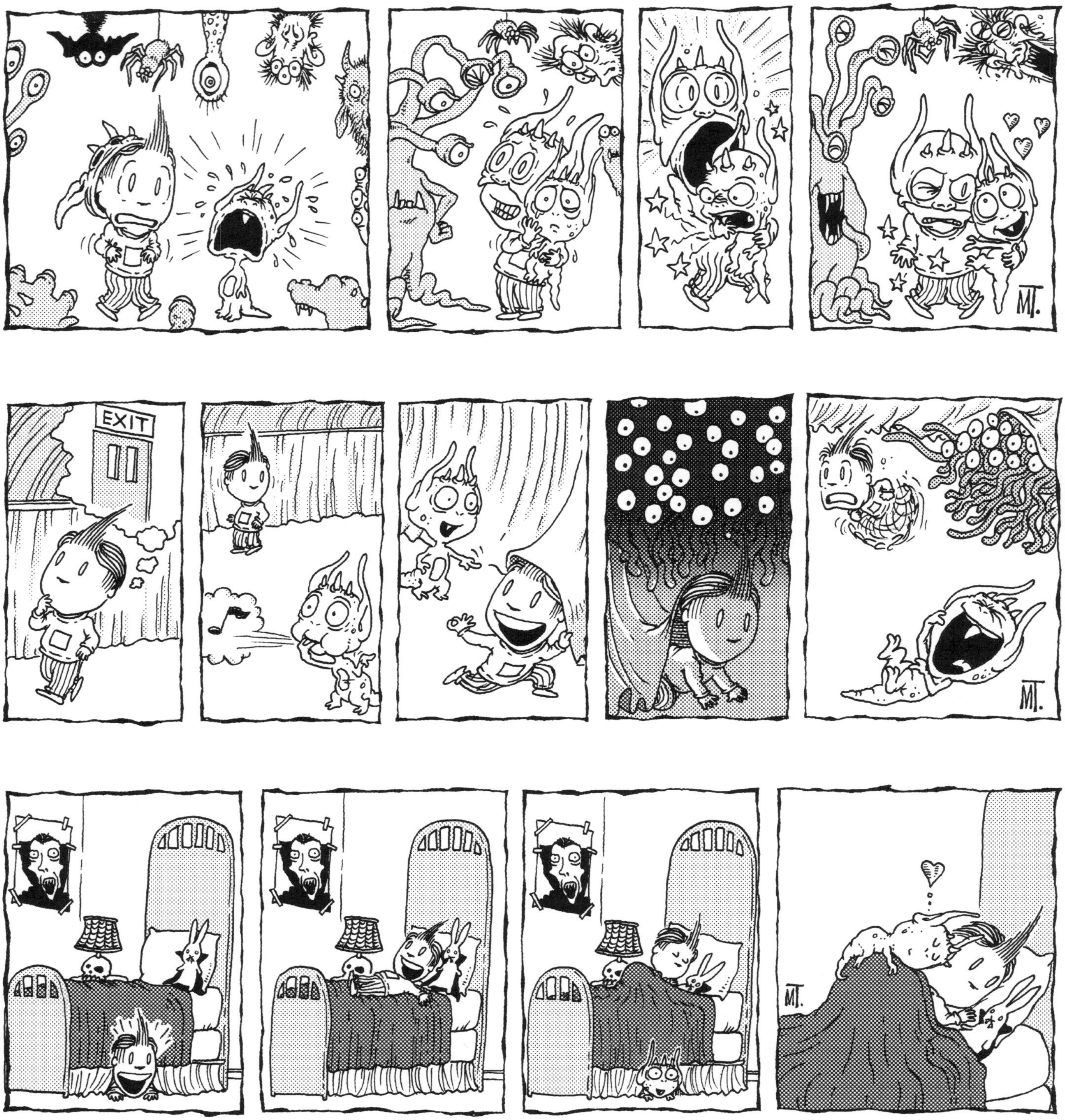
EXIT

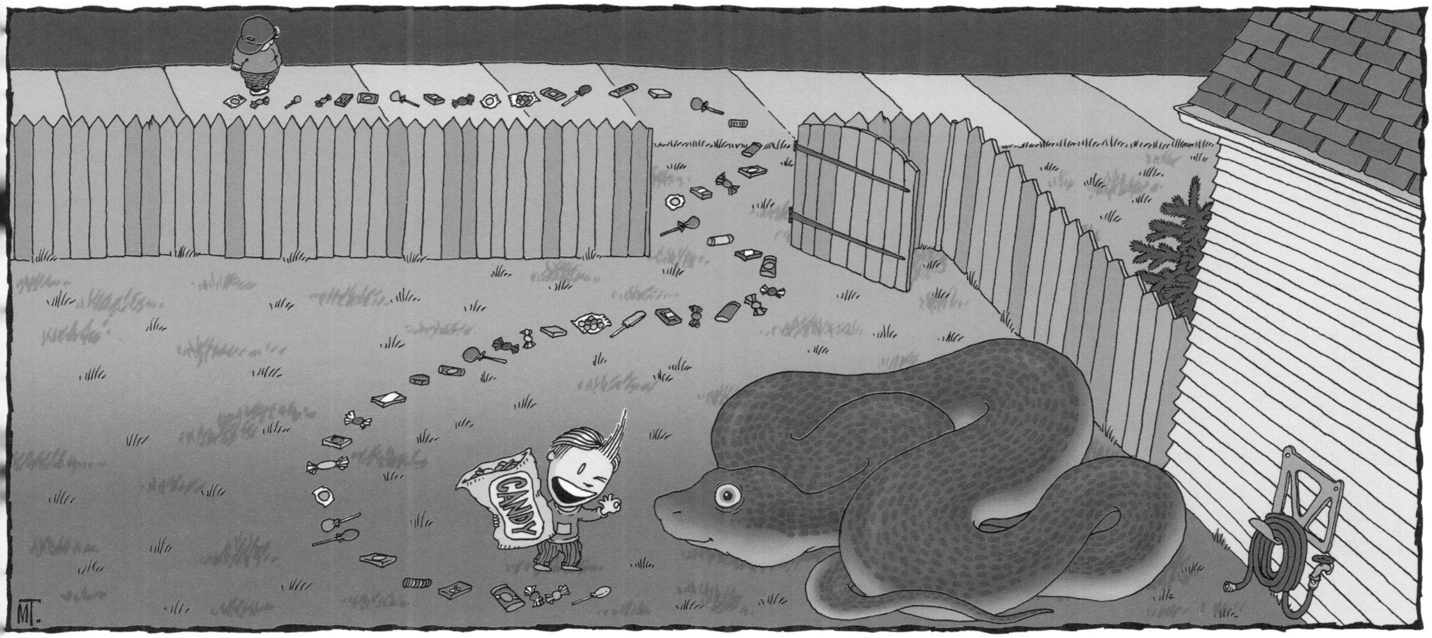
CANDY

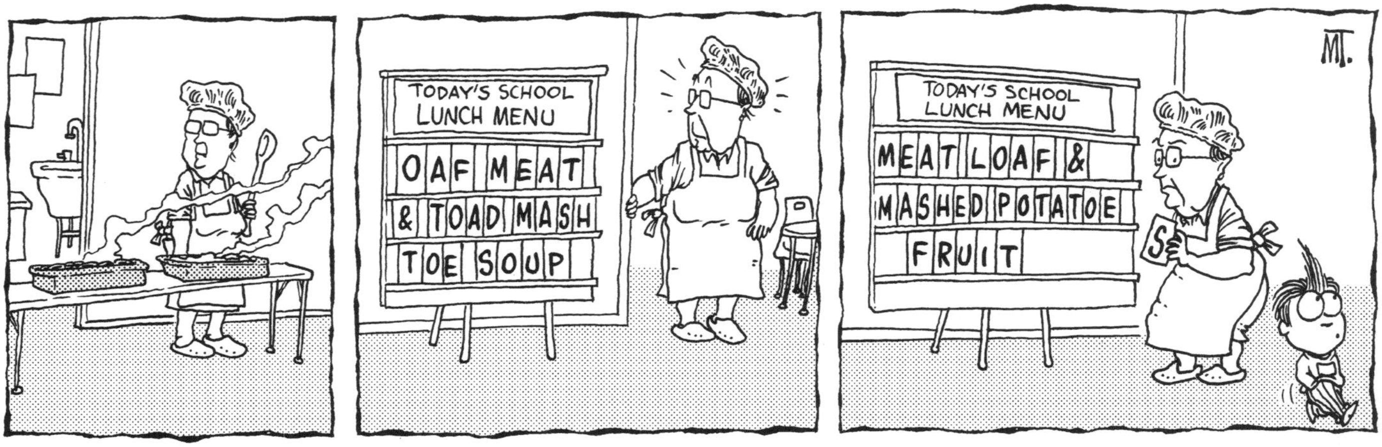

TODAY'S SCHOOL LUNCH MENU
OAF MEAT
& TOAD MASH
TOE SOUP
TODAY'S SCHOOL LUNCH MENU
MEAT LOAF &
MASHED POTATOE
FRUIT
S

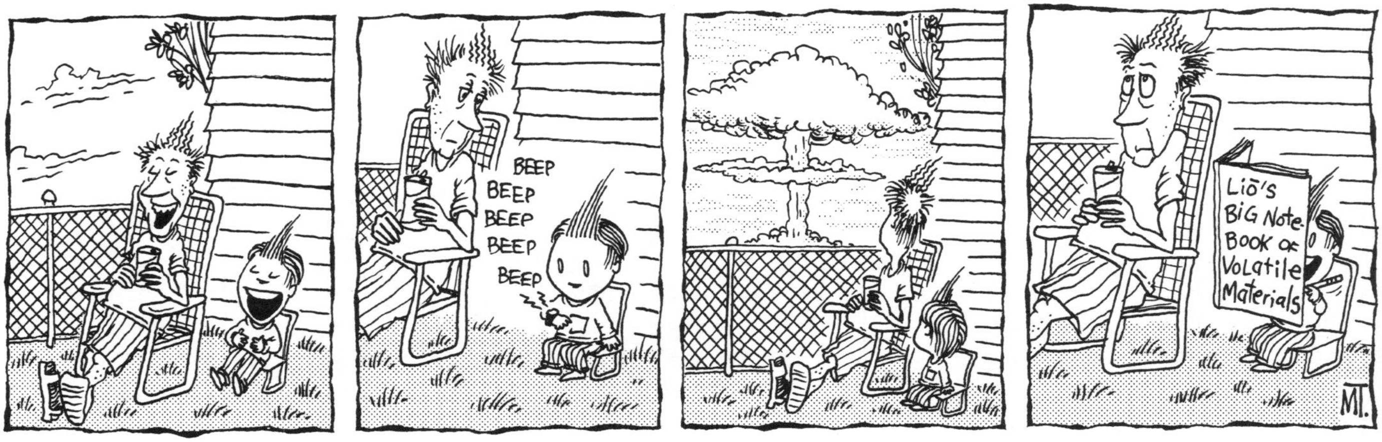

BEEP
BEEP
BEEP
BEEP
BEEP
Lio's Big Note Book of Volatile Materials

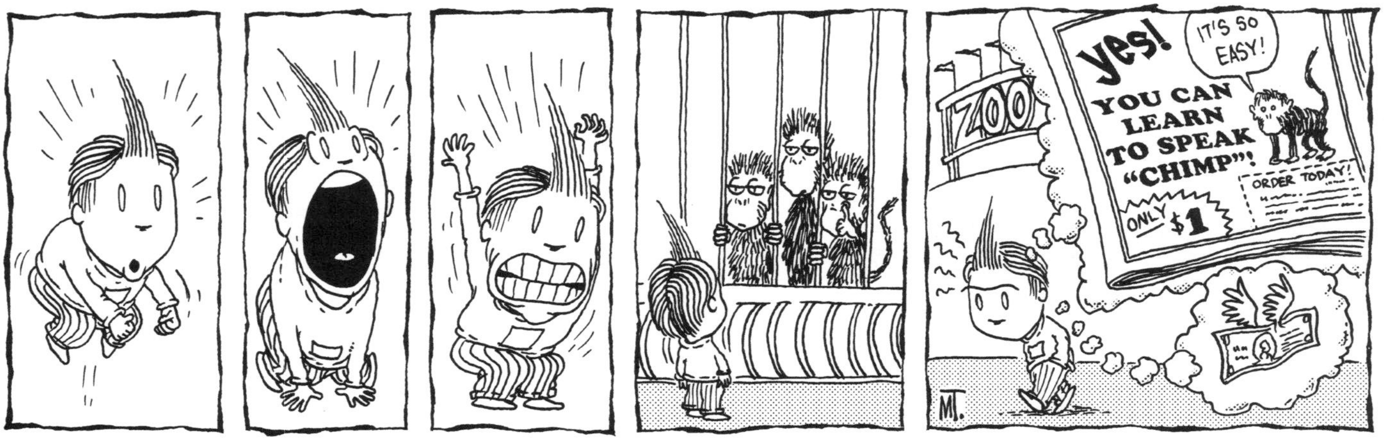

ZOO
Yes!
YOU CAN LEARN TO SPEAK "CHIMP"!
IT'S SO EASY!
ORDER TODAY!
ONLY $1

REPORT CARD Liō

Liō'S DITCHES 4-CHEAP

REPORT CARD Liō

THE DAILY TRUMPETER

LOCAL BOY INVENTS DITCH-DIGGING ROBOT

Teachers thought he would amount to nothing

REPORT

THE WALL STREET JOURNAL.

LIŌ DITCH KING-- COMPANY 'DITCHTECH' GOES PUBLIC - STOCK SOARS

FISH SUPPLIES

PET EMPORIUM

FLOATING CREATURE FLAKES
• PROMOTES COLOR
• BALANCED DIET

Welcome to THE BLACK LAGOON

The New York Times.

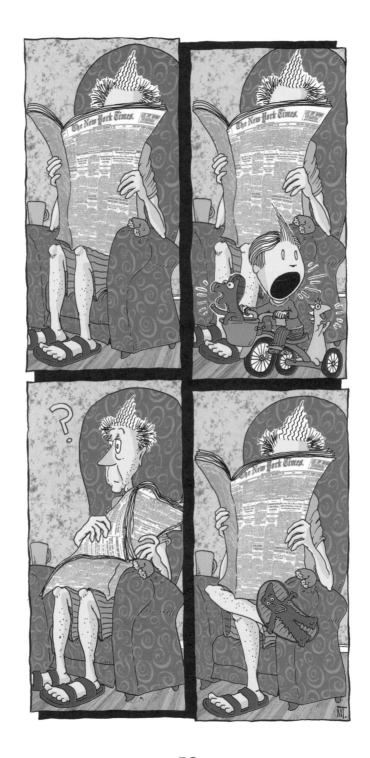

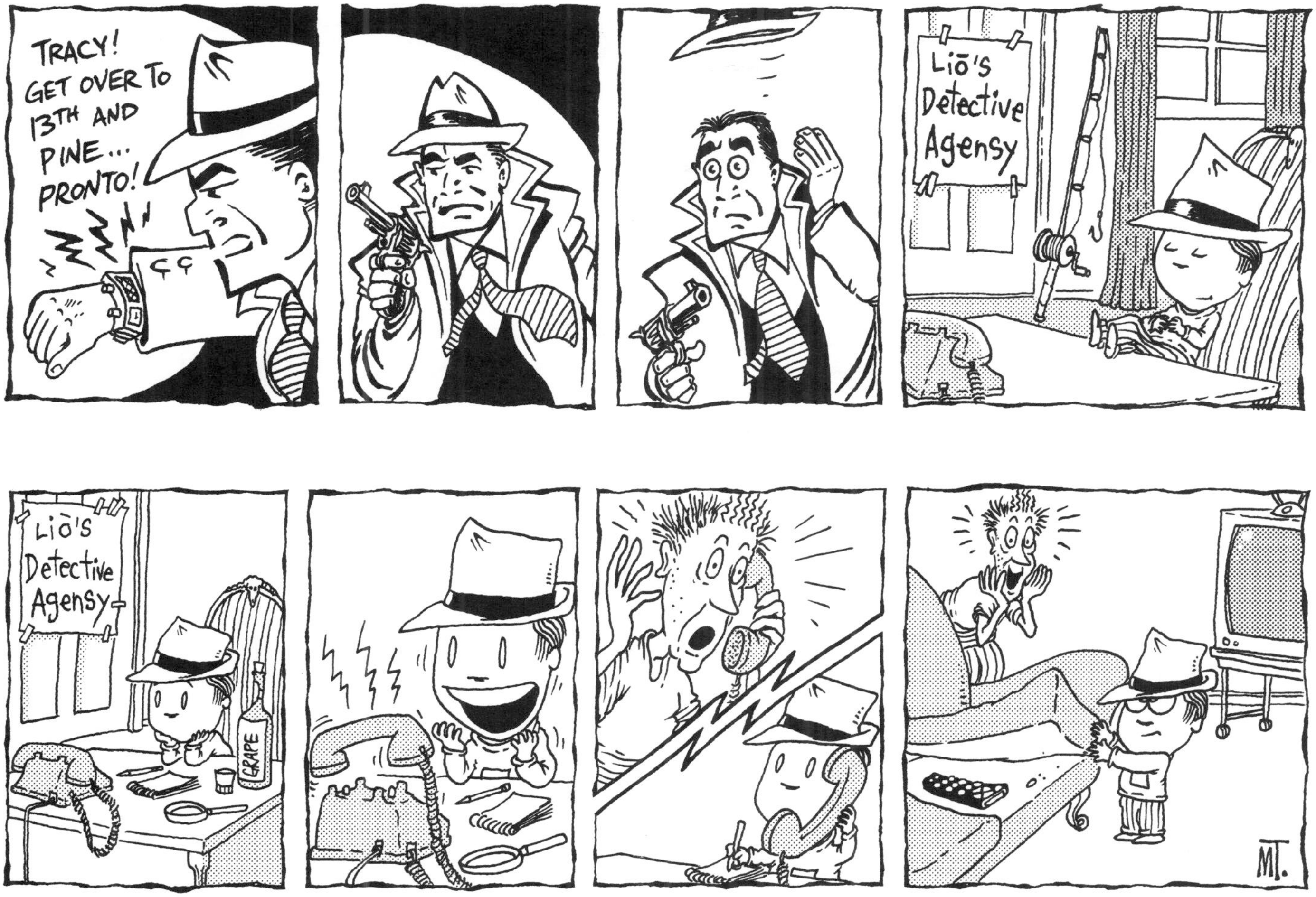
TRACY! GET OVER TO 13TH AND PINE... PRONTO!
Liō's Detective Agensy
Liō's Detective Agensy
GRAPE
MT.

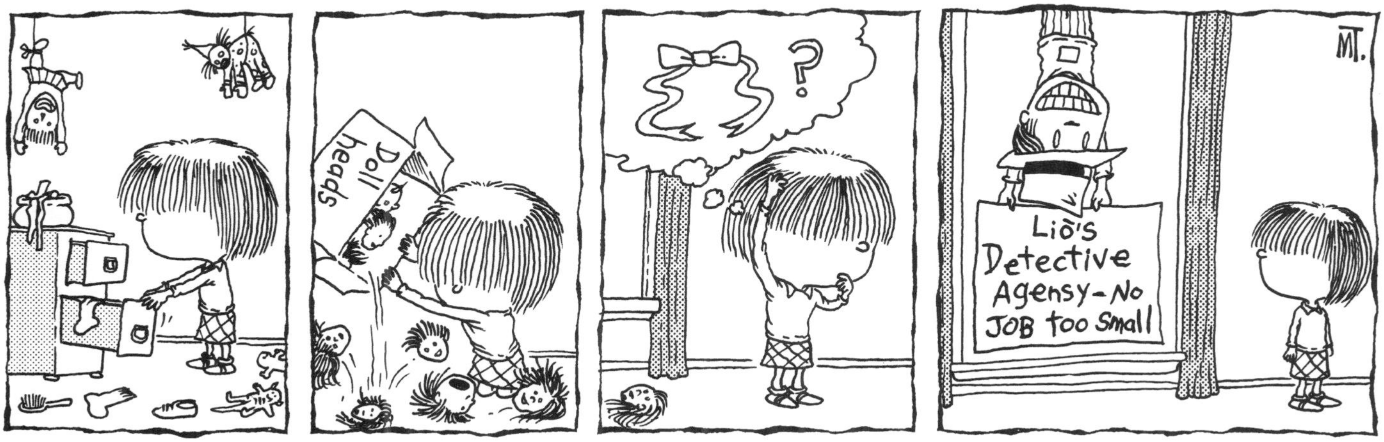
Doll heads
?
Liō's Detective Agensy - No JOB too Small
MT.

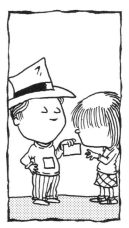

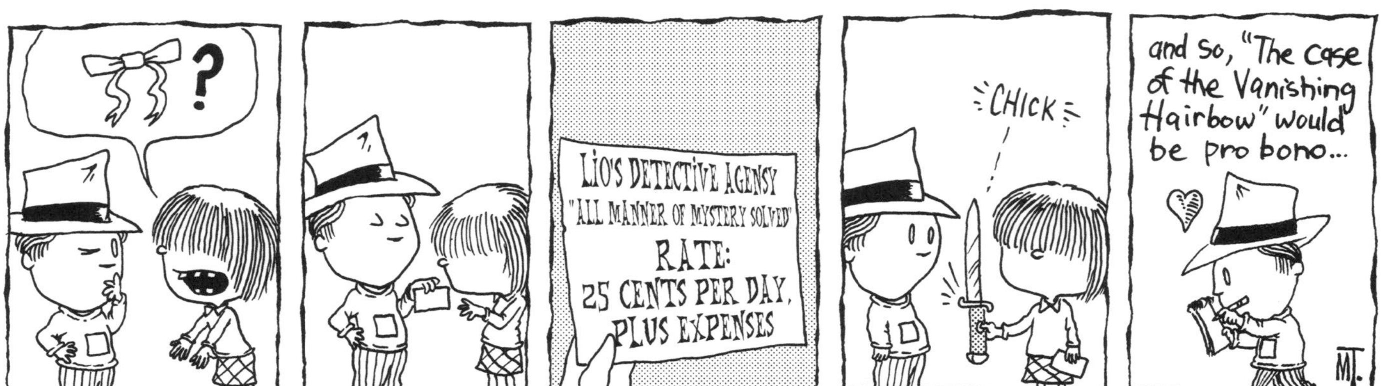
?
LIO'S DETECTIVE AGENSY
"ALL MANNER OF MYSTERY SOLVED"
RATE:
25 CENTS PER DAY,
PLUS EXPENSES
CHICK
and so, "The case of the Vanishing Hairbow" would be pro bono...
MT.

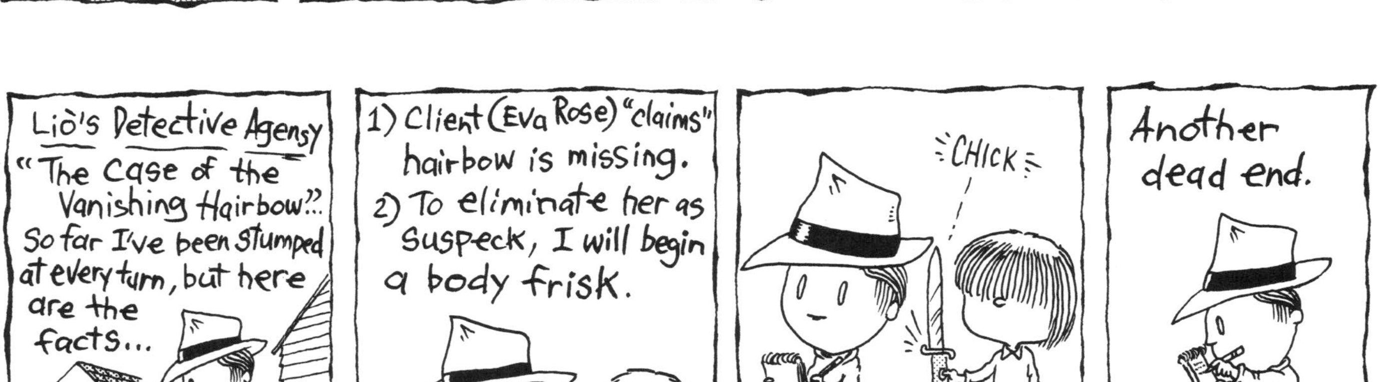
Lio's Detective Agensy
"The case of the Vanishing Hairbow"...
So far I've been stumped at every turn, but here are the facts...
1) Client (Eva Rose) "claims" hairbow is missing.
2) To eliminate her as suspeck, I will begin a body frisk.
CHICK
Another dead end.
MT.

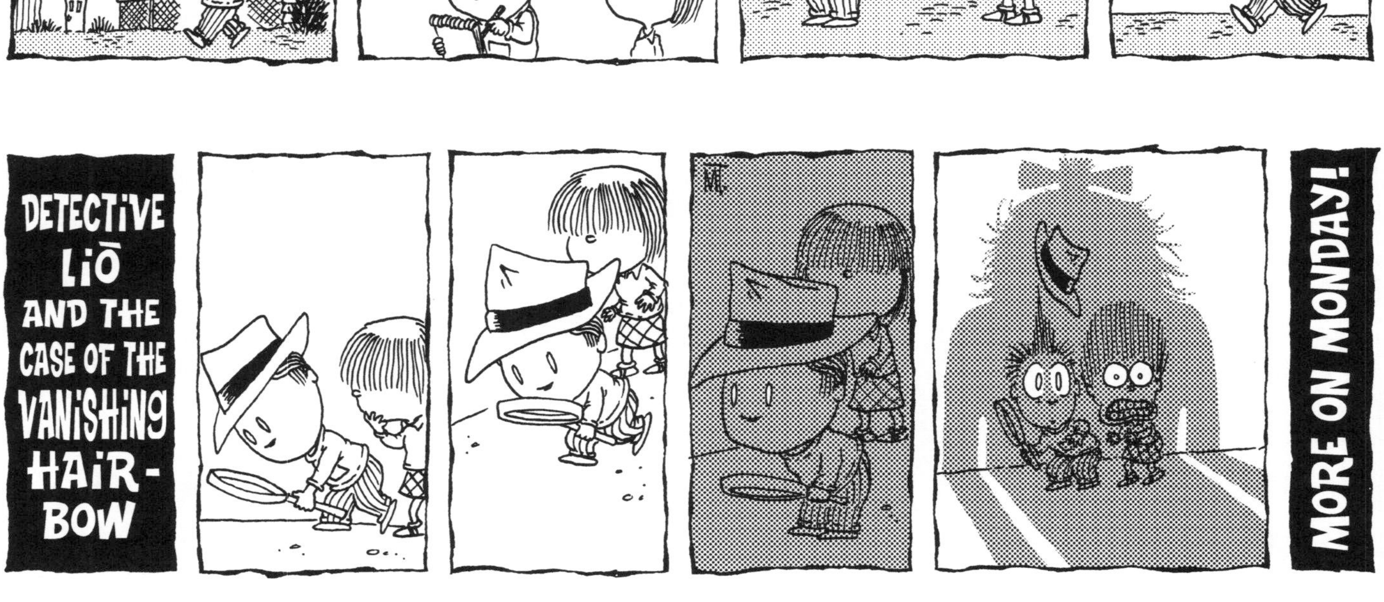
DETECTIVE LIŌ AND THE CASE OF THE VANISHING HAIR-BOW
MT.
MORE ON MONDAY!

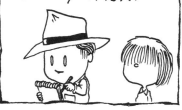

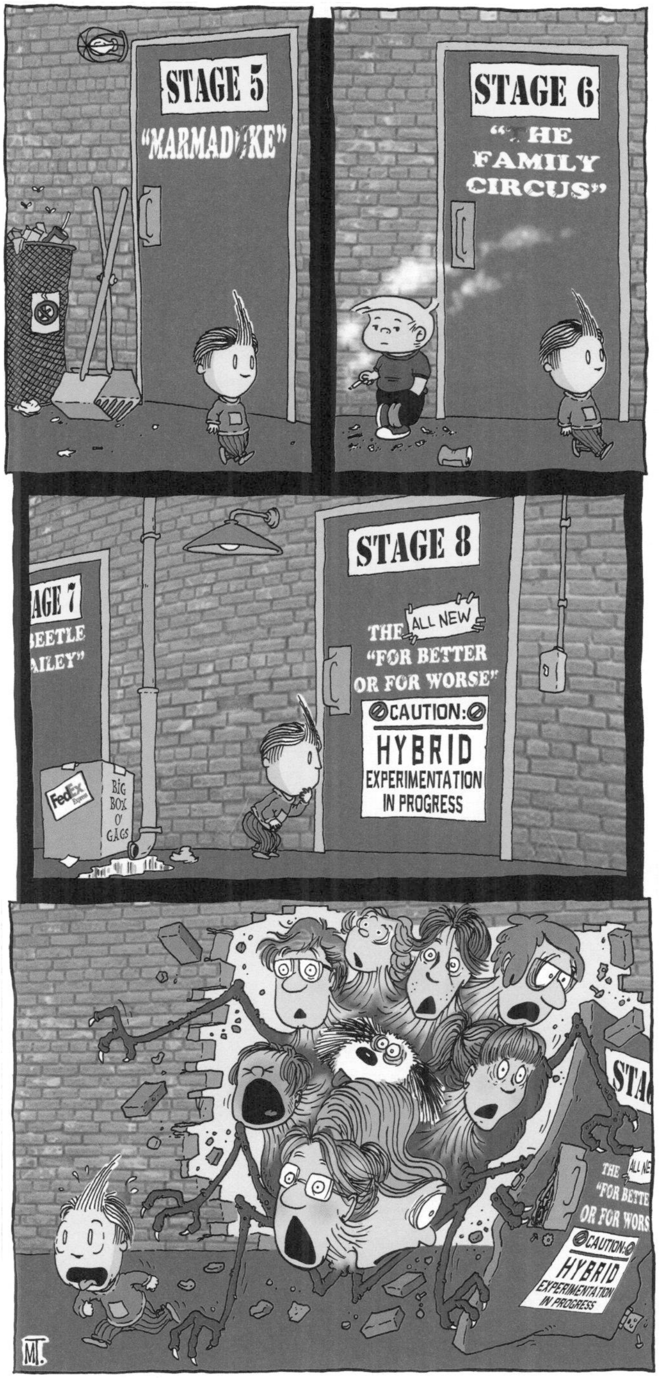
STAGE 5
STAGE 6
STAGE 8
THE ALL NEW "FOR BETTER OR FOR WORSE"
CAUTION:
HYBRID
EXPERIMENTATION IN PROGRESS
FedEx
BIG BOX O' GAGS
CAUTION:
HYBRID
EXPERIMENTATION IN PROGRESS

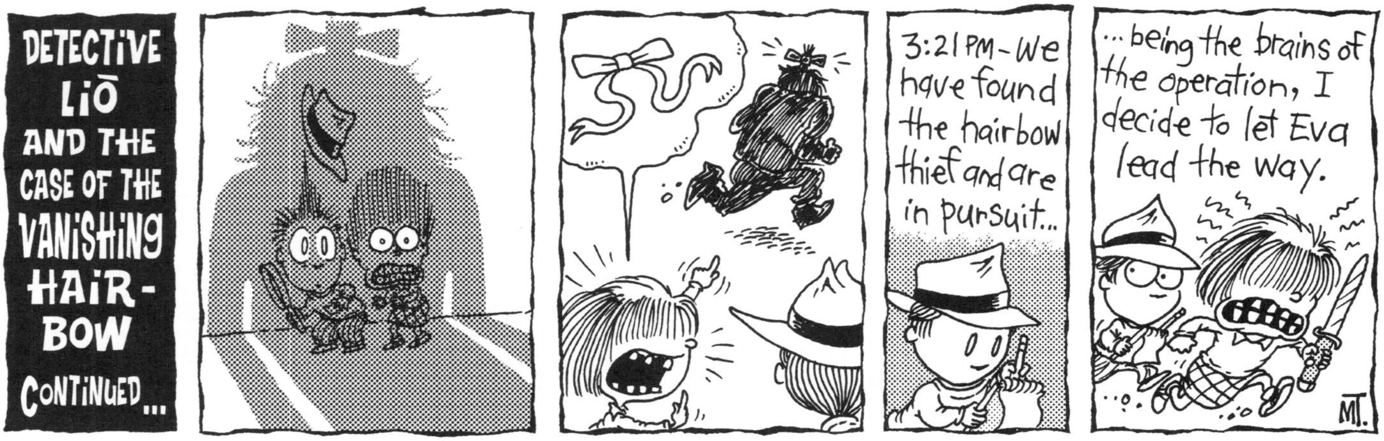
DETECTIVE LIŌ AND THE CASE OF THE VANISHING HAIR-BOW CONTINUED...
3:21 PM - We have found the hairbow thief and are in pursuit...
... being the brains of the operation, I decide to let Eva lead the way.

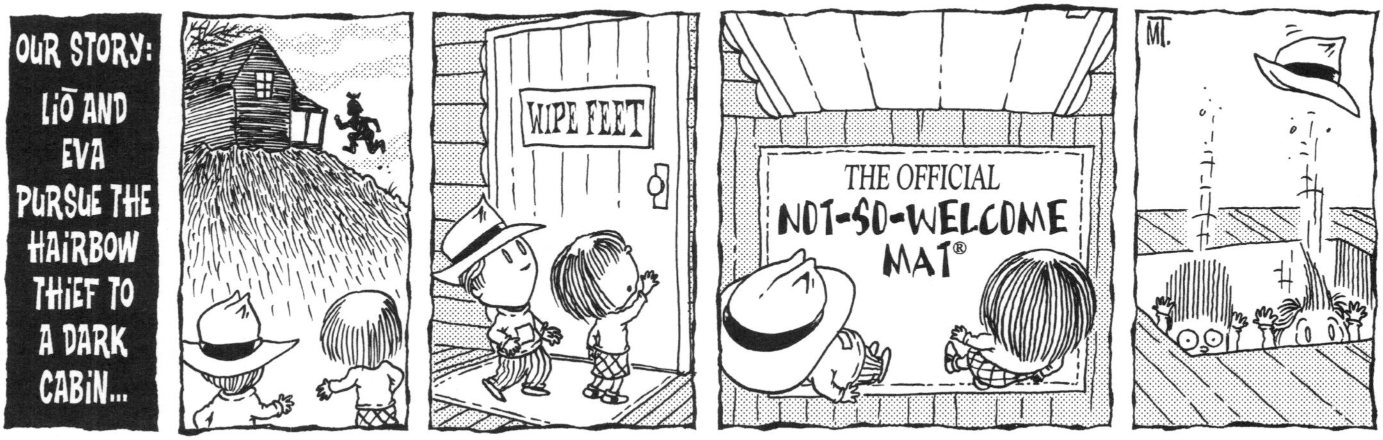
OUR STORY: LIŌ AND EVA PURSUE THE HAIRBOW THIEF TO A DARK CABIN...
WIPE FEET
THE OFFICIAL NOT-SO-WELCOME MAT®

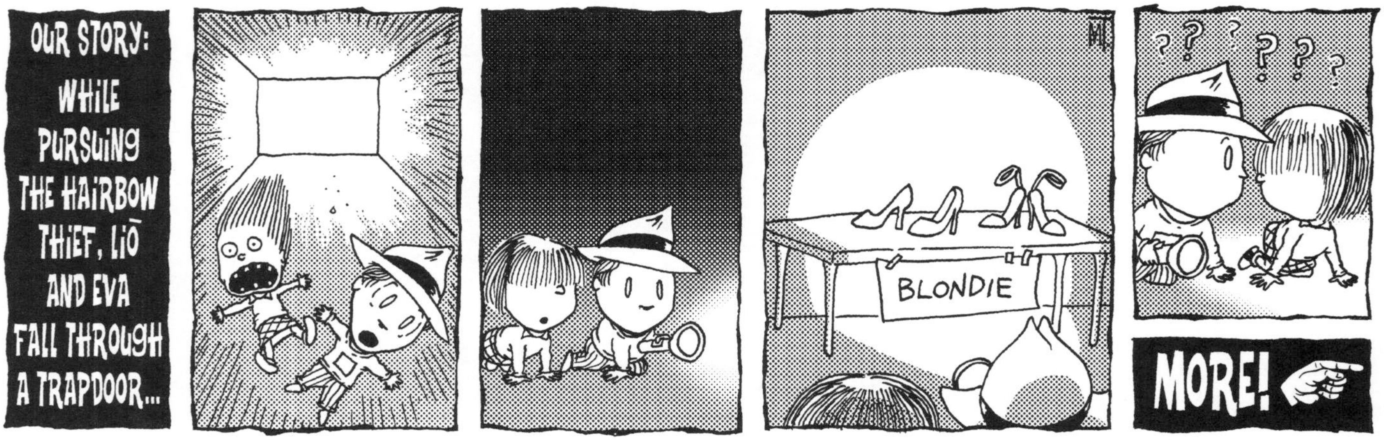
OUR STORY: WHILE PURSUING THE HAIRBOW THIEF, LIŌ AND EVA FALL THROUGH A TRAPDOOR...
BLONDIE
MORE!

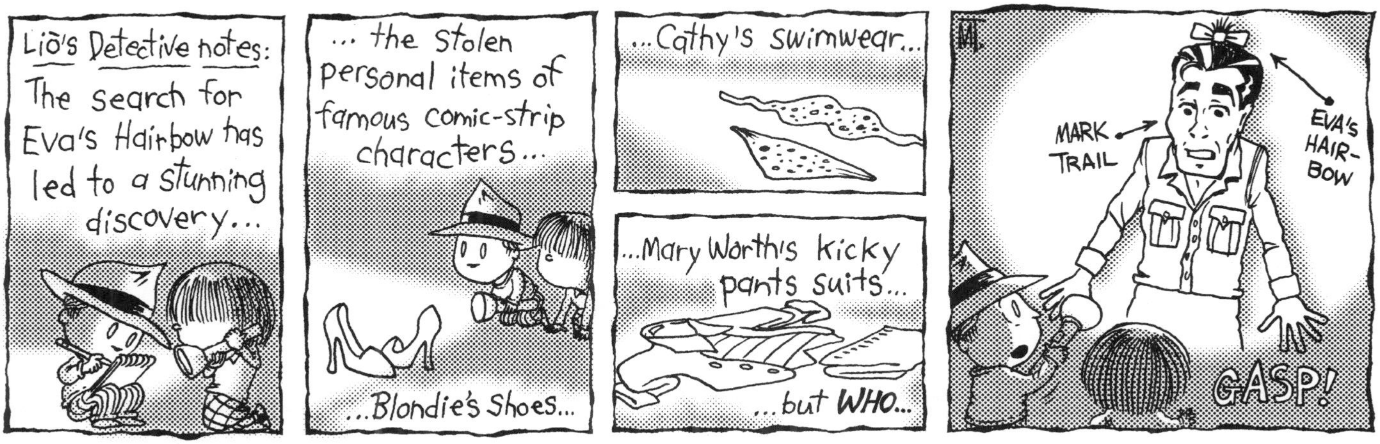
Liō's Detective notes:
The search for Eva's Hairbow has led to a stunning discovery...
... the stolen personal items of famous comic-strip characters...
...Blondie's Shoes...
...Cathy's swimwear...
...Mary Worth's kicky pants suits...
...but WHO...
MT.
MARK TRAIL
EVA'S HAIR-BOW
GASP!

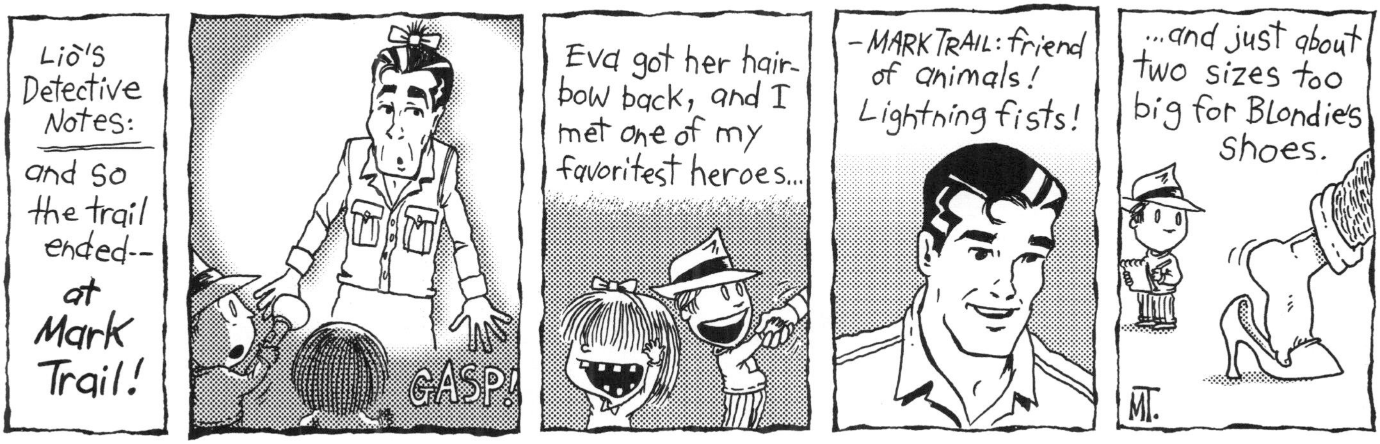
Liō's Detective Notes:
and so the trail ended-- at Mark Trail!
GASP!
Eva got her hair-bow back, and I met one of my favoritest heroes...
-MARK TRAIL: friend of animals! Lightning fists!
...and just about two sizes too big for Blondie's shoes.
MT.

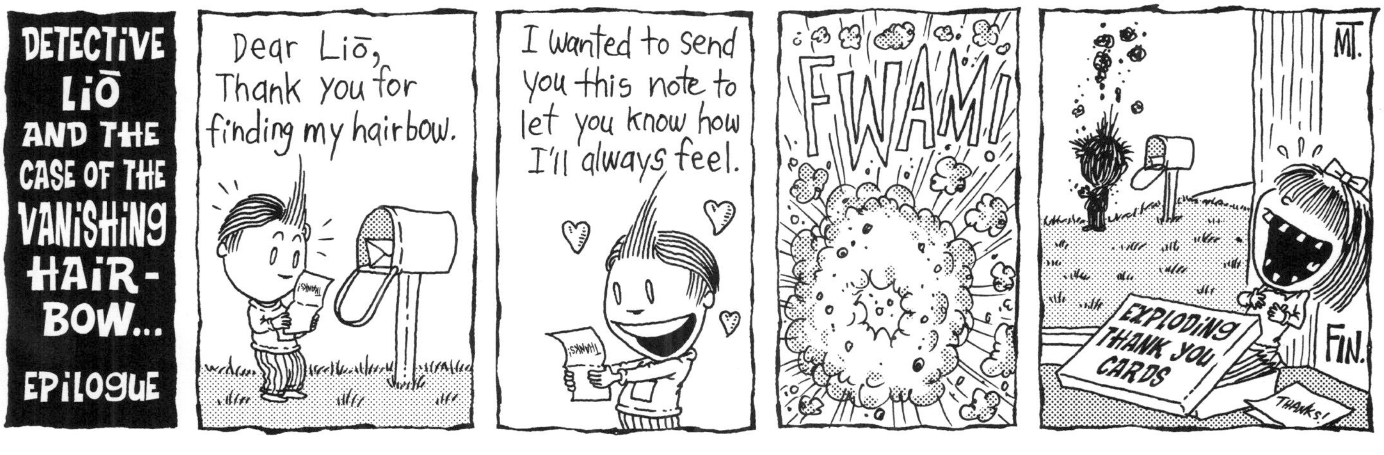
DETECTIVE LIŌ AND THE CASE OF THE VANISHING HAIR-BOW... EPILOGUE
Dear Liō,
Thank you for finding my hairbow.
I wanted to send you this note to let you know how I'll always feel.
FWAM!
MT.
EXPLODING THANK YOU CARDS
THANKS!
FIN.

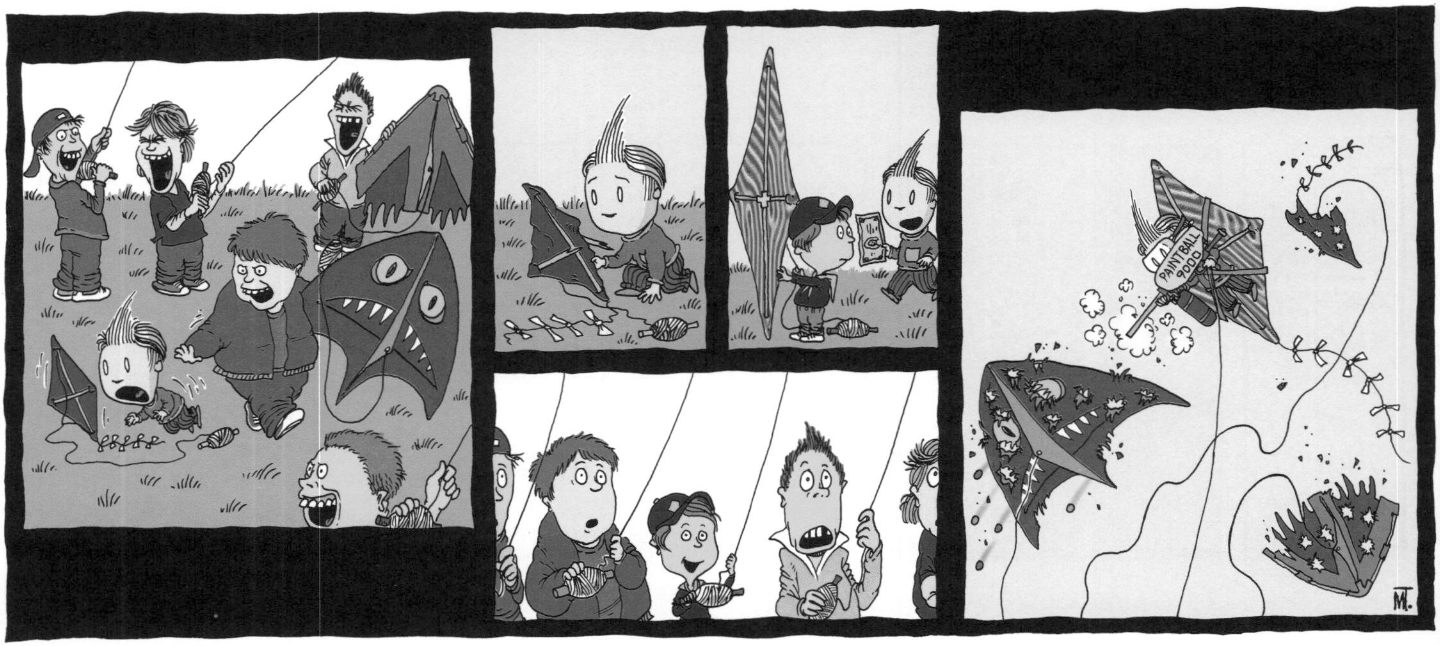
PAINTBALL
9000

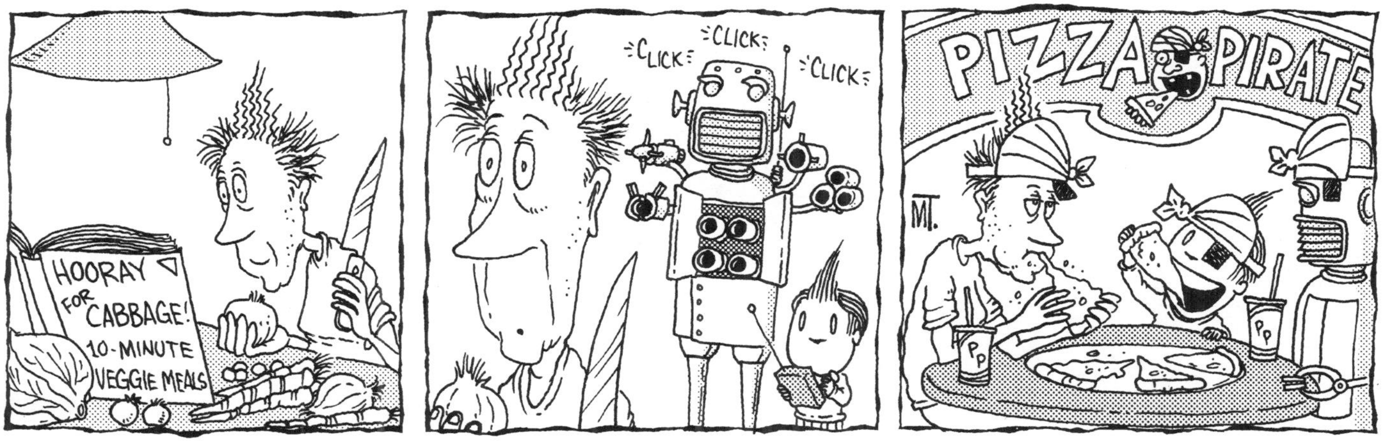
HOORAY FOR CABBAGE!
10-MINUTE VEGGIE MEALS
CLICK
CLICK
CLICK
PIZZA PIRATE
MT.

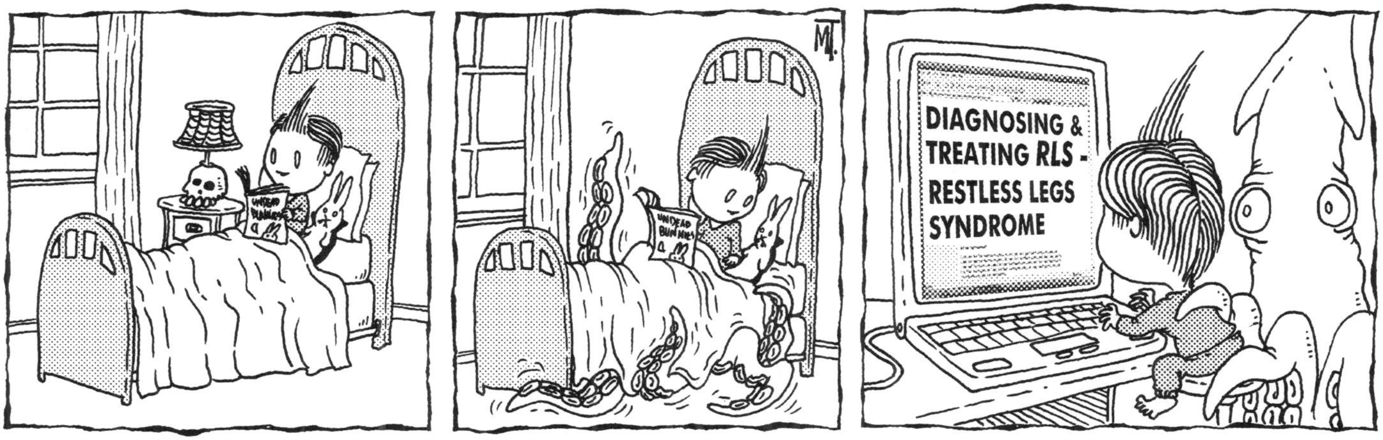
MT.
DIAGNOSING & TREATING RLS - RESTLESS LEGS SYNDROME

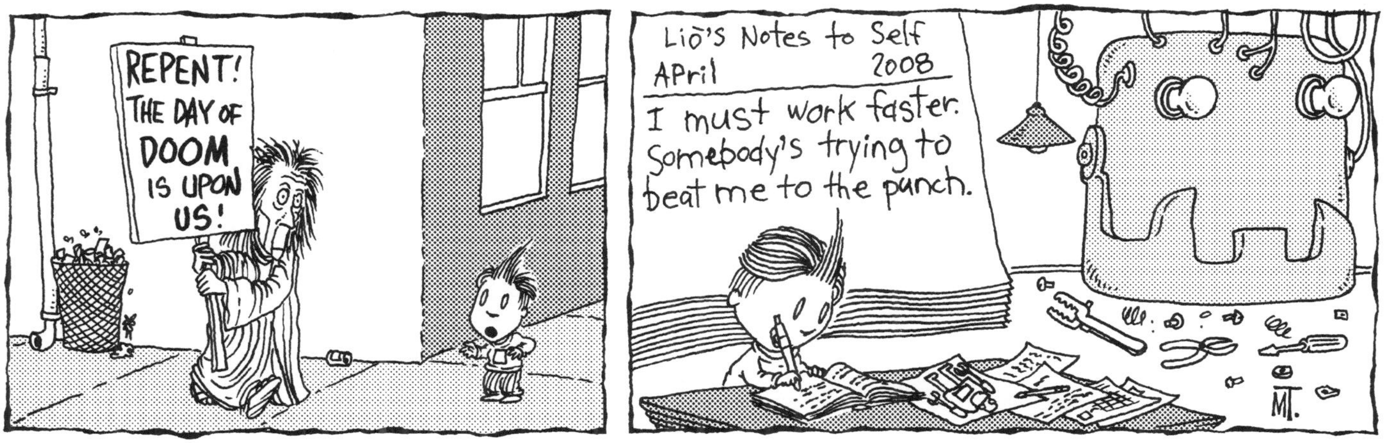
REPENT! THE DAY OF DOOM IS UPON US!
Lio's Notes to Self
April 2008
I must work faster. Somebody's trying to beat me to the punch.
MT.

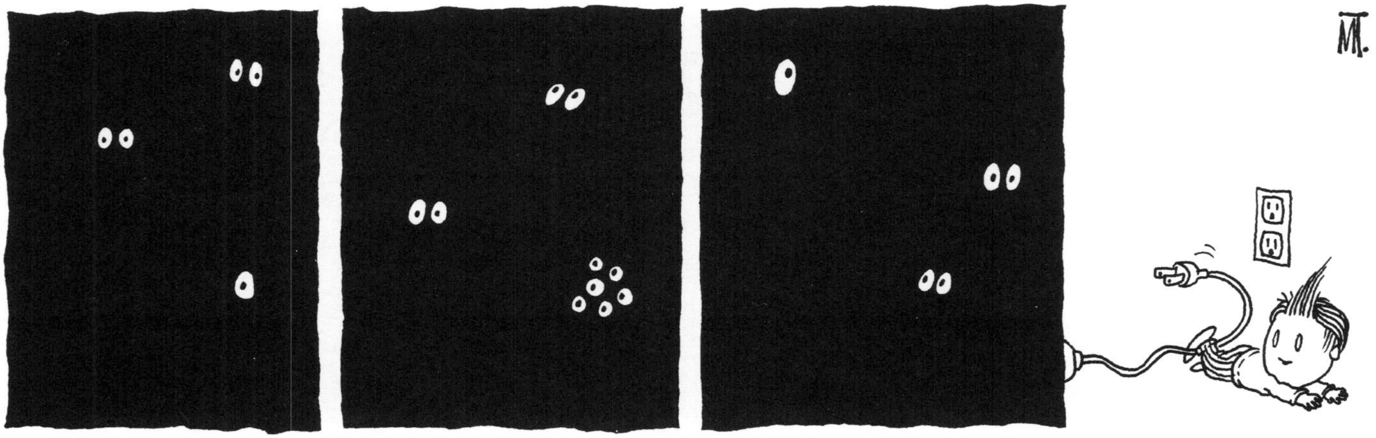

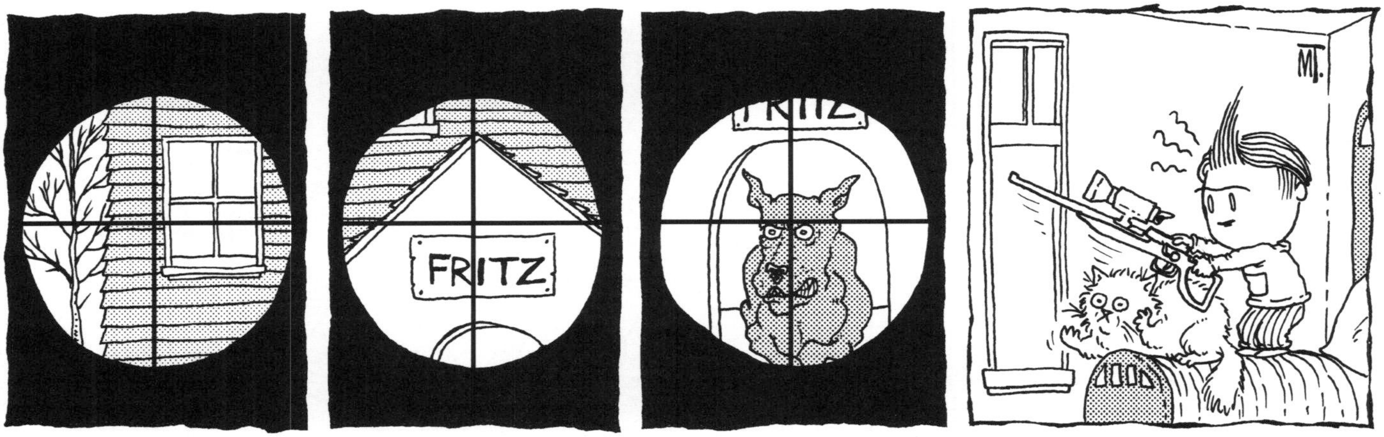
FRITZ
FRITZ

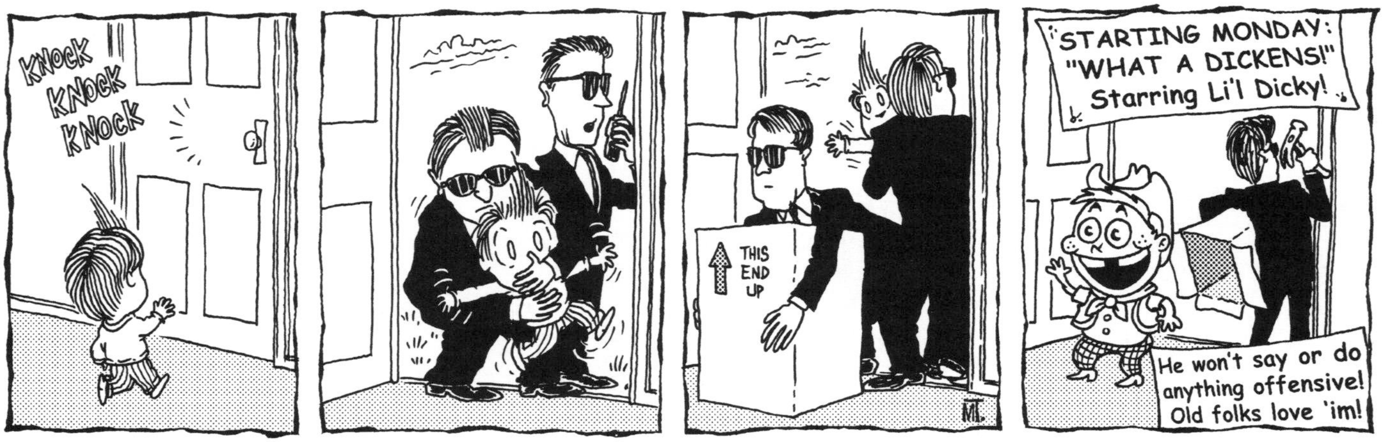
KNOCK KNOCK KNOCK
THIS END UP
STARTING MONDAY: "WHAT A DICKENS!" Starring Li'l Dicky!
He won't say or do anything offensive! Old folks love 'im!

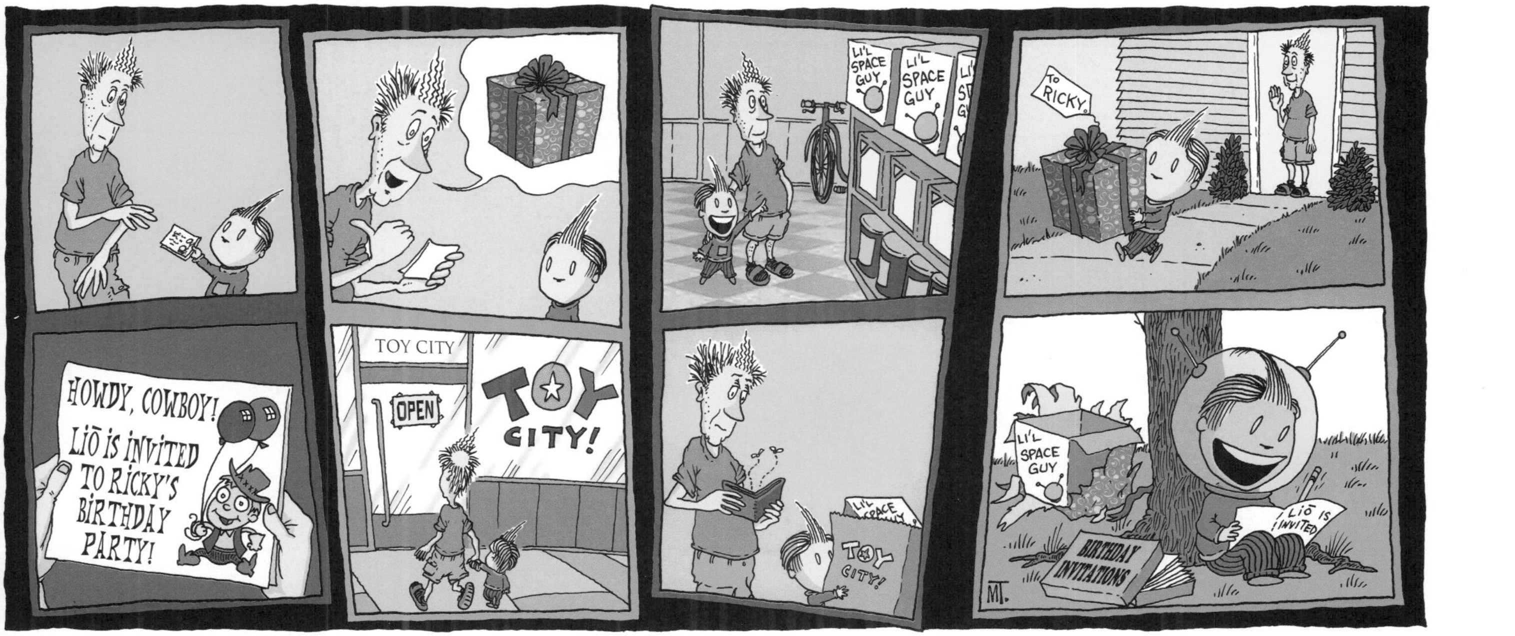
HOWDY, COWBOY!
LIŌ IS INVITED TO RICKY'S BIRTHDAY PARTY!
TOY CITY
OPEN
TOY CITY!
LI'L SPACE GUY
LI'L SPACE GUY
TOY CITY!
TO RICKY.
LI'L SPACE GUY
LIŌ IS INVITED
BIRTHDAY INVITATIONS

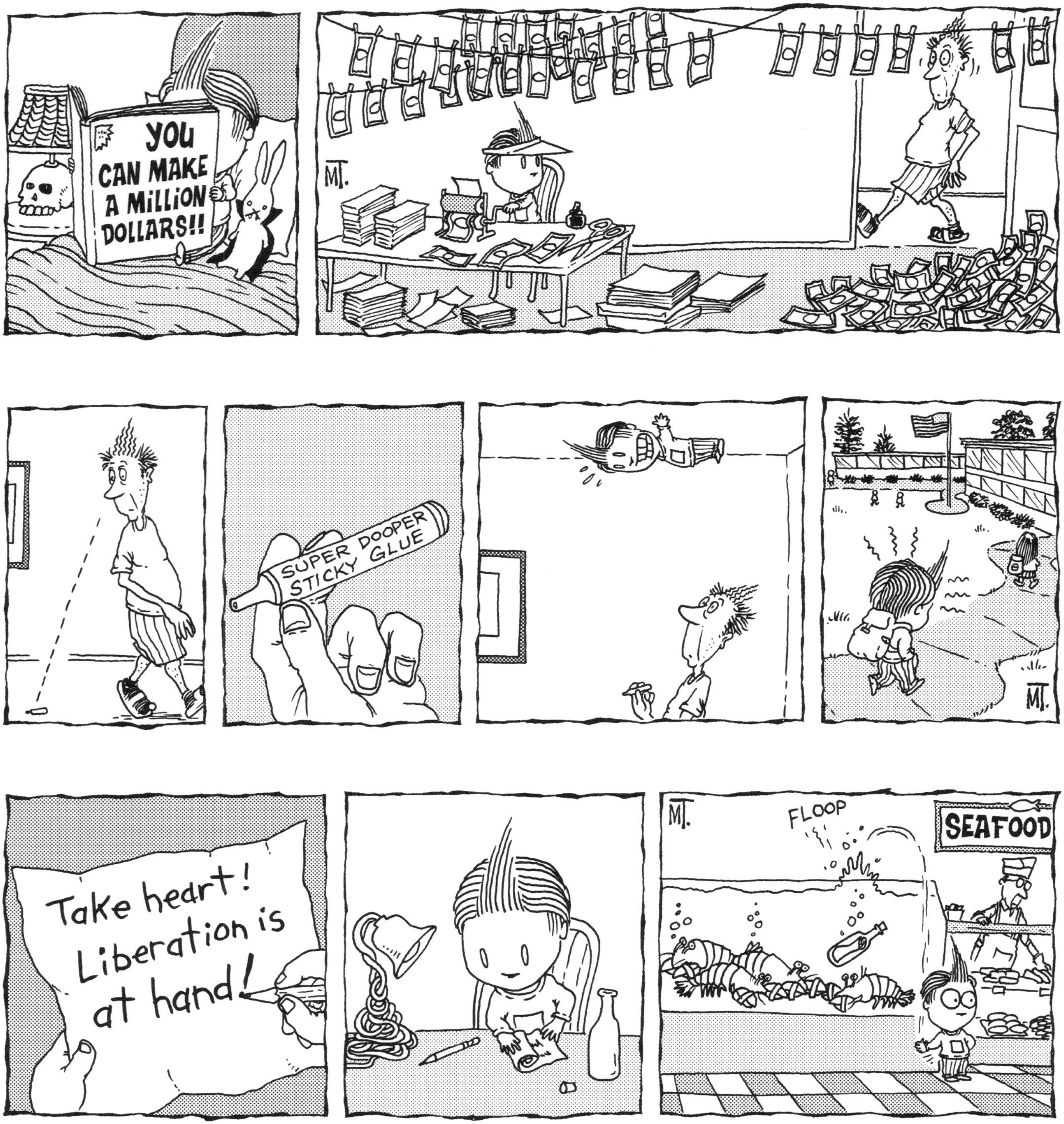
YOU CAN MAKE A MILLION DOLLARS!!
MT.
SUPER DOOPER STICKY GLUE
MT.
Take heart! Liberation is at hand!
MT.
FLOOP
SEAFOOD

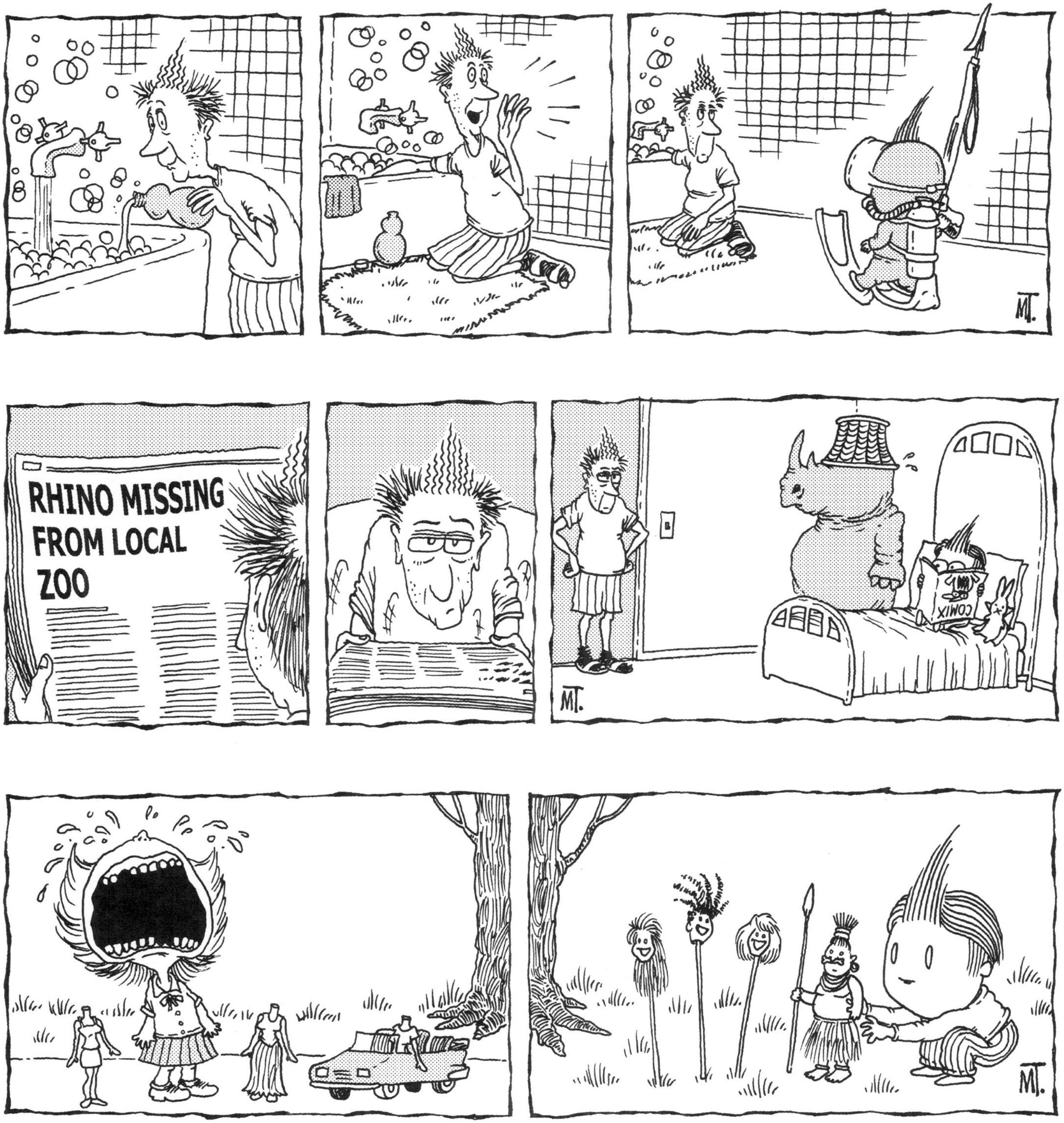
MT.
RHINO MISSING
FROM LOCAL
ZOO
COMIX
MT.
MT.

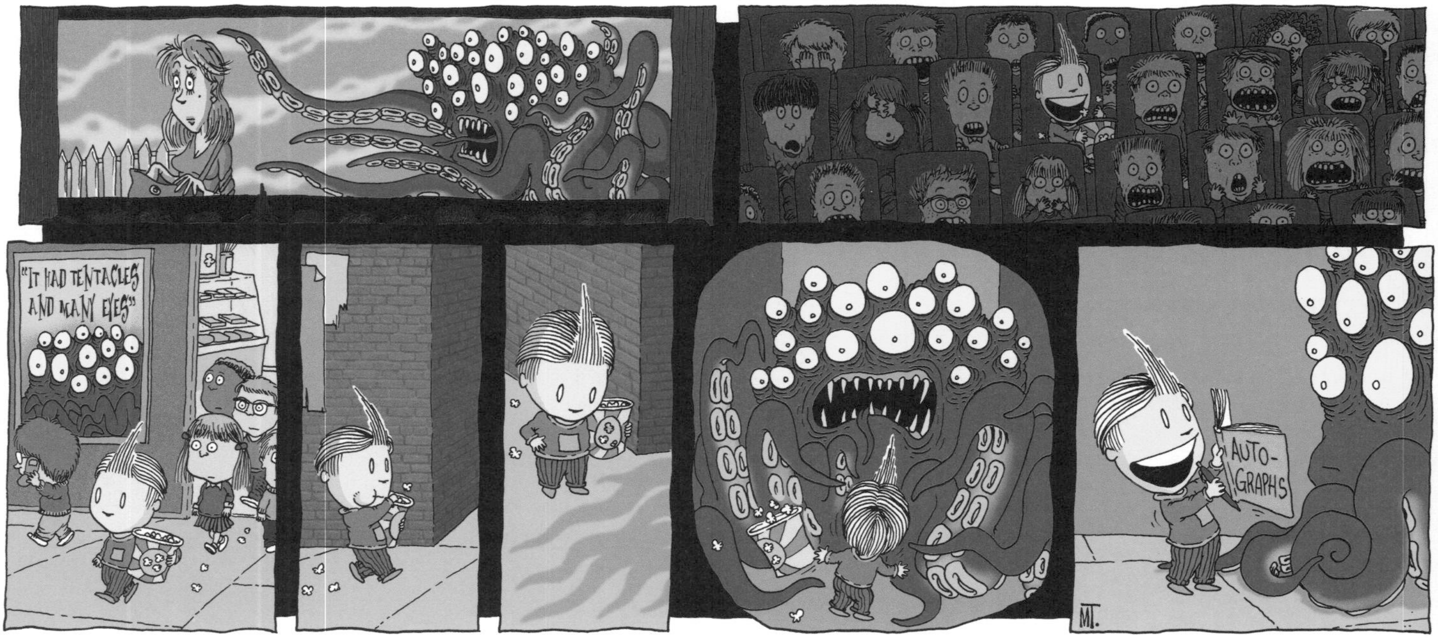
"IT HAD TENTACLES
AND MANY EYES"
AUTO-
GRAPHS
MT.

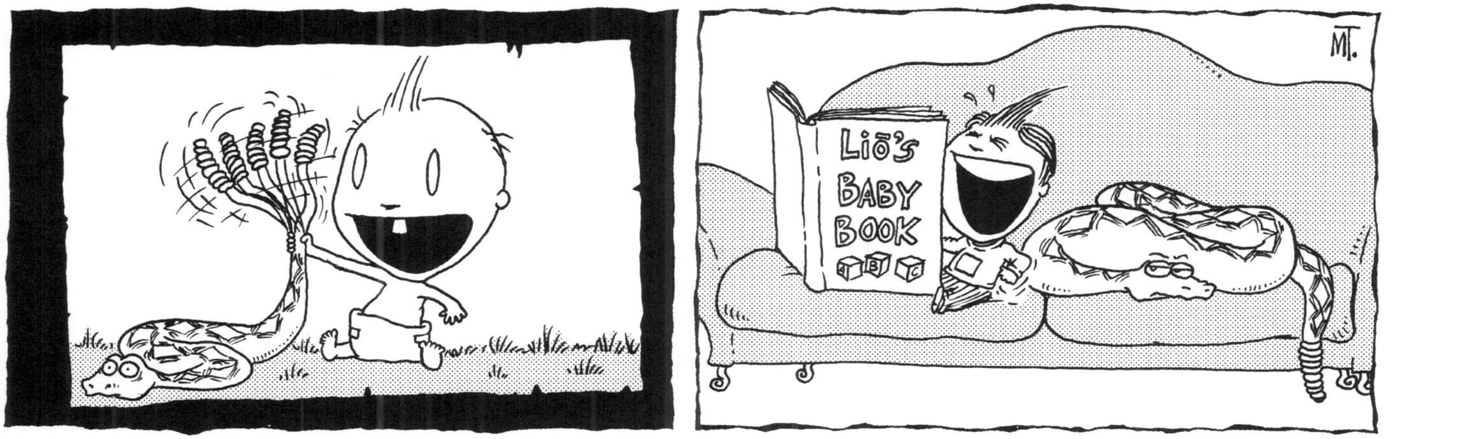
MT.
LIŌ'S
BABY
BOOK
A B C

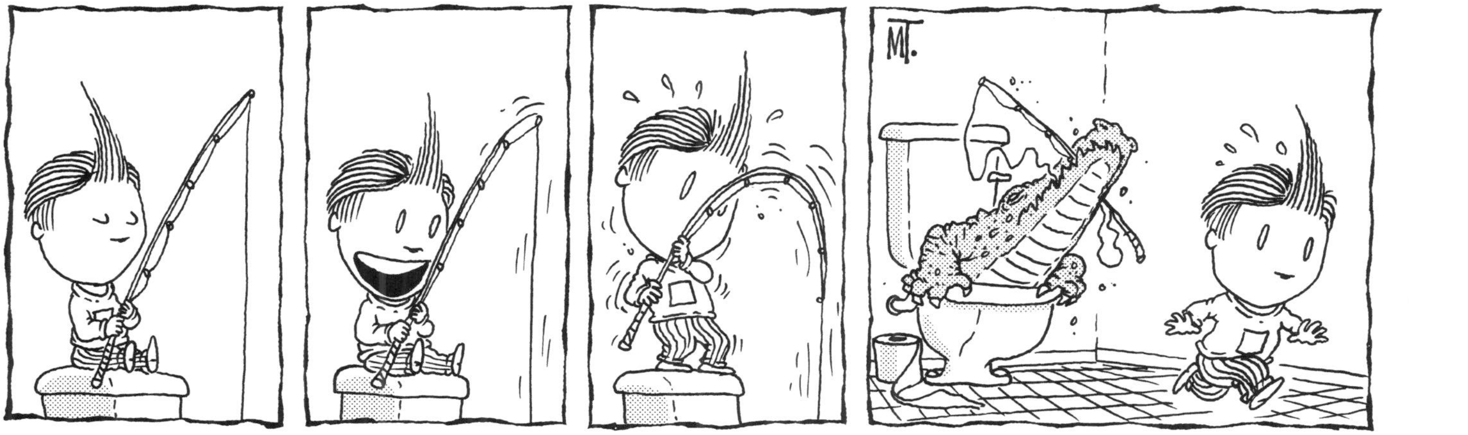
MT.

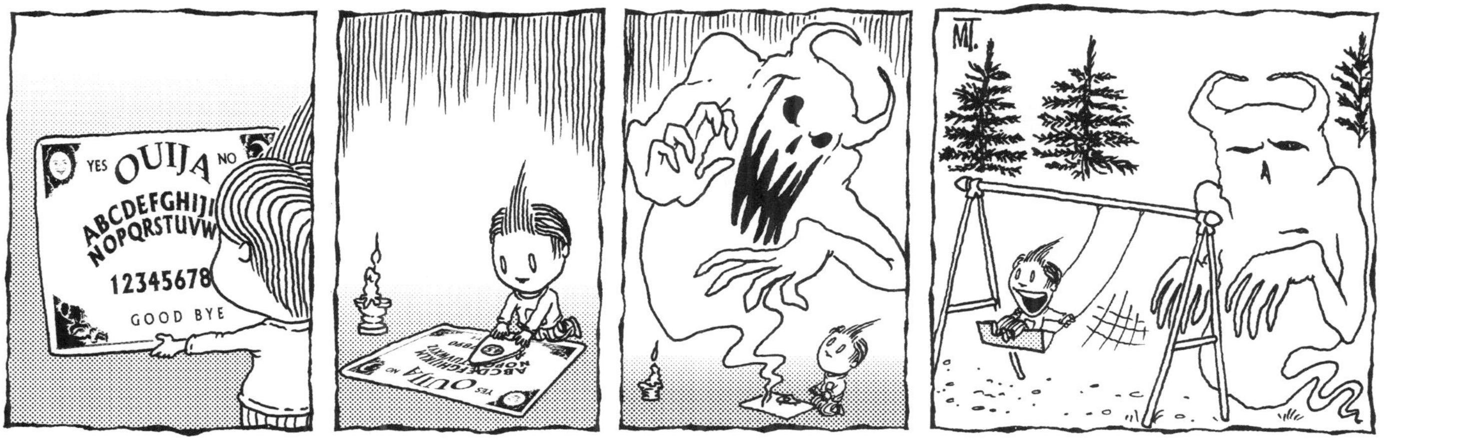
YES OUIJA NO
ABCDEFGHIJ
NOPQRSTUVW
12345678
GOOD BYE
MT.

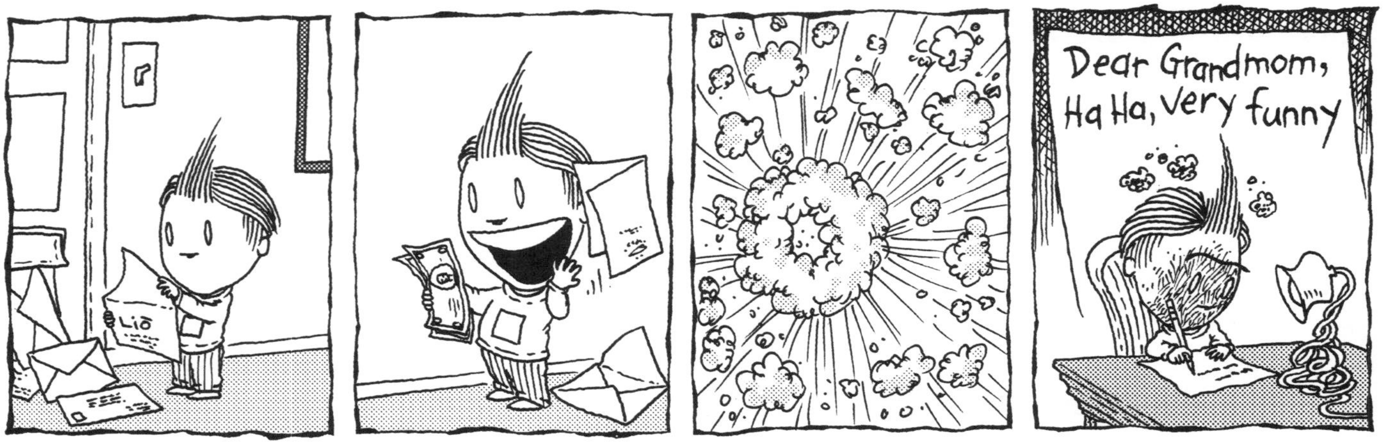
Dear Grandmom,
Ha Ha, very funny

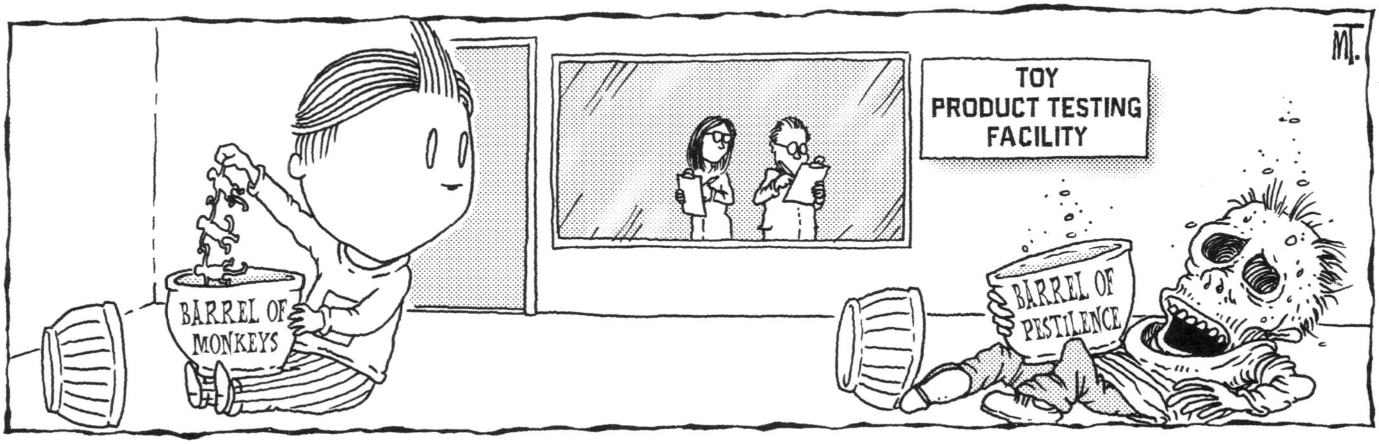
MT.
TOY PRODUCT TESTING FACILITY
BARREL OF MONKEYS
BARREL OF PESTILENCE

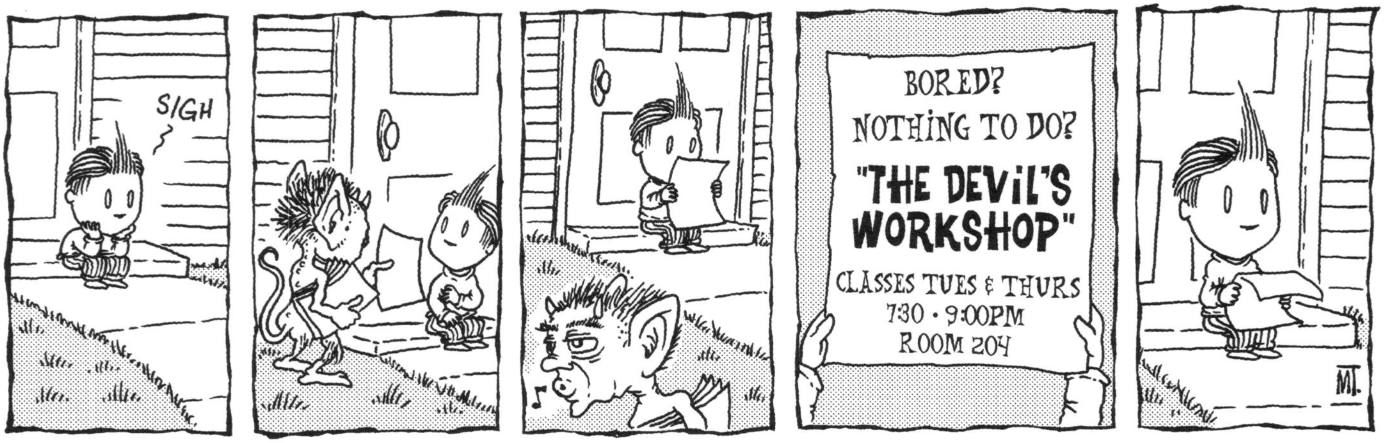
SIGH
BORED?
NOTHING TO DO?
"THE DEVIL'S WORKSHOP"
CLASSES TUES & THURS
7:30 - 9:00PM
ROOM 204
MT.

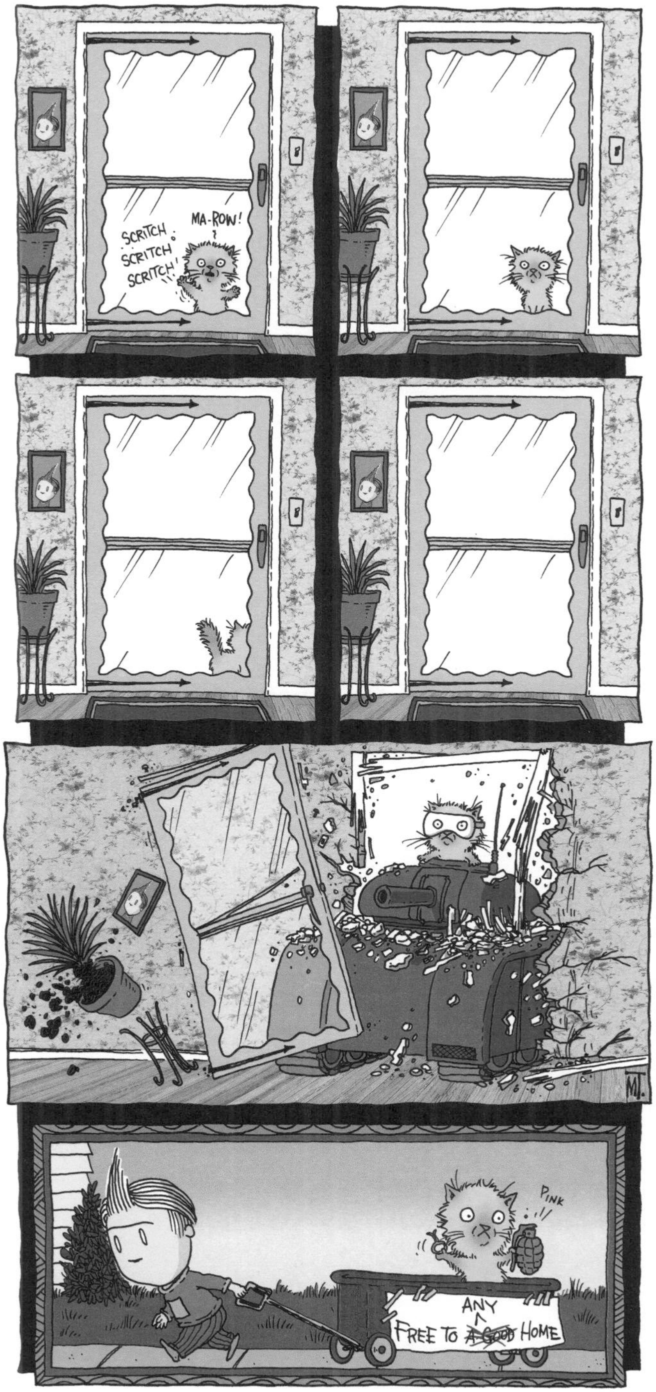
SCRITCH
SCRITCH
SCRITCH!
MA-ROW!
MJ.
PINK
FREE TO ~~A GOOD~~ ANY HOME

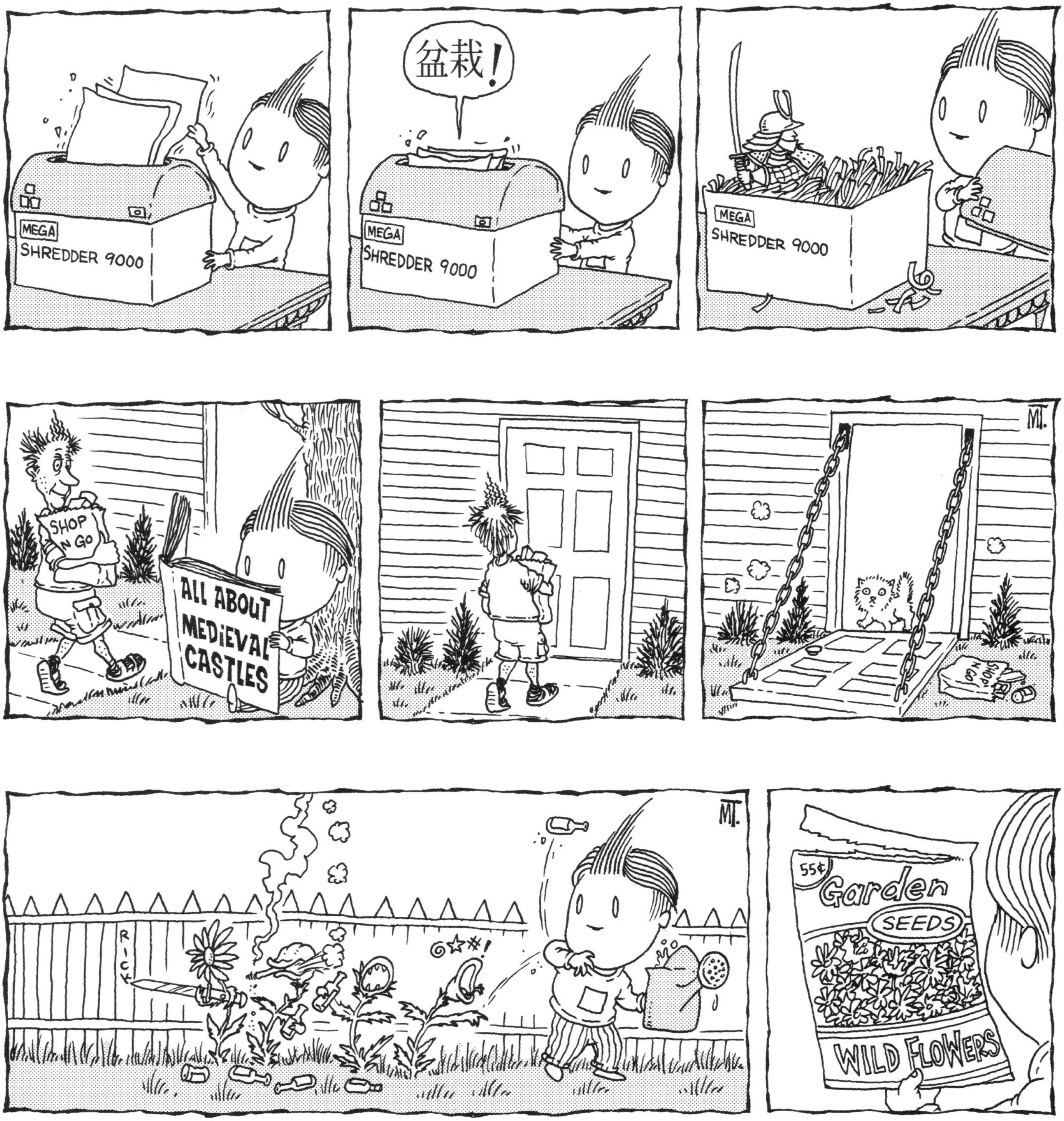
MEGA
SHREDDER 9000
盆栽!
MEGA
SHREDDER 9000
MEGA
SHREDDER 9000
SHOP N GO
ALL ABOUT MEDIEVAL CASTLES
MT.
SHOP N GO
RICK
MT.
55¢
Garden
SEEDS
WILD FLOWERS

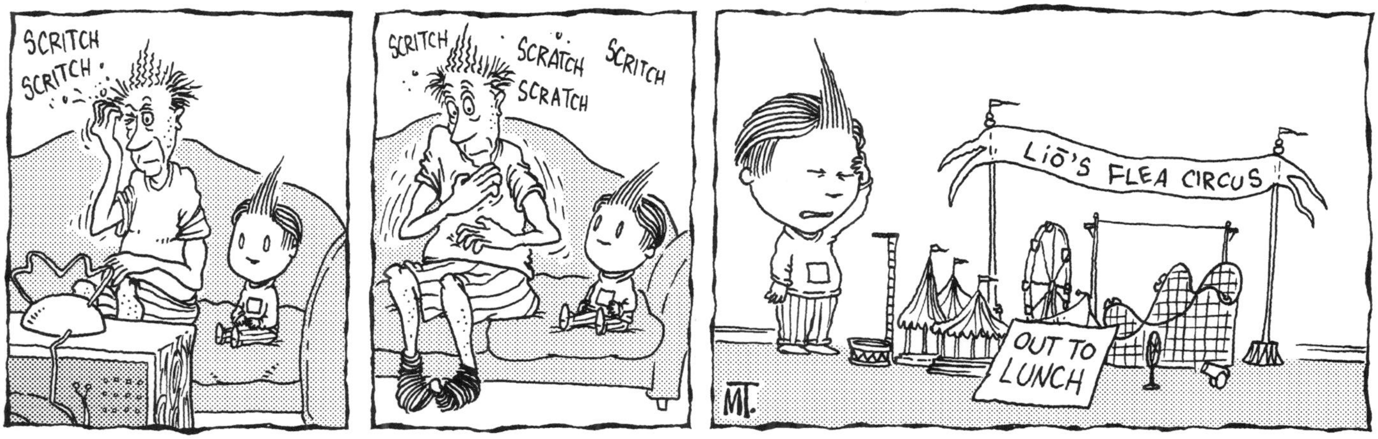
SCRITCH
SCRITCH
SCRITCH
SCRATCH
SCRITCH
SCRATCH
LIŌ'S FLEA CIRCUS
OUT TO LUNCH

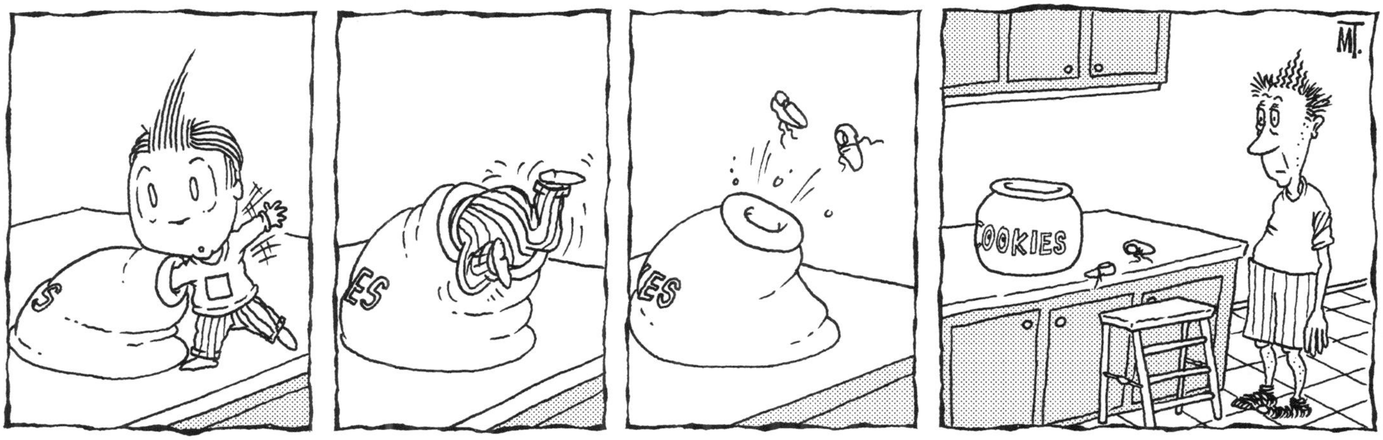
S
ES
ES
OOKIES

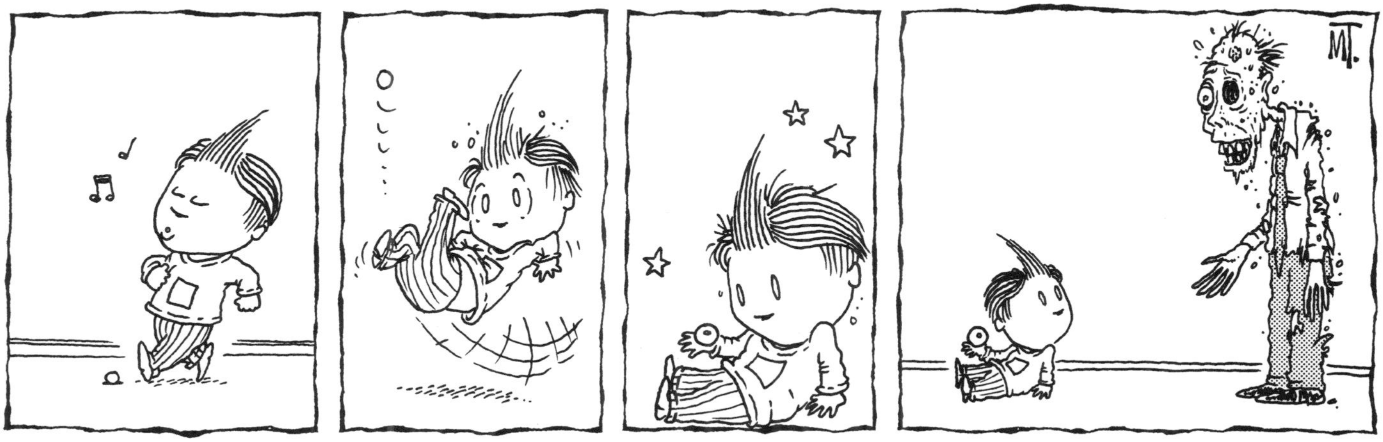

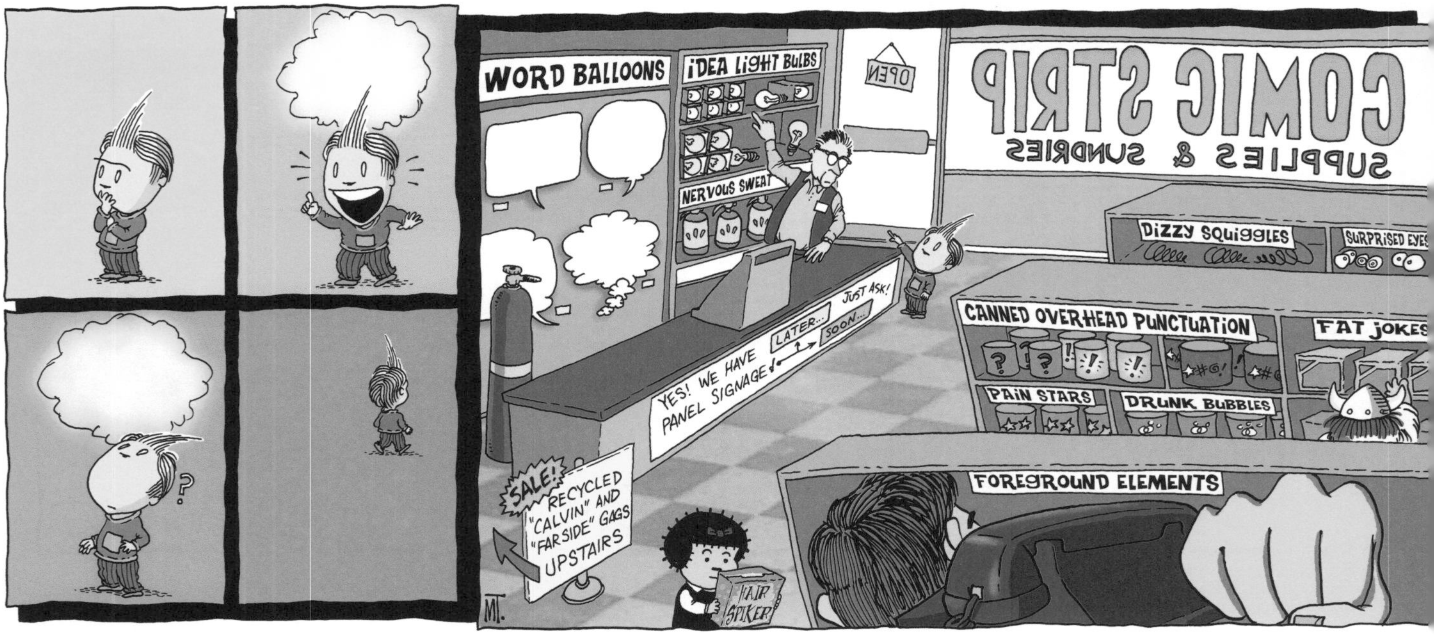
WORD BALLOONS
IDEA LIGHT BULBS
NERVOUS SWEAT
OPEN
COMIC STRIP
SUPPLIES & SUNDRIES
DIZZY SQUIGGLES
SURPRISED EYES
YES! WE HAVE PANEL SIGNAGE!
LATER...
SOON...
JUST ASK!
CANNED OVERHEAD PUNCTUATION
FAT JOKES
PAIN STARS
DRUNK BUBBLES
SALE!
RECYCLED "CALVIN" AND "FARSIDE" GAGS UPSTAIRS
HAIR SPIKER
FOREGROUND ELEMENTS
MT.

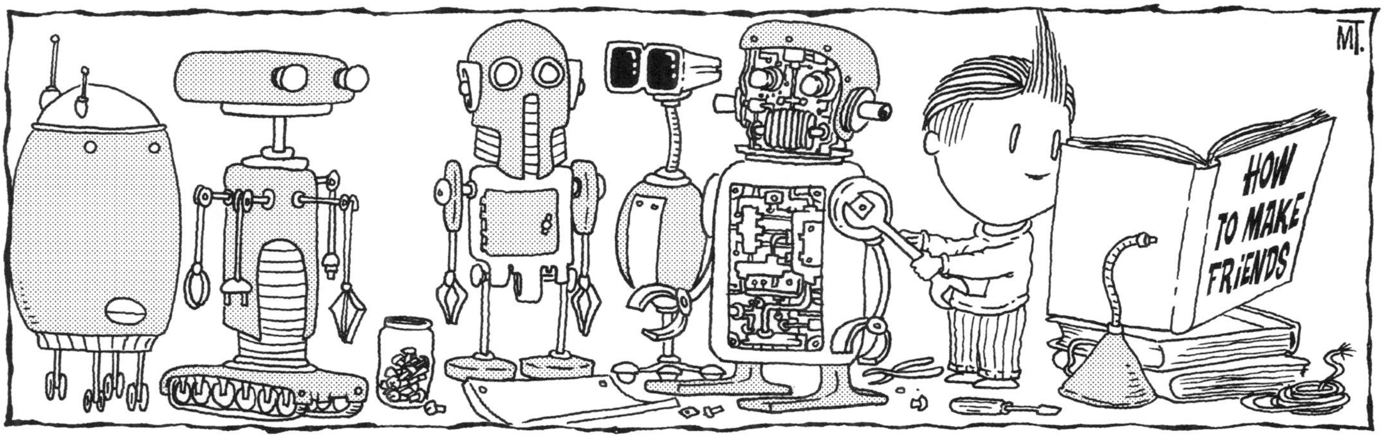
MT.
HOW TO MAKE FRIENDS

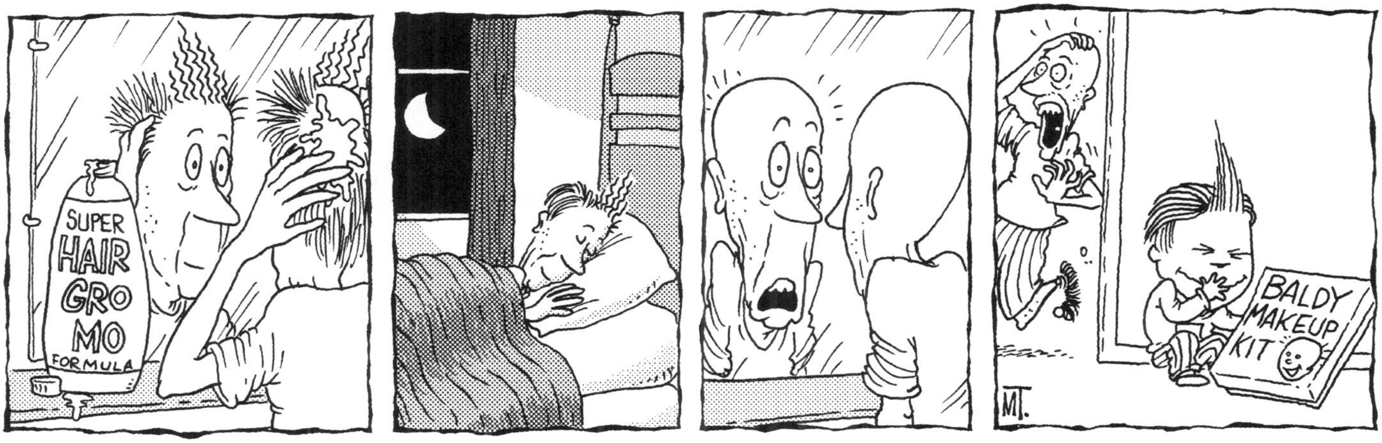
SUPER HAIR GRO MO FORMULA
BALDY MAKEUP KIT
MT.

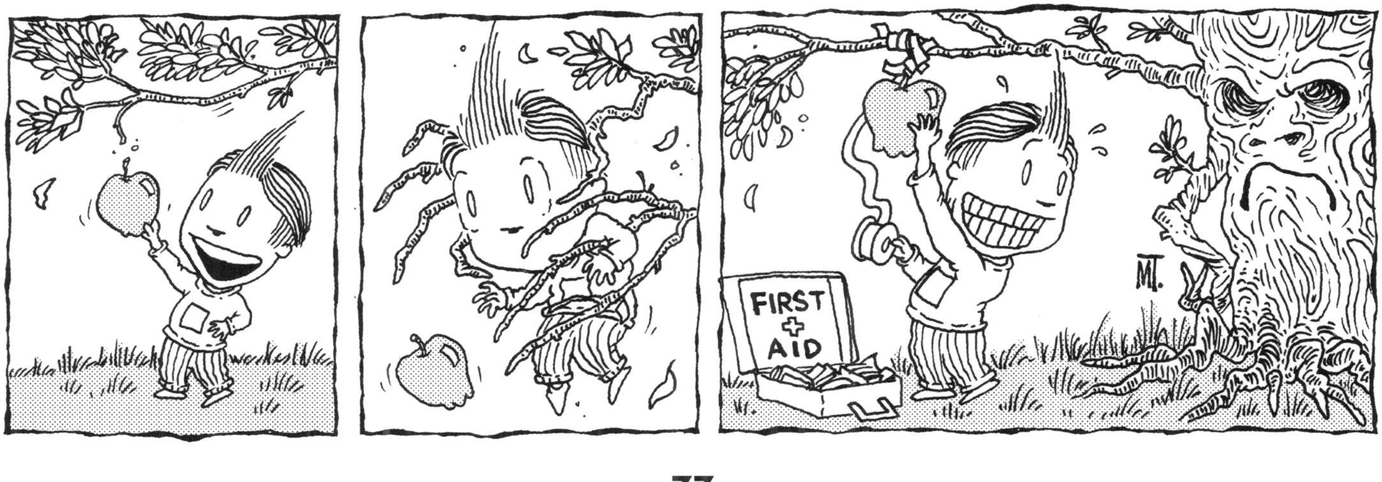
FIRST + AID
MT.

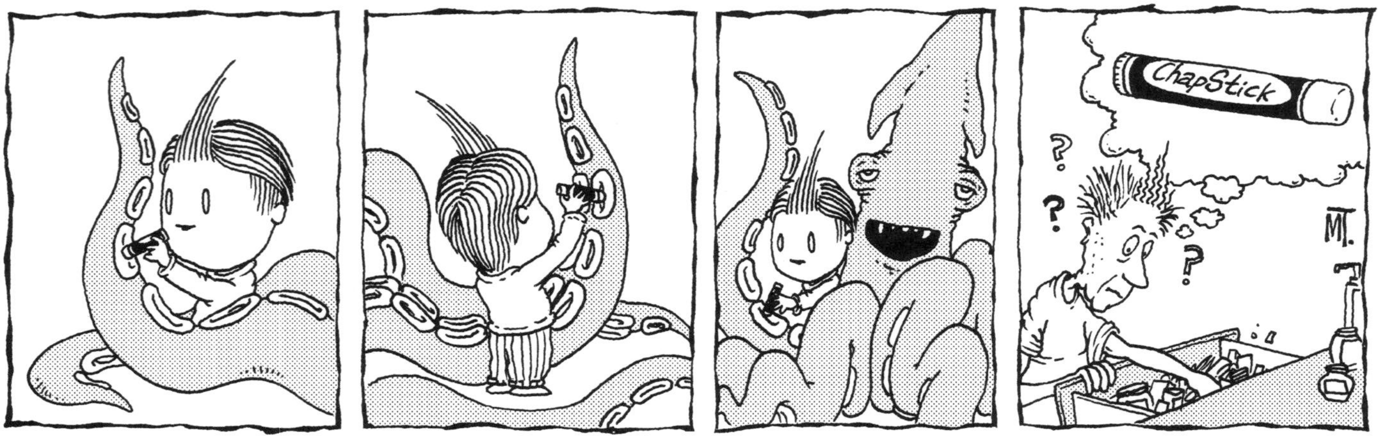
ChapStick

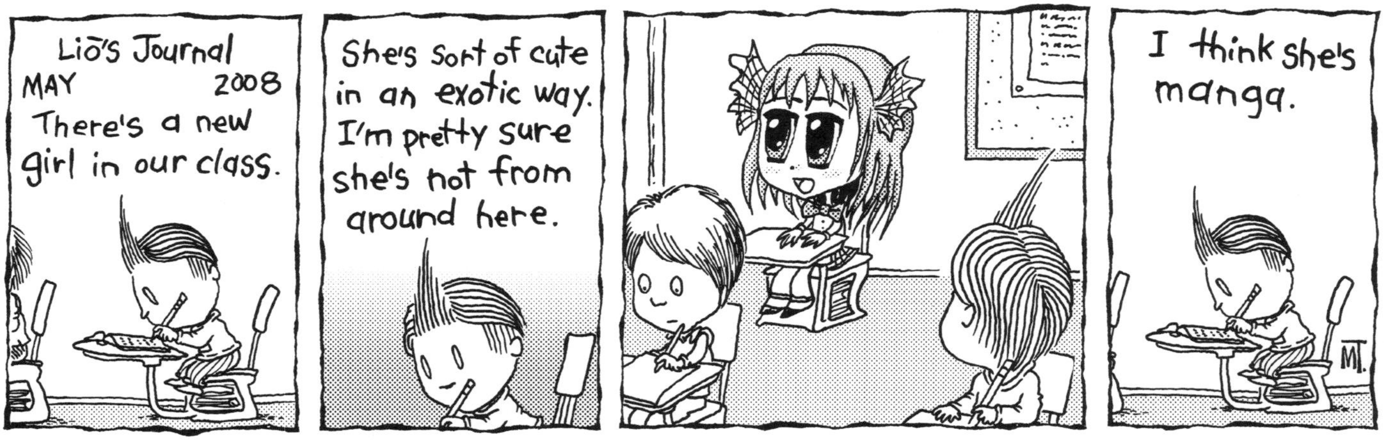
Lio's Journal
MAY 2008
There's a new girl in our class.
She's sort of cute in an exotic way. I'm pretty sure she's not from around here.
I think she's manga.

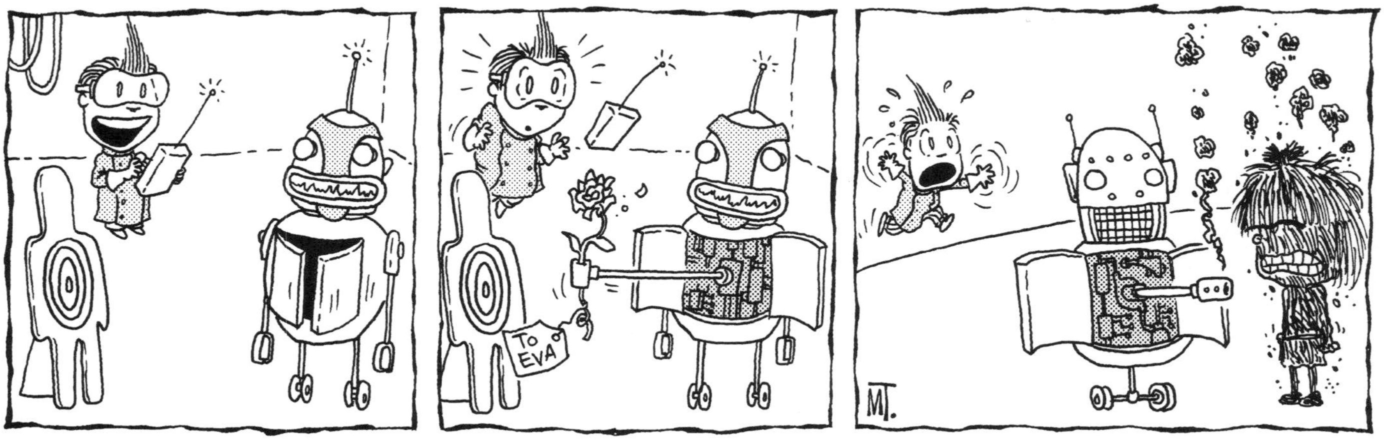
To EVA

LIŌ
SET PIECE 118
“SUNRISE” - 09B

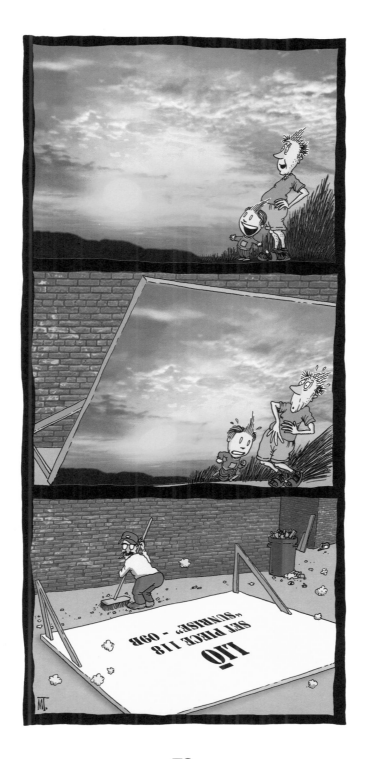

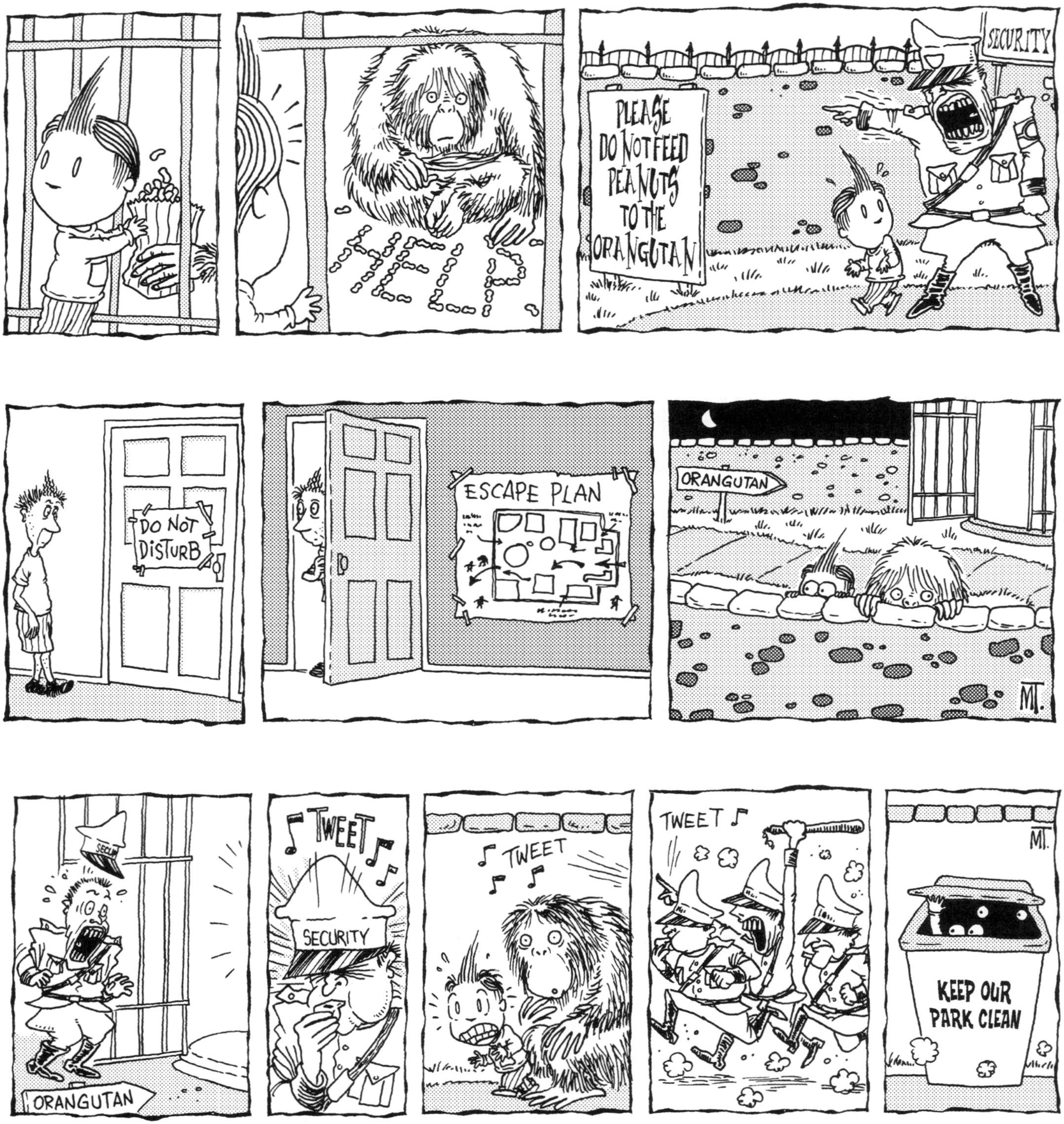
HELP
SECURITY
PLEASE DO NOT FEED PEANUTS TO THE ORANGUTAN
DO NOT DISTURB
ESCAPE PLAN
ORANGUTAN
MT.
ORANGUTAN
TWEET
SECURITY
TWEET
TWEET
MT.
KEEP OUR PARK CLEAN

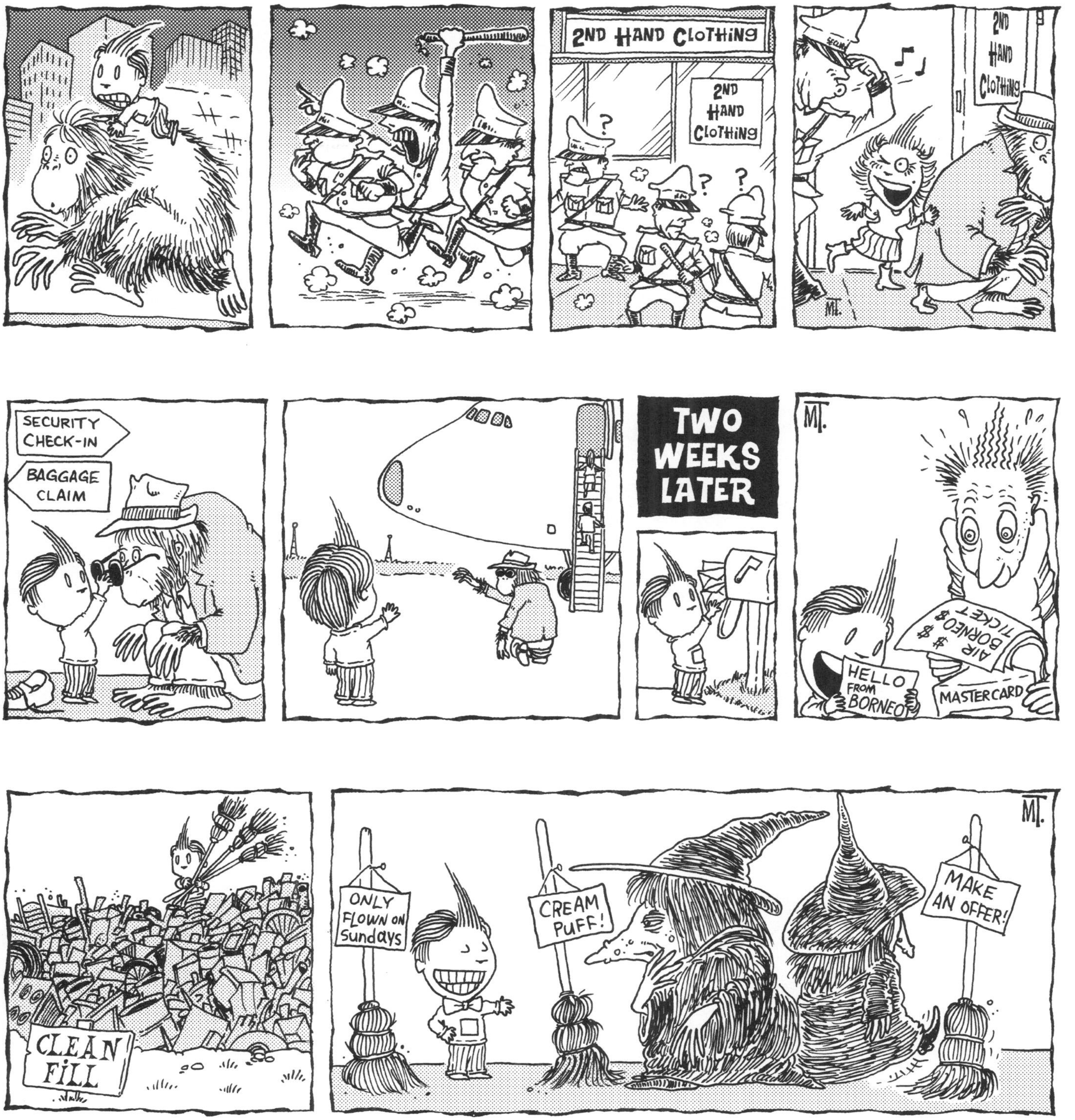
2ND HAND CLOTHING
2ND HAND CLOTHING
?
? ?
2ND HAND CLOTHING
MT.
SECURITY CHECK-IN
BAGGAGE CLAIM
TWO WEEKS LATER
MT.
AIR BORNEO $ $ TICKET
HELLO FROM BORNEO
MASTERCARD
CLEAN FILL
MT.
ONLY FLOWN ON Sundays
CREAM PUFF!
MAKE AN OFFER!

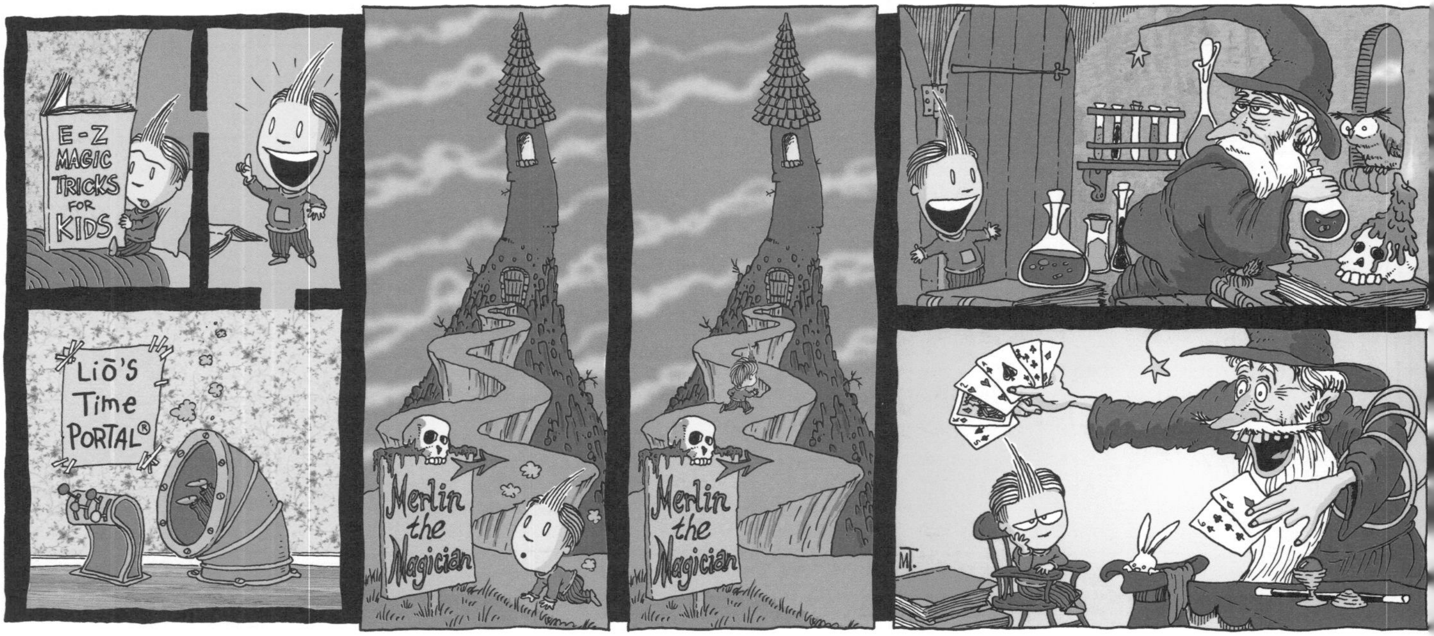
E-Z MAGIC TRICKS FOR KIDS
LIO'S Time PORTAL®
Merlin the Magician
Merlin the Magician
MT.

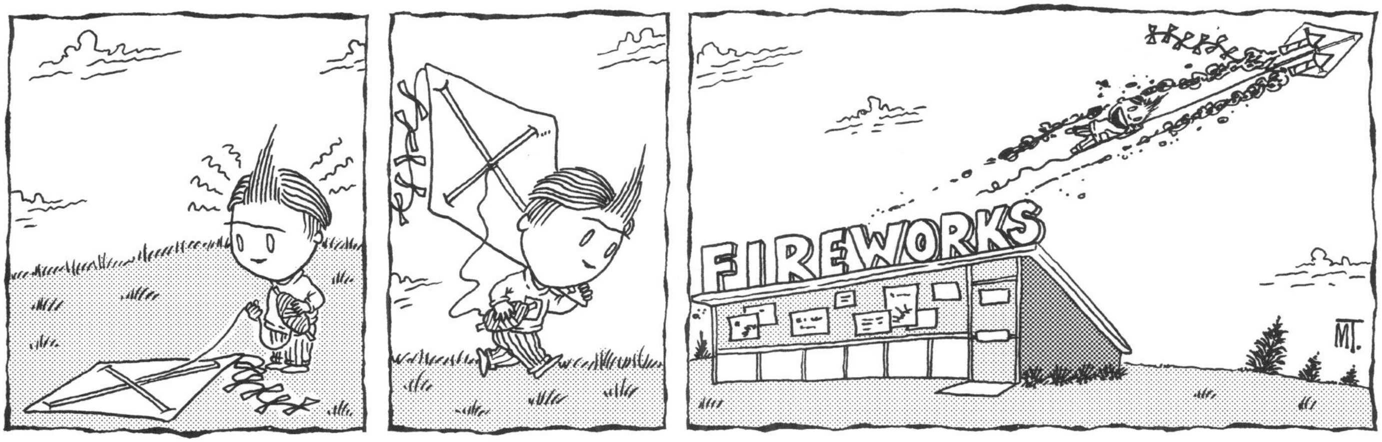
FIREWORKS

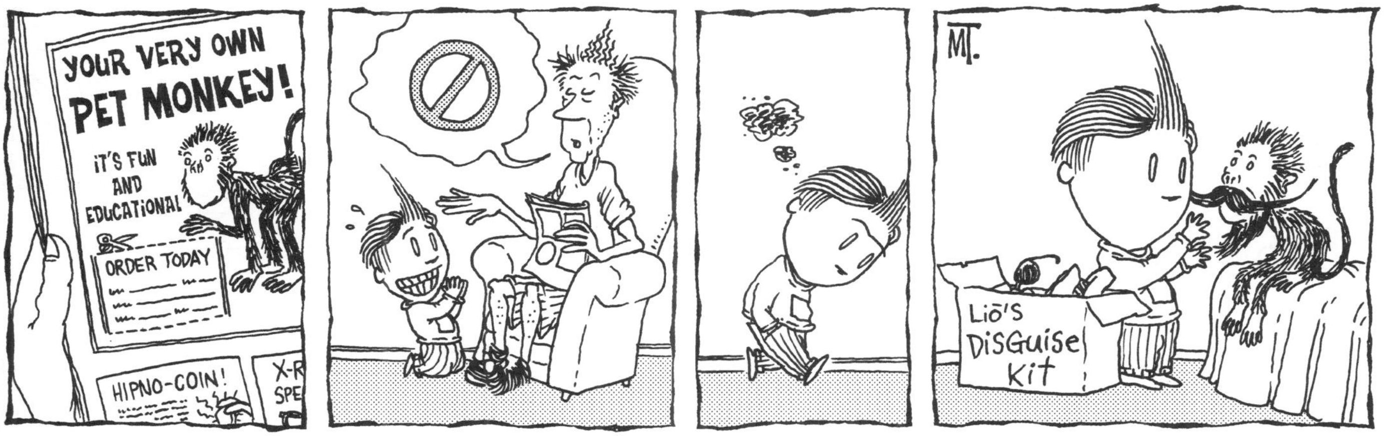
YOUR VERY OWN
PET MONKEY!
IT'S FUN AND EDUCATIONAL
ORDER TODAY
HIPNO-COIN!
LIŌ'S DISGUISE KIT

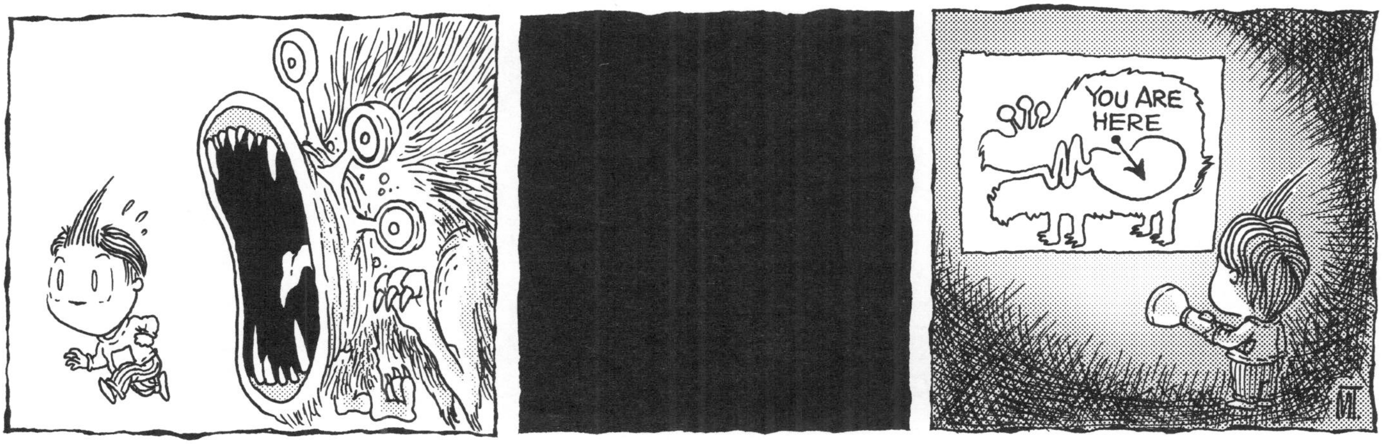
YOU ARE HERE

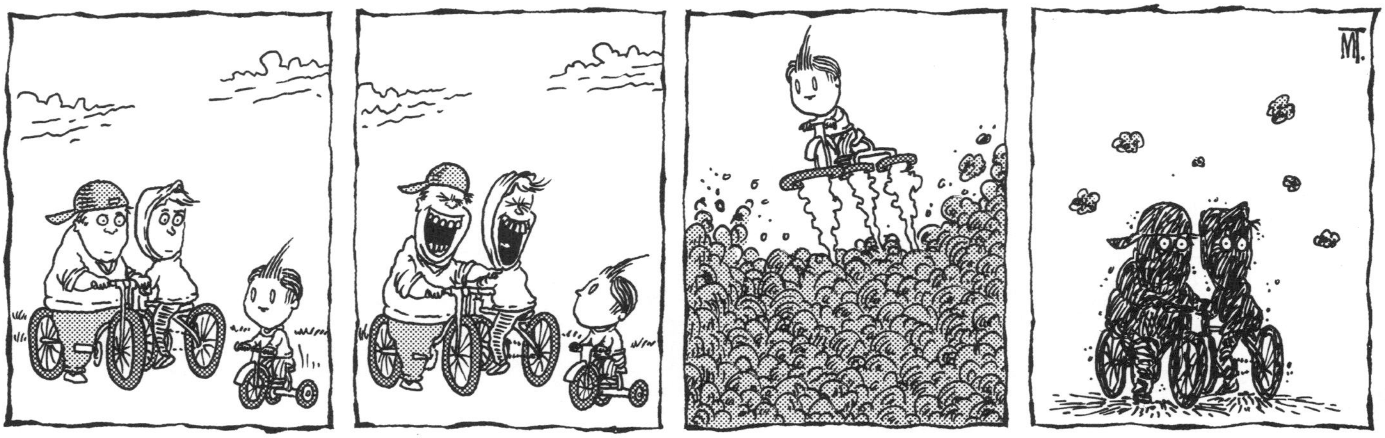

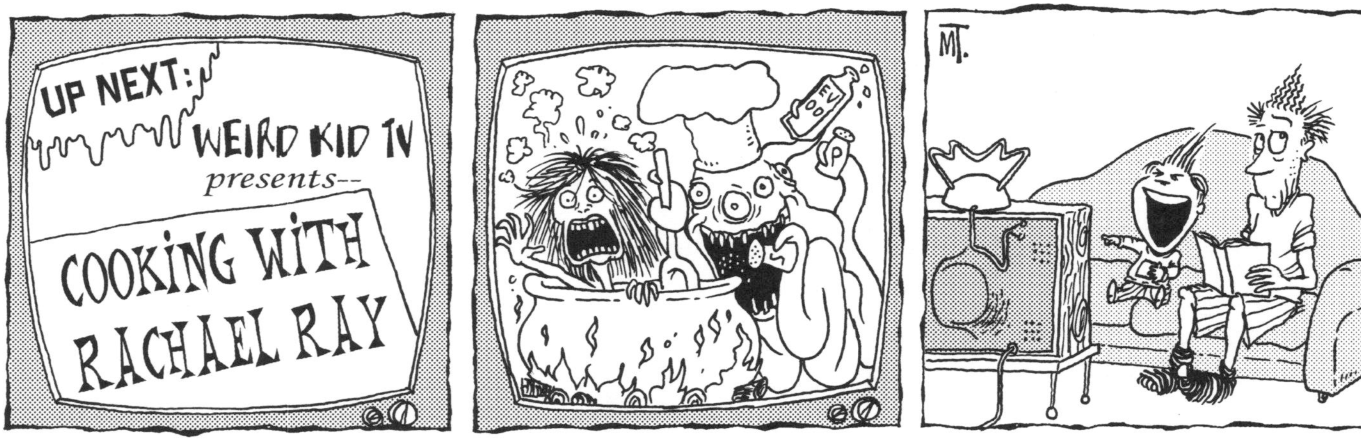
UP NEXT:
WEIRD KID TV
presents--
COOKING WITH RACHAEL RAY

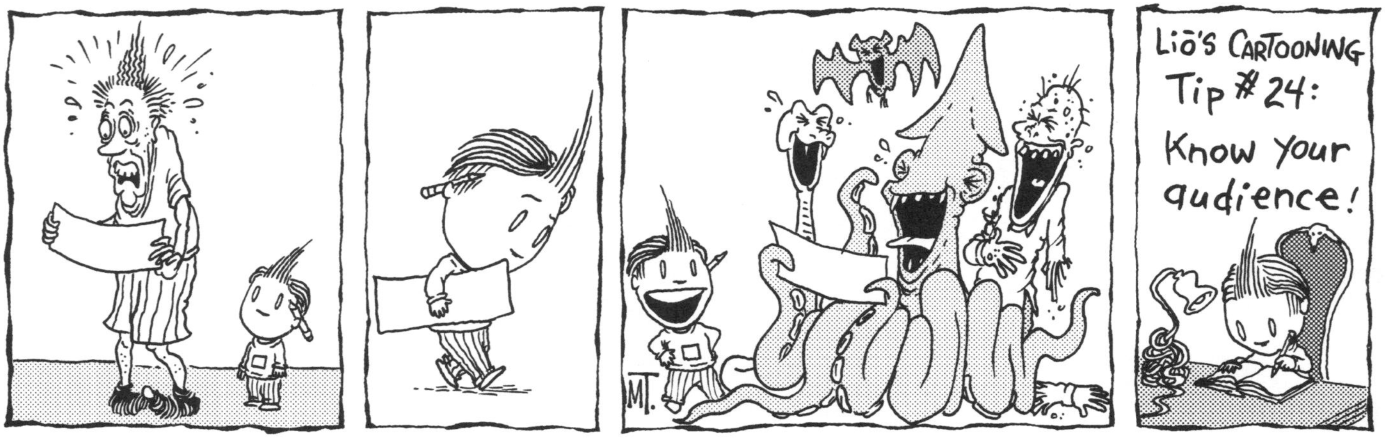
LIŌ'S CARTOONING Tip #24: Know your audience!

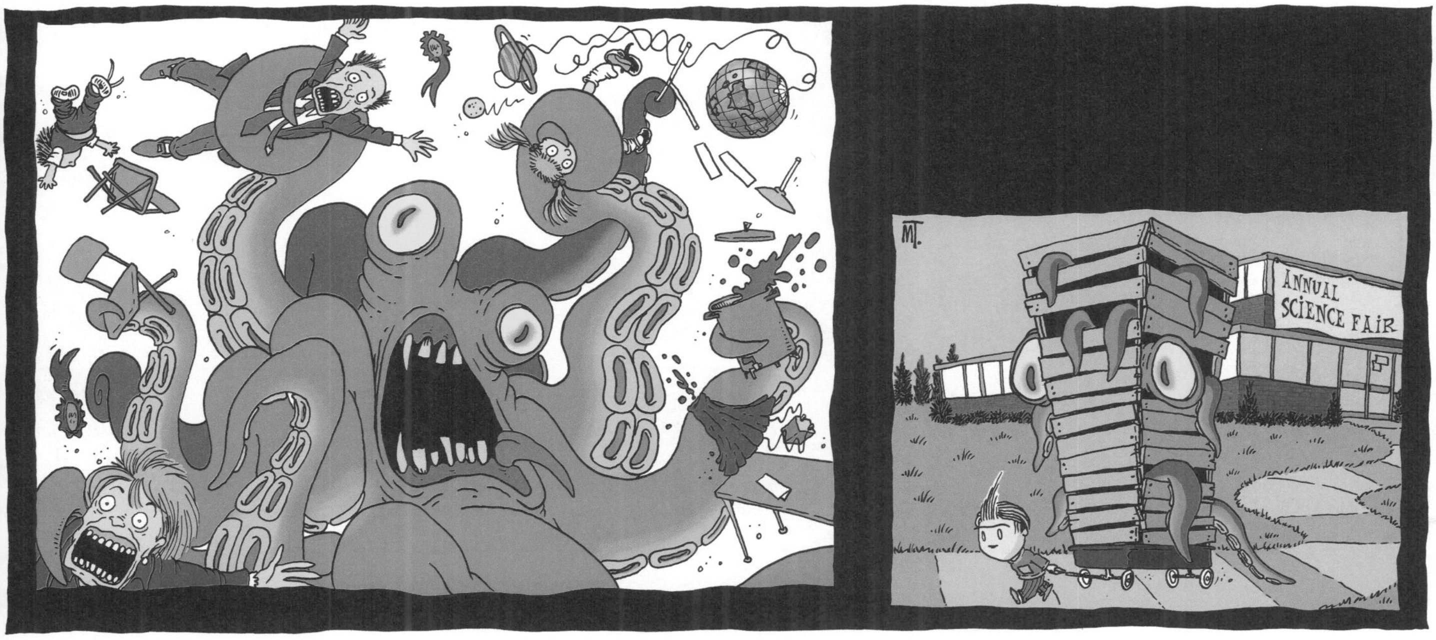
ANNUAL
SCIENCE FAIR

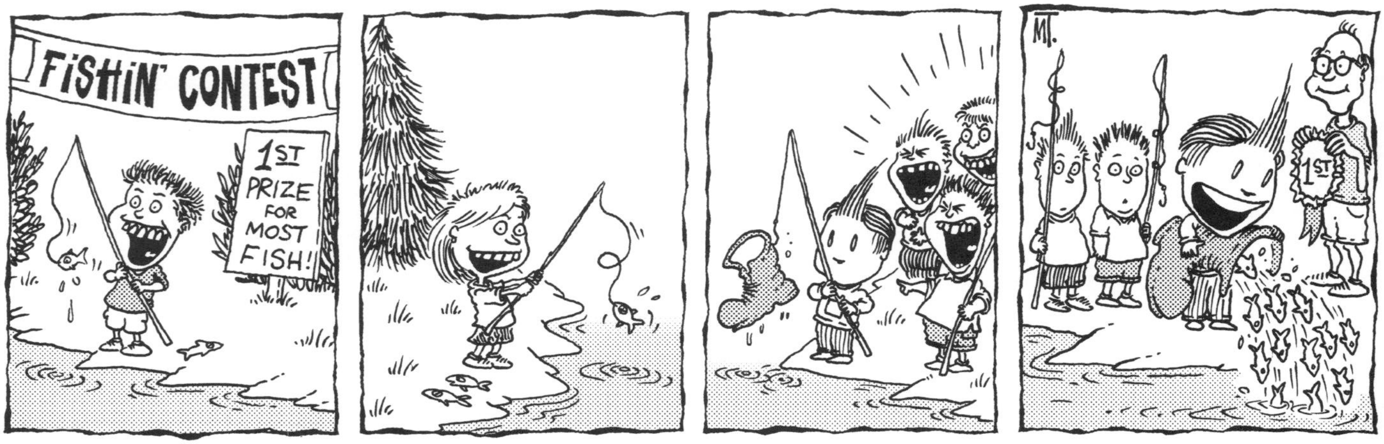
FiSHIN' CONTEST
1ST PRIZE FOR MOST FISH!
MT.
1ST

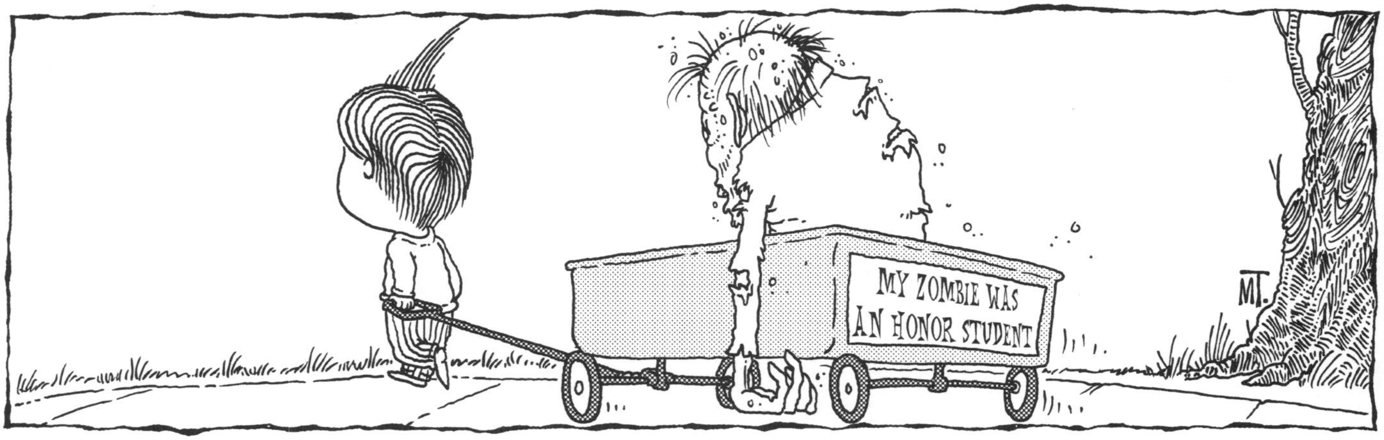
MY ZOMBIE WAS AN HONOR STUDENT
MT.

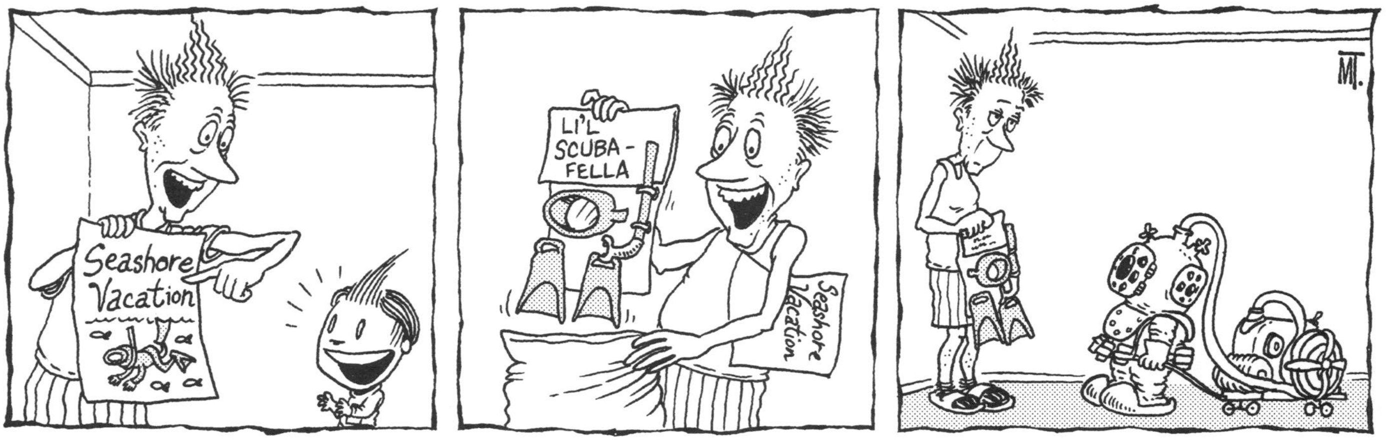
Seashore Vacation
LI'L SCUBA-FELLA
Seashore Vacation
MT.

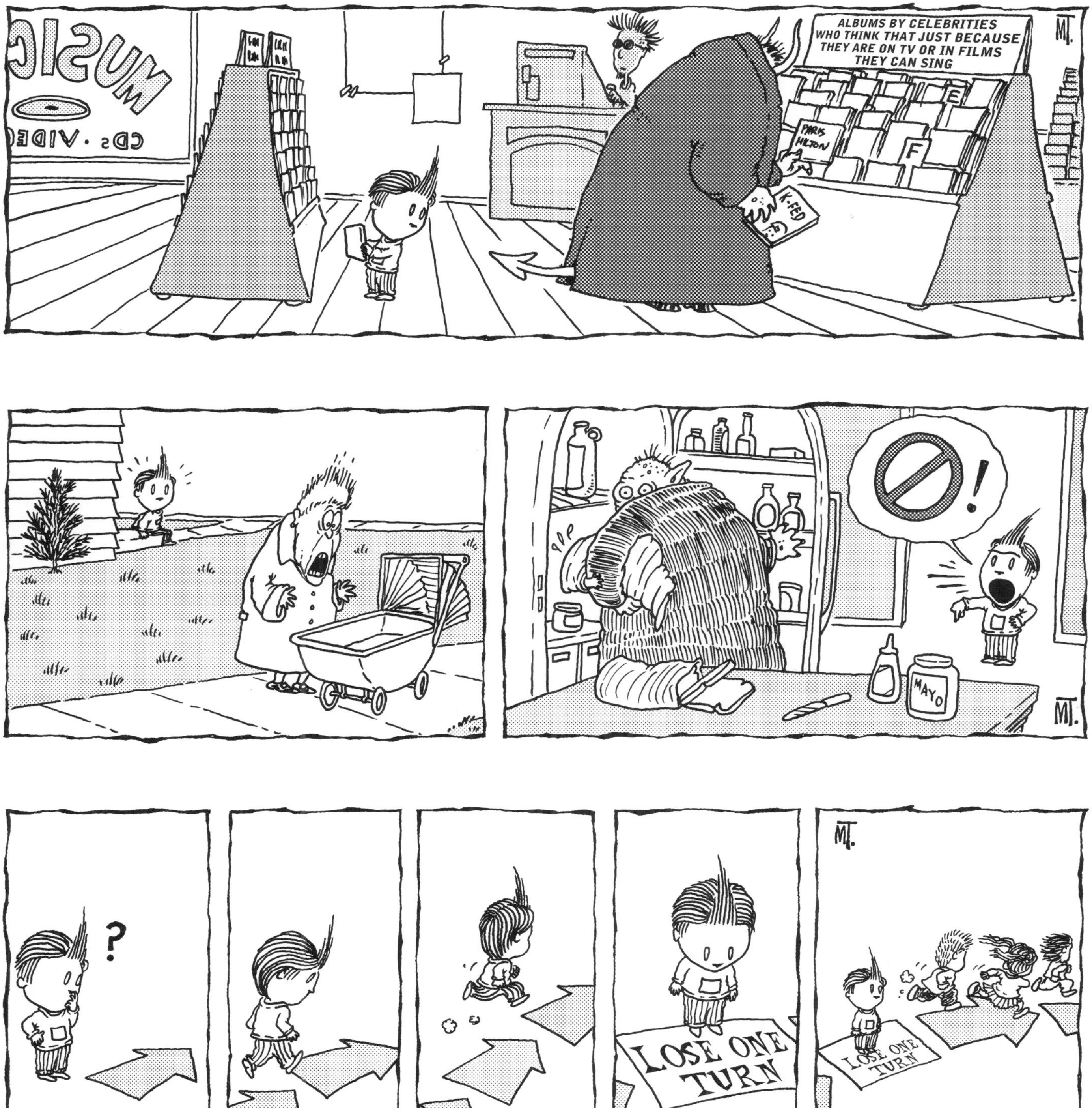

ALBUMS BY CELEBRITIES WHO THINK THAT JUST BECAUSE THEY ARE ON TV OR IN FILMS THEY CAN SING
PARIS HILTON
K-FED
E
F
MAYO
!
?
LOSE ONE TURN
LOSE ONE TURN

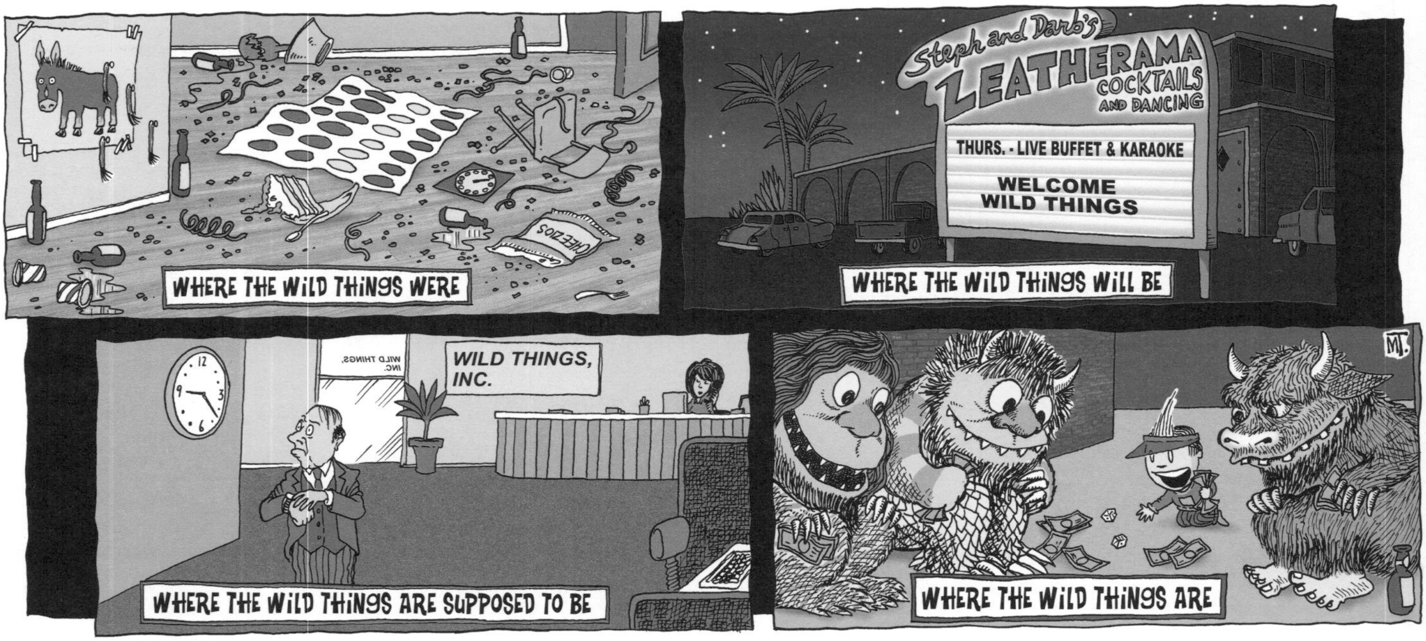

CHEEZOS
WHERE THE WILD THINGS WERE
Steph and Darb's
LEATHERAMA
COCKTAILS
AND DANCING
THURS. - LIVE BUFFET & KARAOKE
WELCOME
WILD THINGS
WHERE THE WILD THINGS WILL BE
WILD THINGS,
INC.
WHERE THE WILD THINGS ARE SUPPOSED TO BE
MT.
WHERE THE WILD THINGS ARE

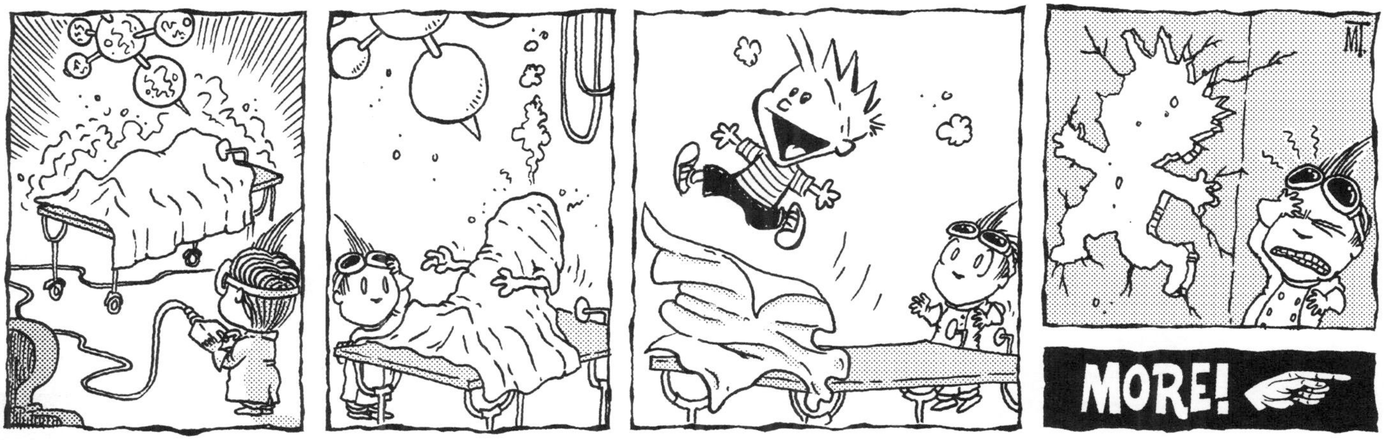

MORE!

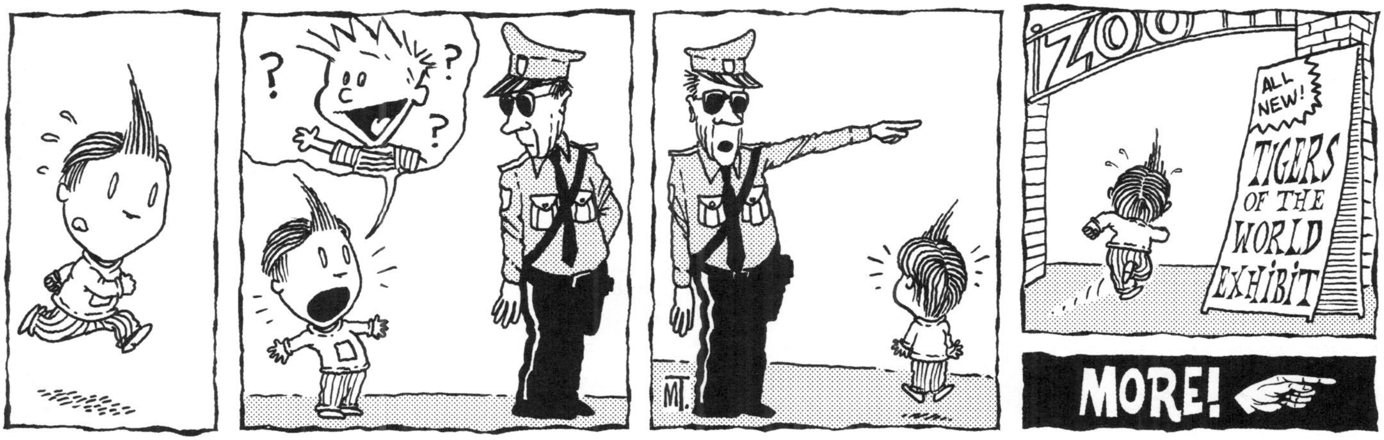

? ? ?
ZOO
ALL NEW!
TIGERS OF THE WORLD EXHIBIT
MORE!

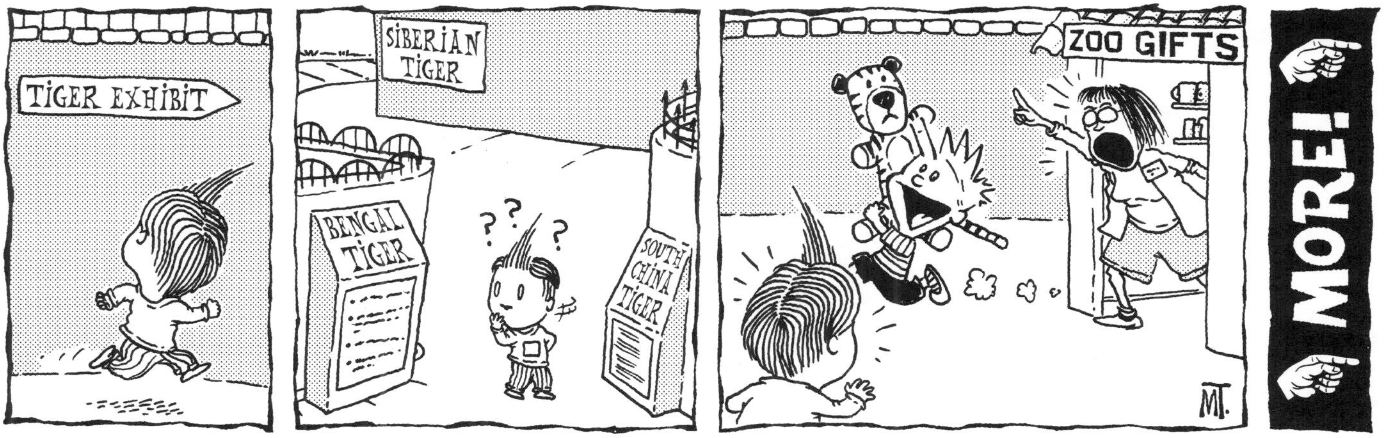

TIGER EXHIBIT
SIBERIAN TIGER
BENGAL TIGER
? ? ?
SOUTH CHINA TIGER
ZOO GIFTS
MORE!

TOYS
TRANSMOGRIFIER GUN
HA HA HA
MORE!
FFFOOOOOOOOOo
oOOOoTHOOMP!
THE COMPLETE CALVIN AND HOBBES
FIN.
EPILOGUE...
THE COMPLETE CALVIN AND HOBBES
HA HA HA HA

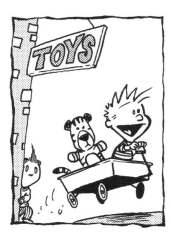

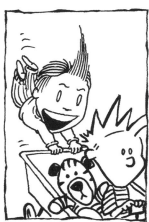

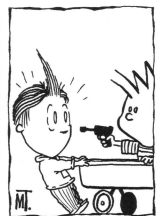

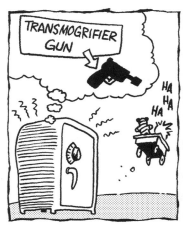

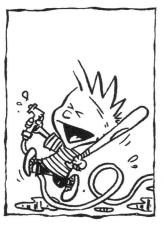

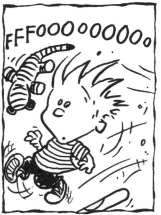

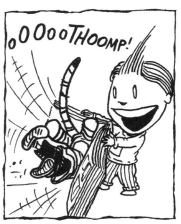

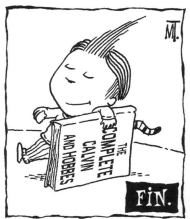

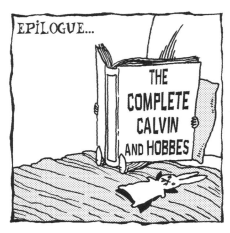

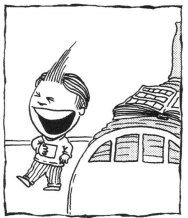

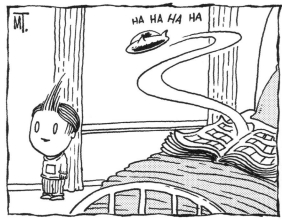

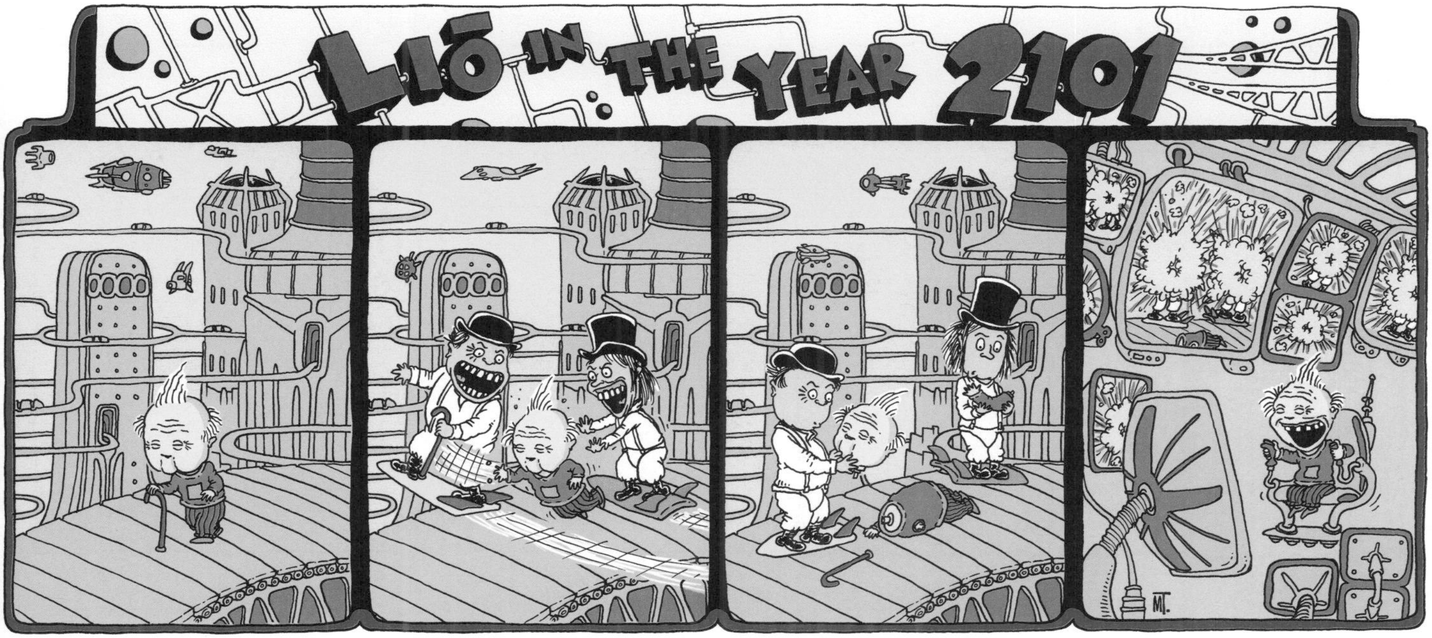
LIŌ IN THE YEAR 2101
MT.

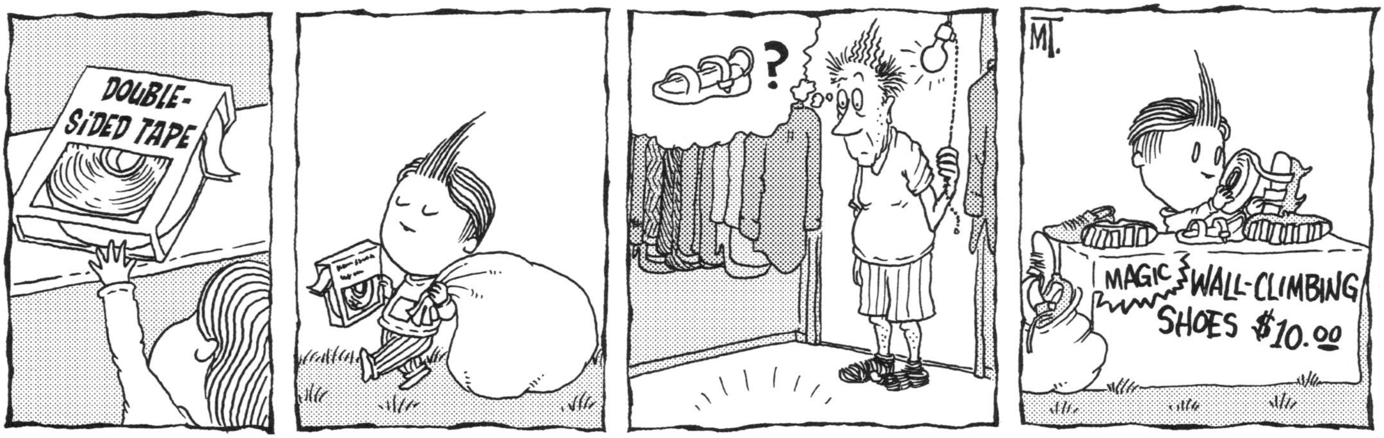
DOUBLE-SIDED TAPE
?
MAGIC WALL-CLIMBING SHOES $10.00

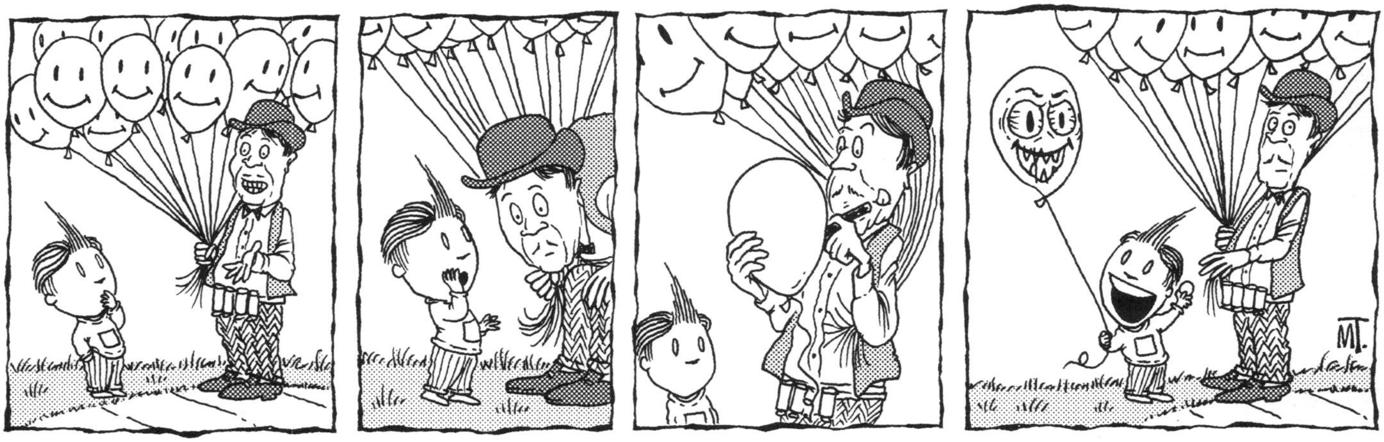

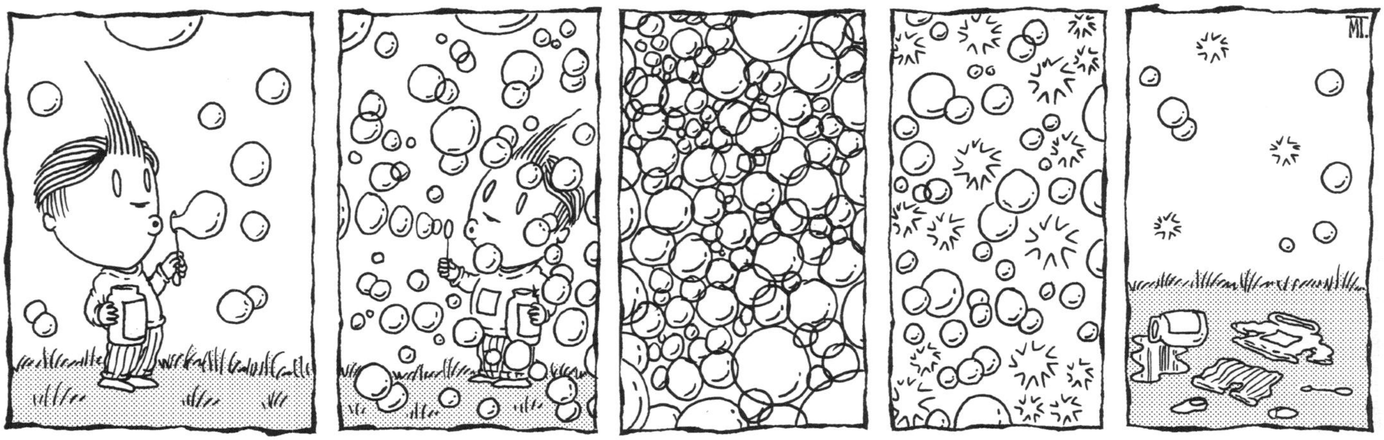

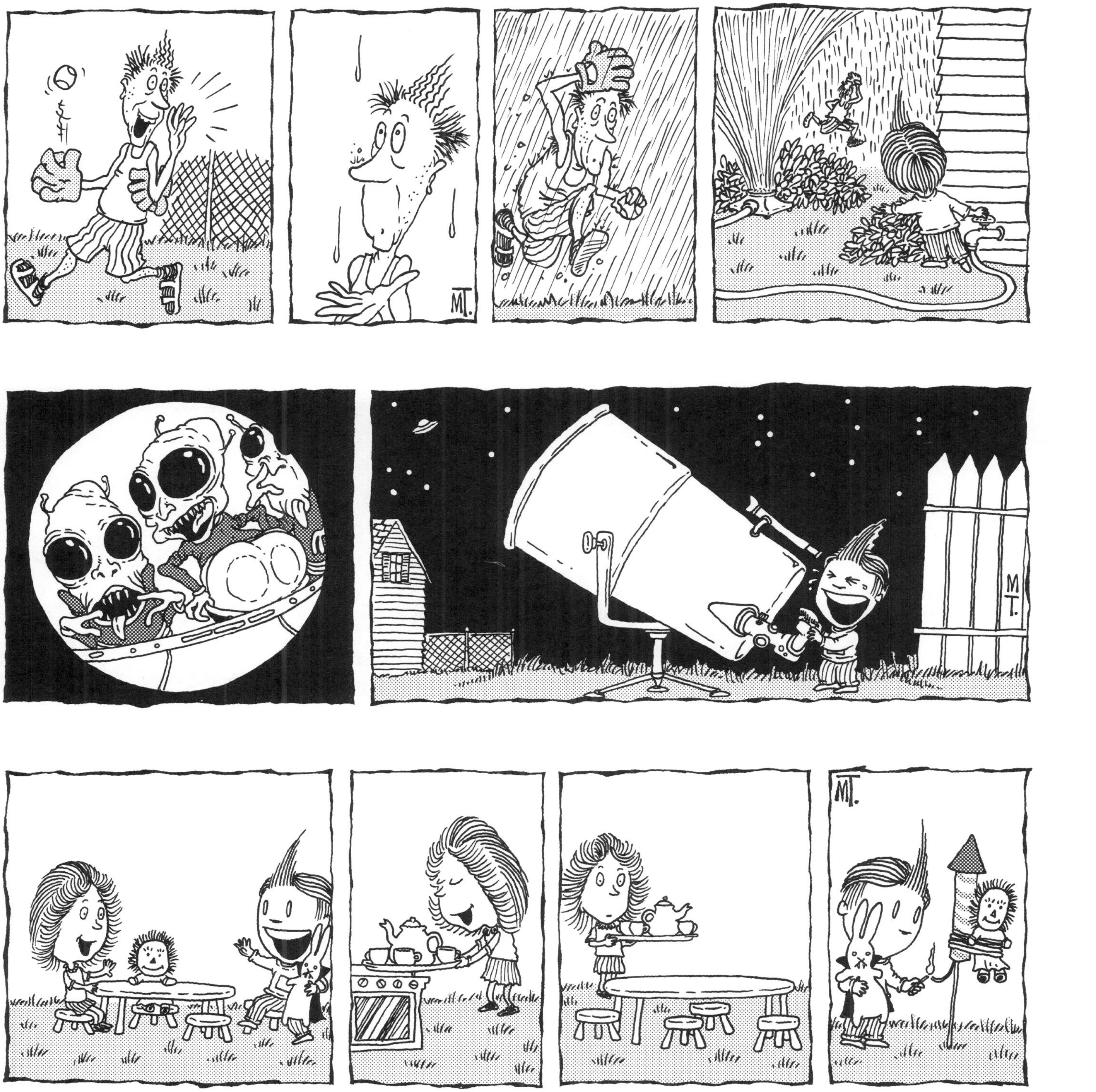

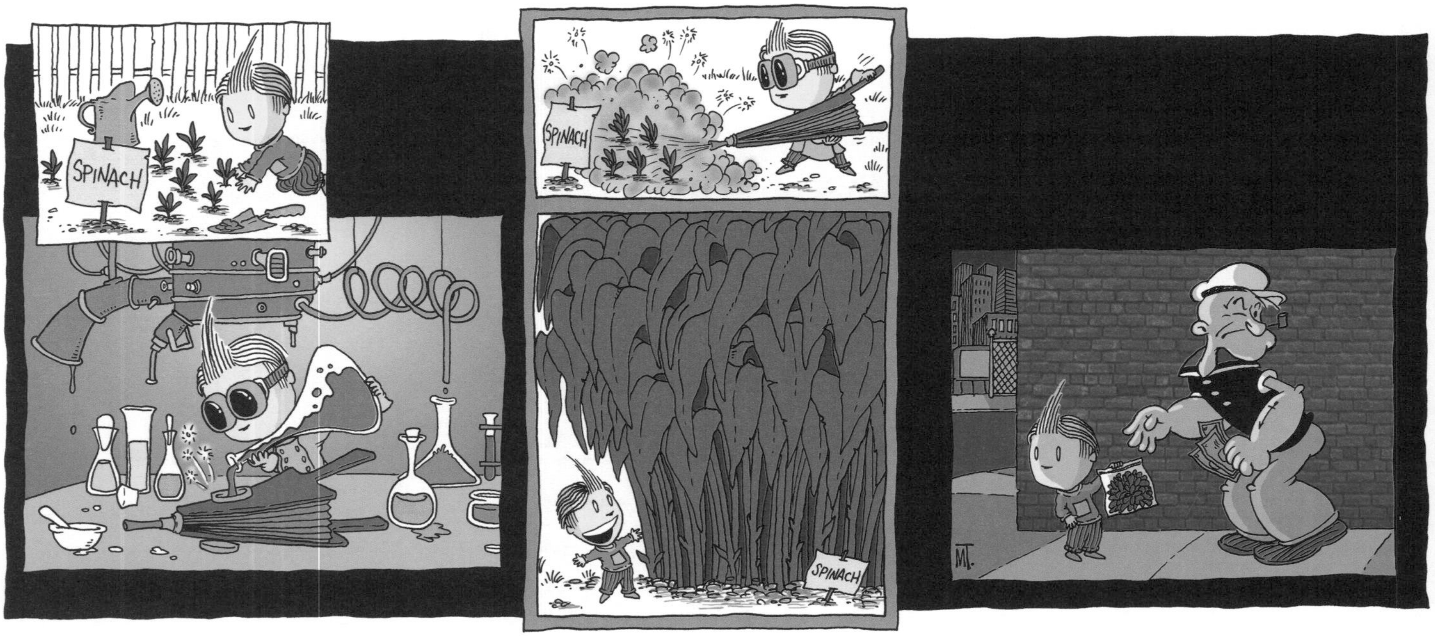
SPINACH
SPINACH
SPINACH

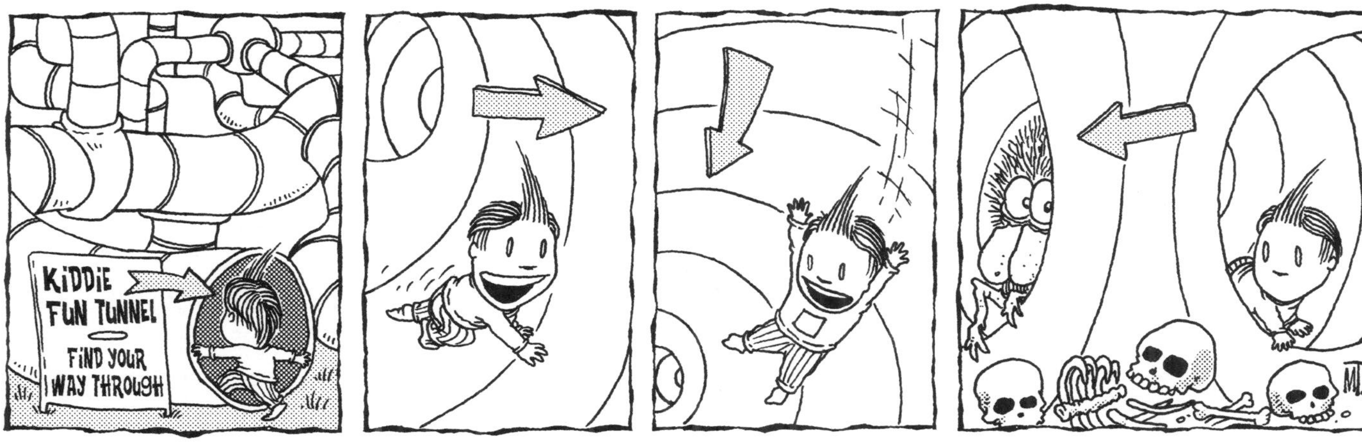
KIDDIE FUN TUNNEL
FIND YOUR WAY THROUGH
MT.

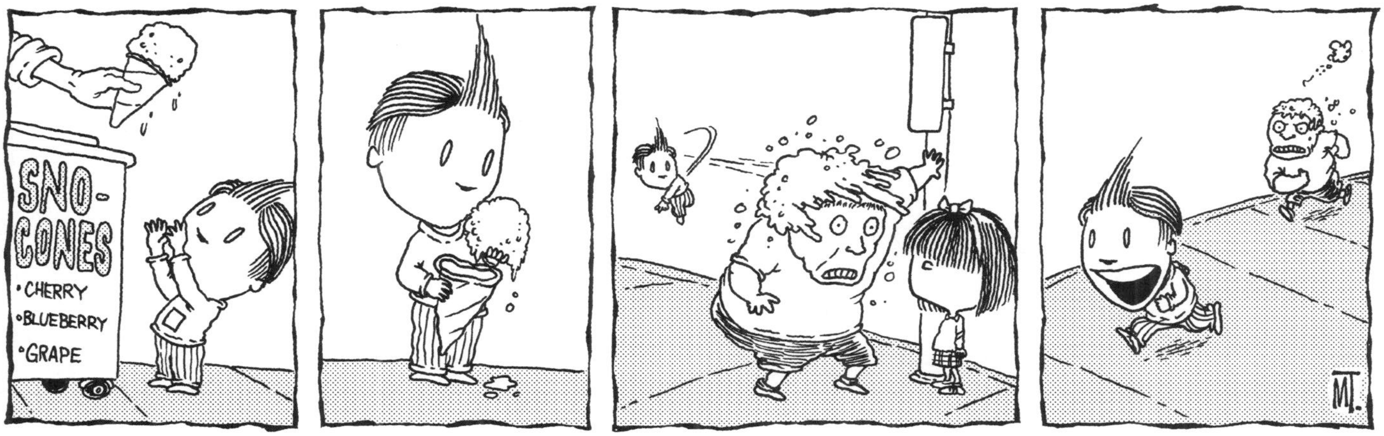
SNO-CONES
• CHERRY
• BLUEBERRY
• GRAPE
MT.

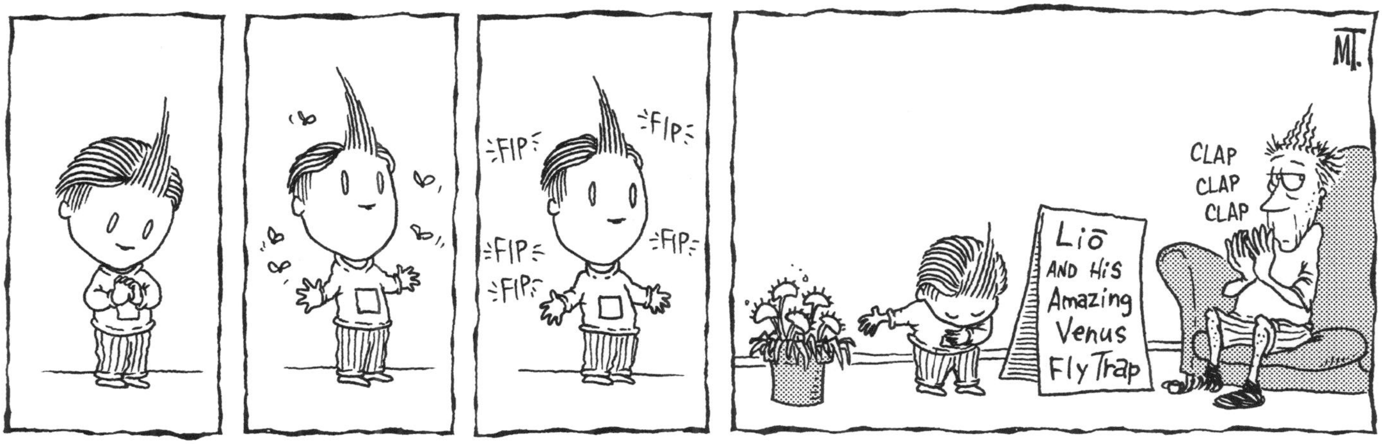
MT.
FIP
FIP
FIP
FIP
FIP
CLAP
CLAP
CLAP
Liō AND His Amazing Venus FlyTrap

MT.
THE ART OF SELF-MINIATUR-IZATION
MT.
AACHOO! ACHOO!!
UNDEAD BUNNIES
SSSNNURFLE
FLIF
TISSUES
TISSUES
UNDEAD BUNNIES
MT.
SNIFF!

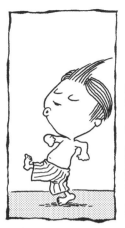

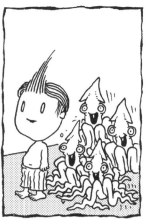

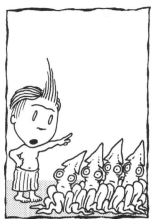

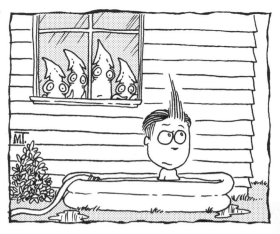

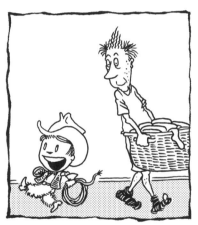

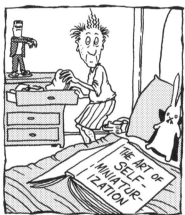

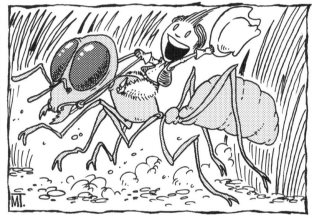

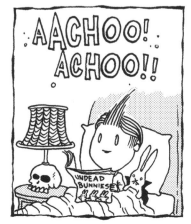

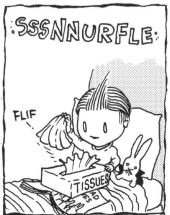

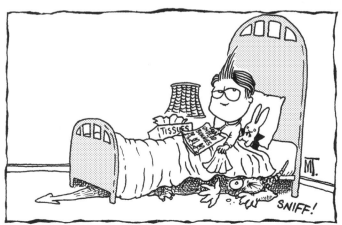

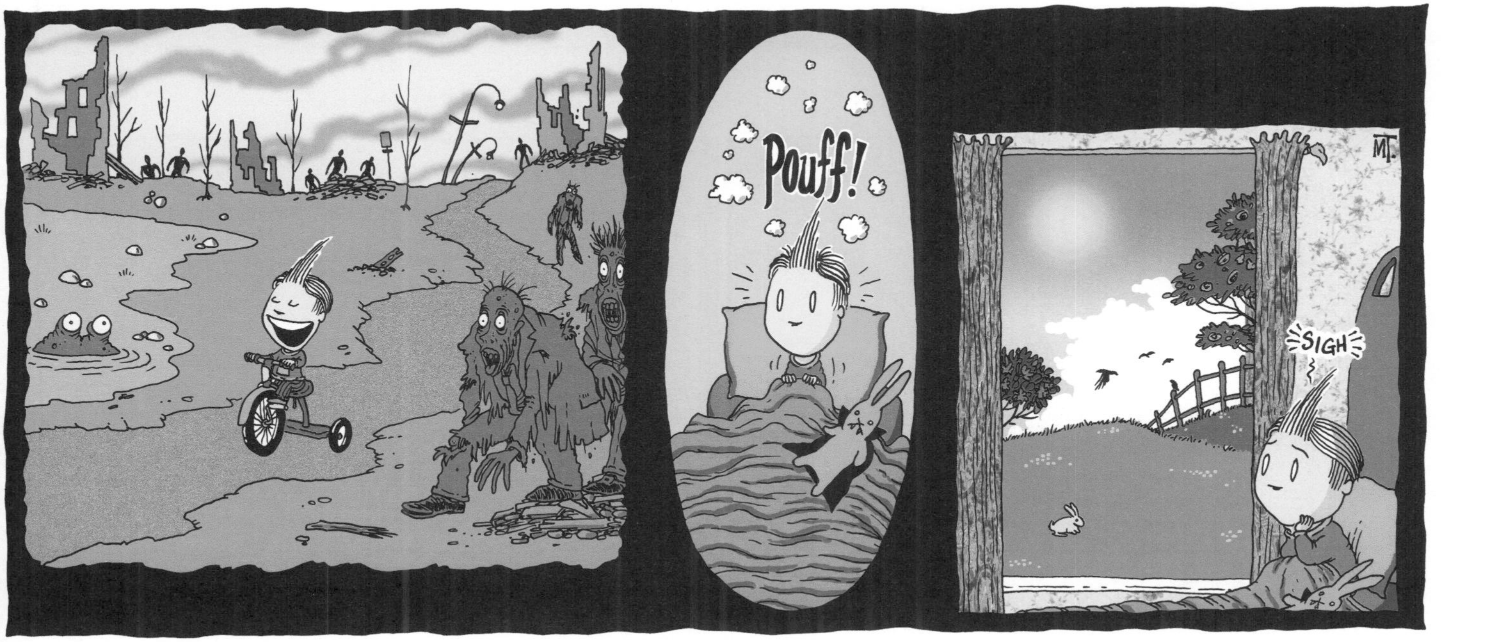
Pouff!
SIGH
MT.

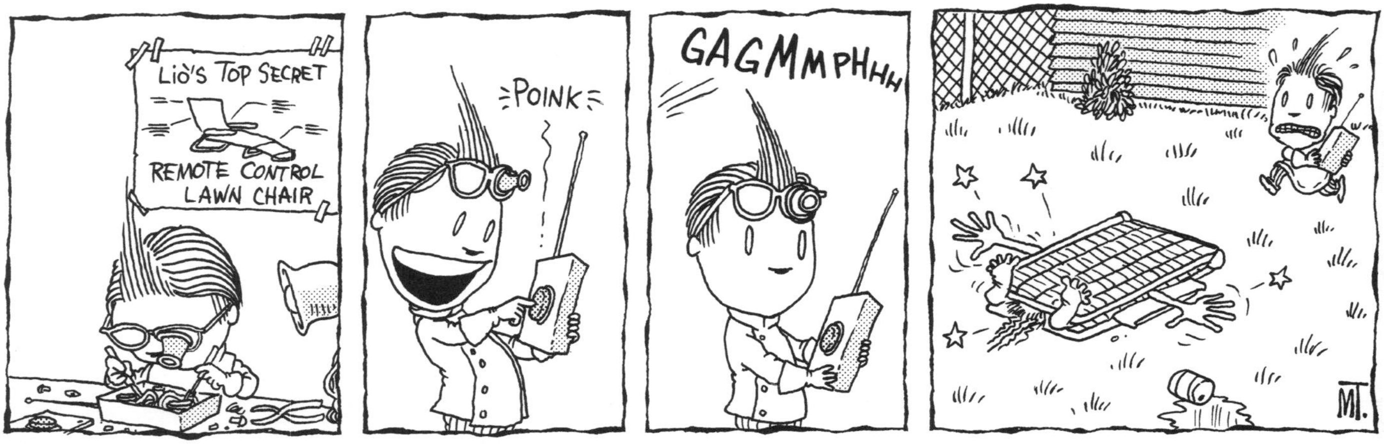
LIO'S TOP SECRET
REMOTE CONTROL LAWN CHAIR
POINK
GAGMMPHHH

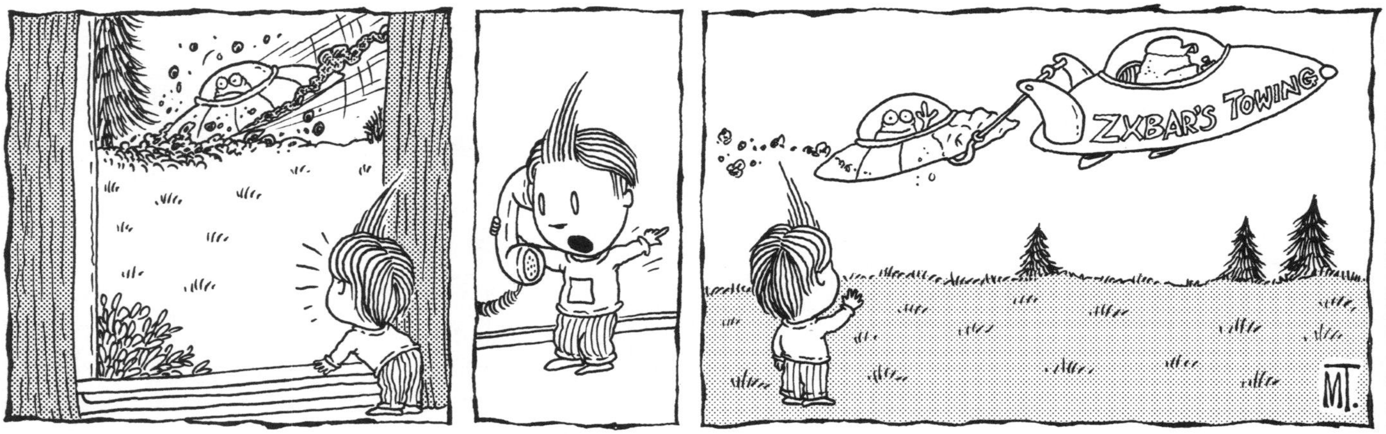
ZXBAR'S TOWING

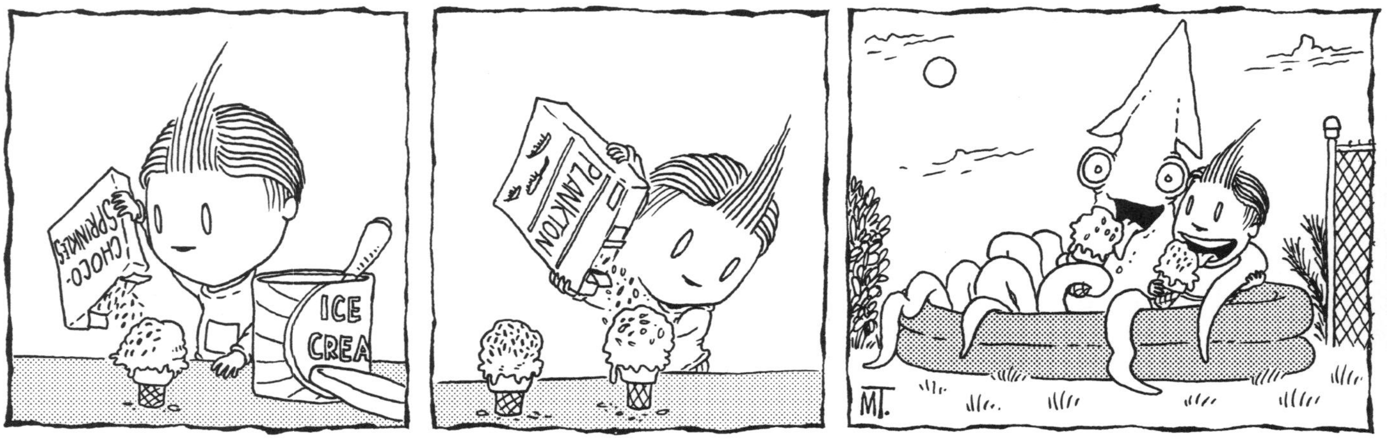
CHOCO-SPRINKLES
ICE CREA
PLANKTON

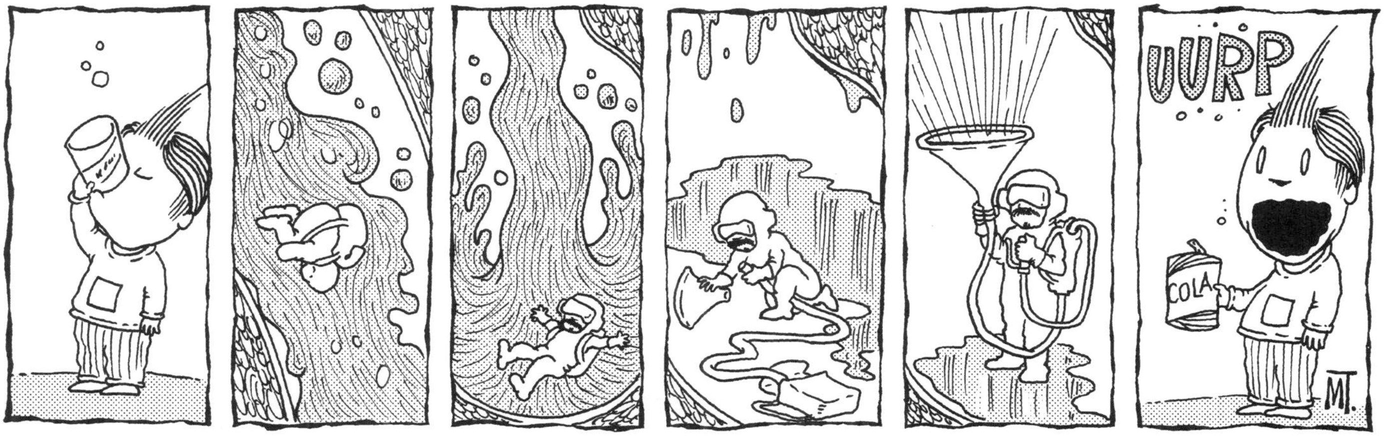
UURP
COLA

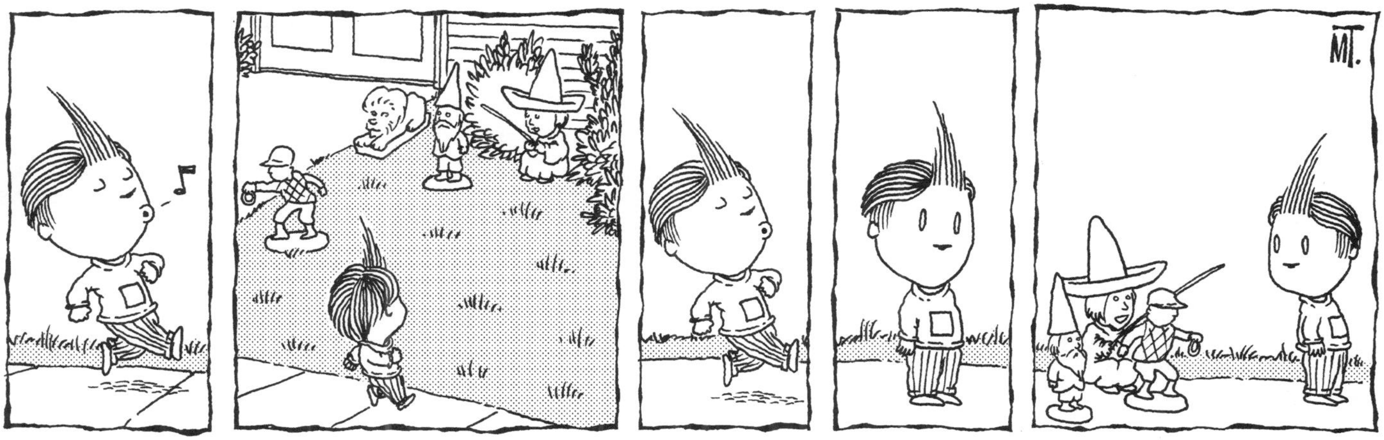

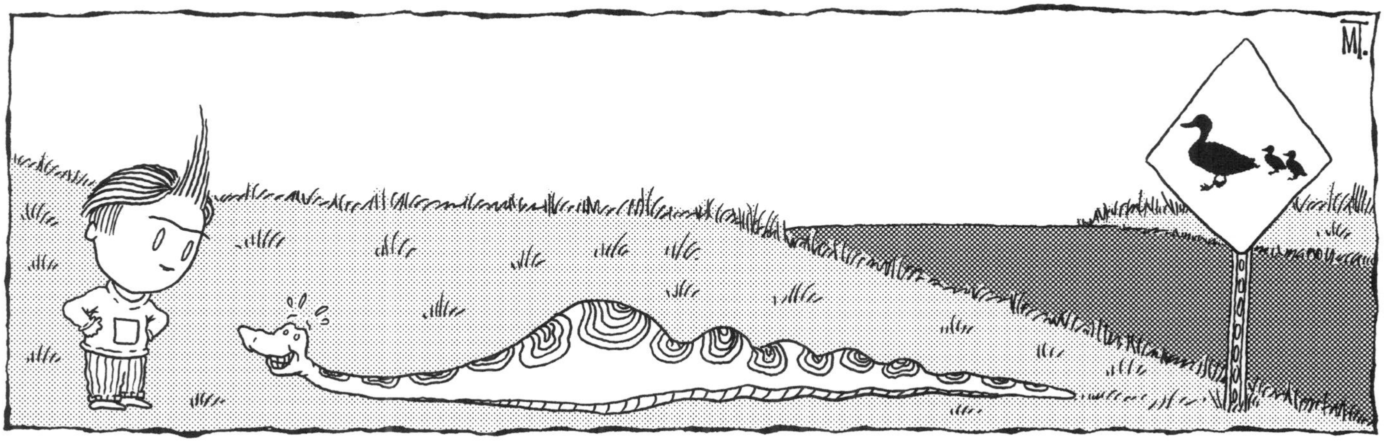

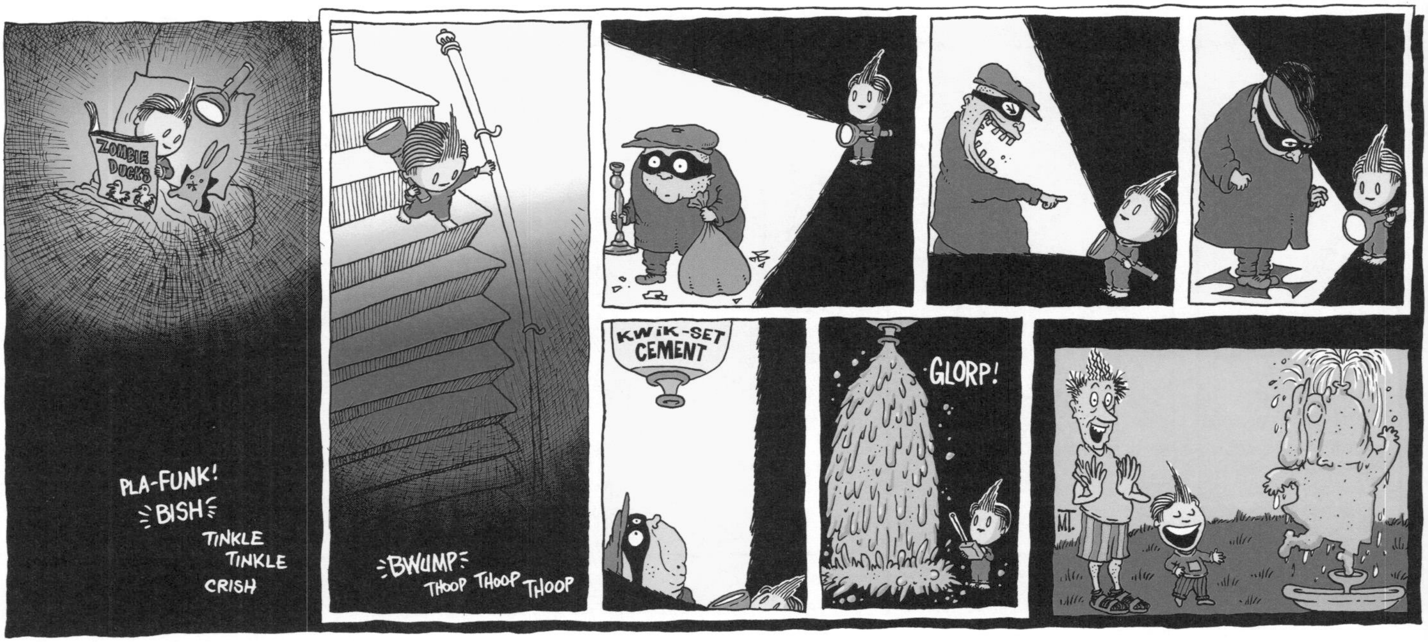
ZOMBIE DUCKS
PLA-FUNK!
BISH
TINKLE
TINKLE
CRISH
BWUMP
THOOP THOOP THOOP
KWIK-SET CEMENT
GLORP!
M.T.

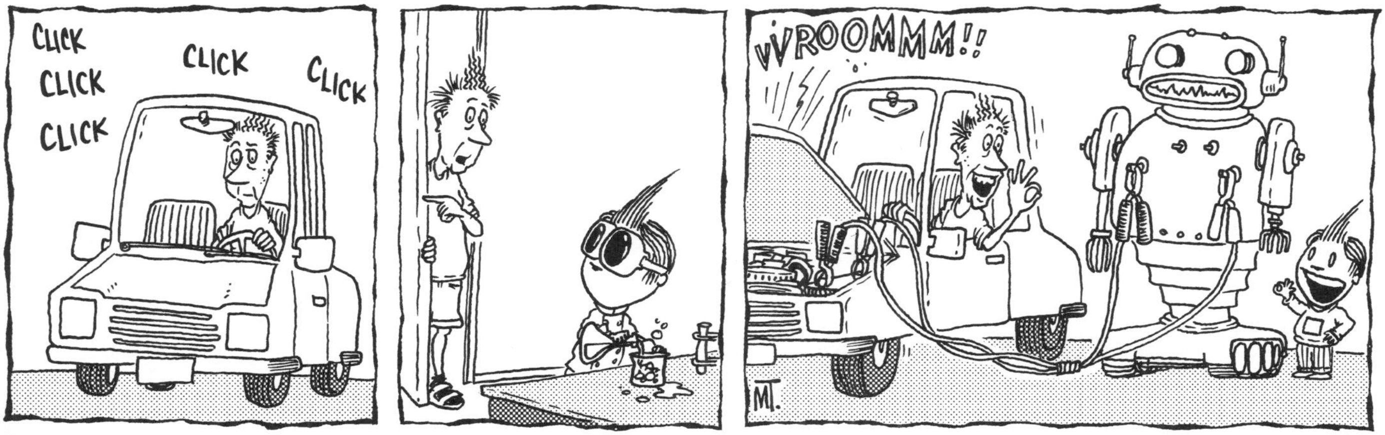
CLICK
CLICK
CLICK
CLICK
CLICK
VVROOMMM!!

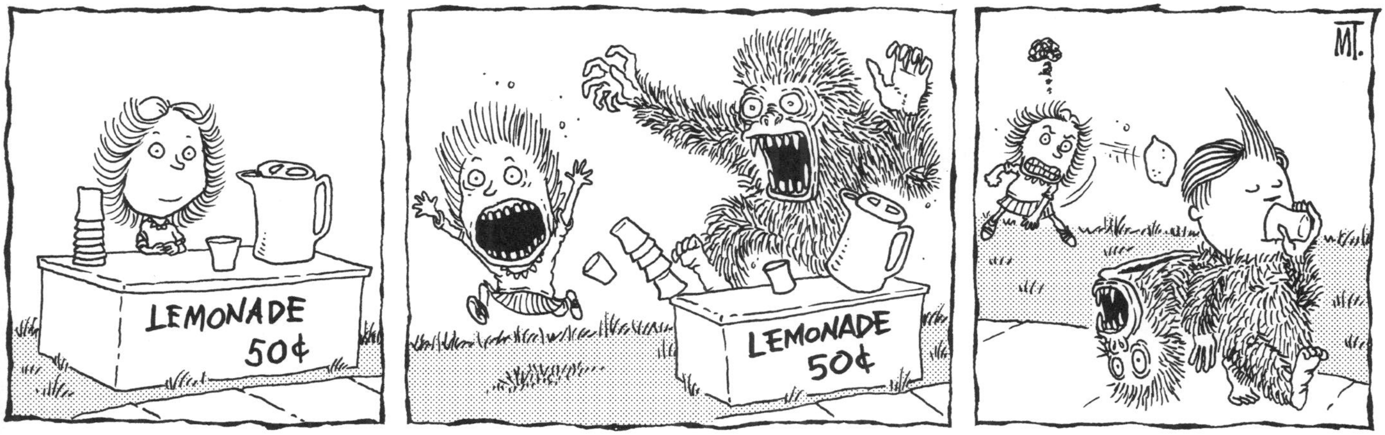
LEMONADE 50¢
LEMONADE 50¢

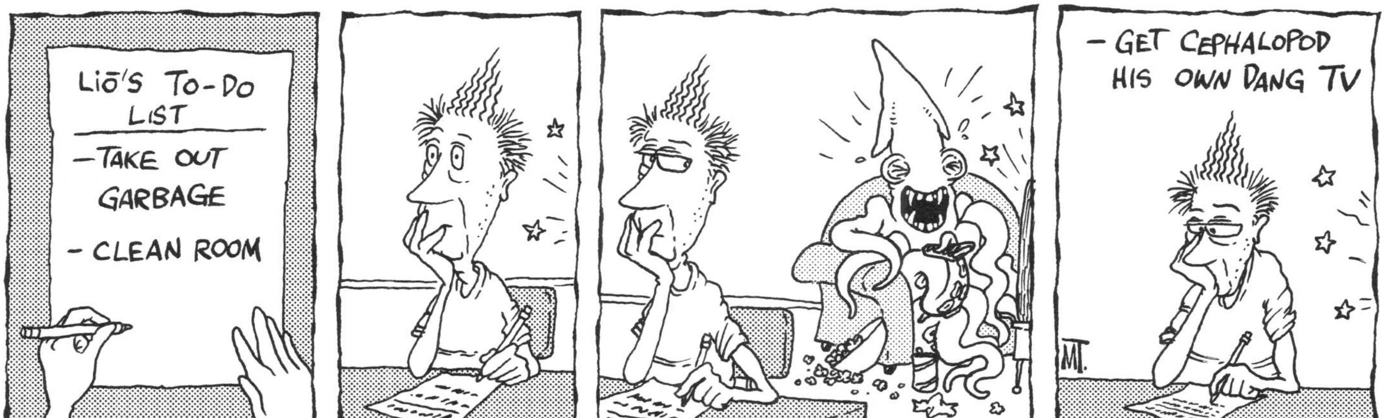
LIO'S TO-DO LIST
-TAKE OUT GARBAGE
- CLEAN ROOM
- GET CEPHALOPOD HIS OWN DANG TV

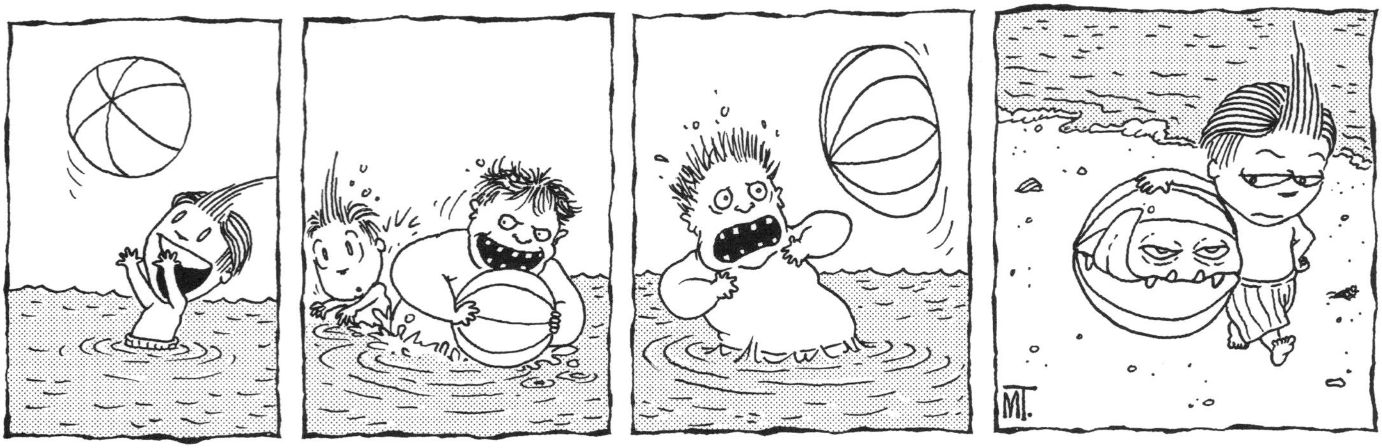

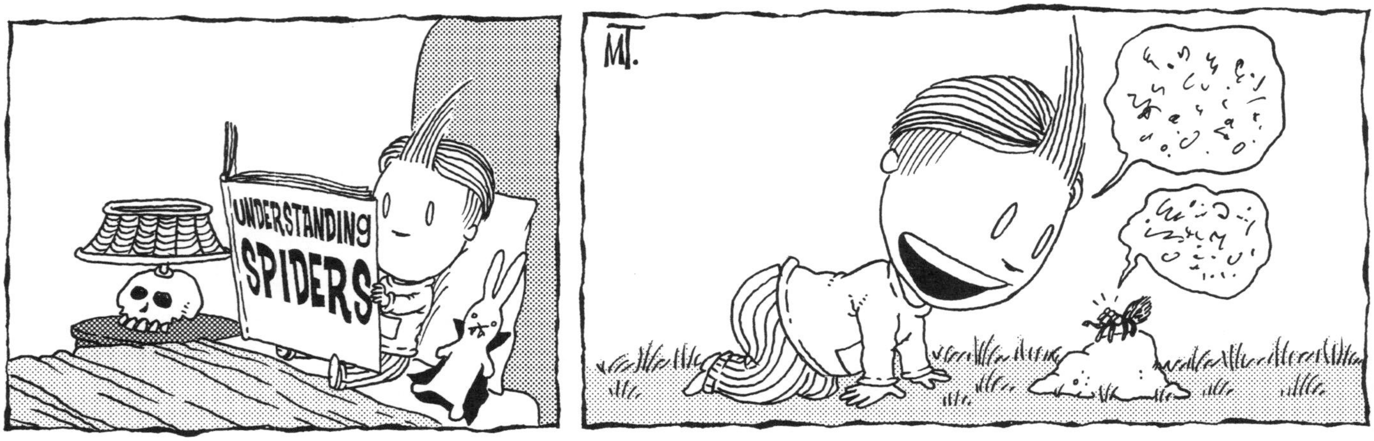
UNDERSTANDING
SPIDERS

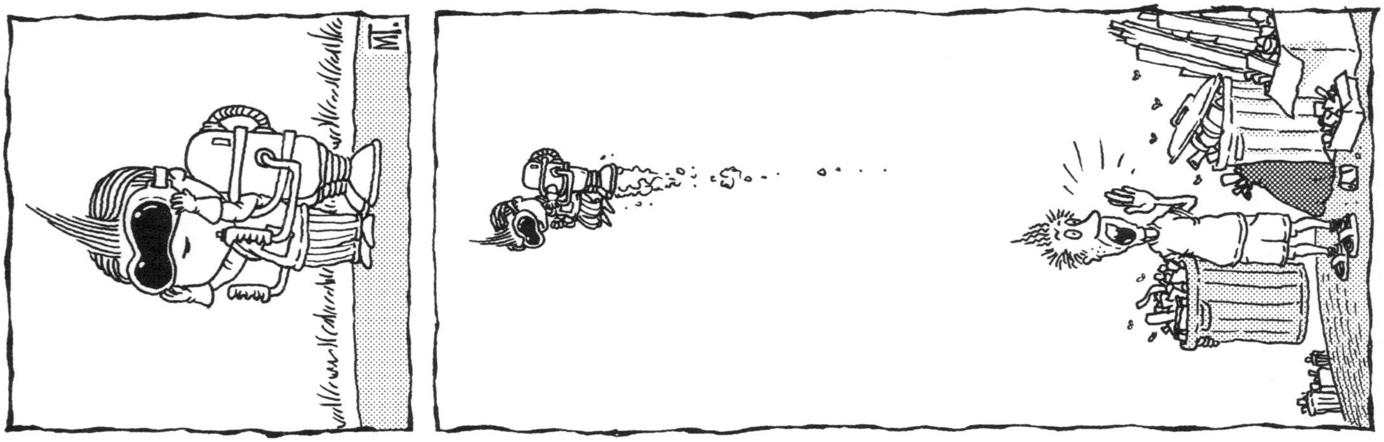

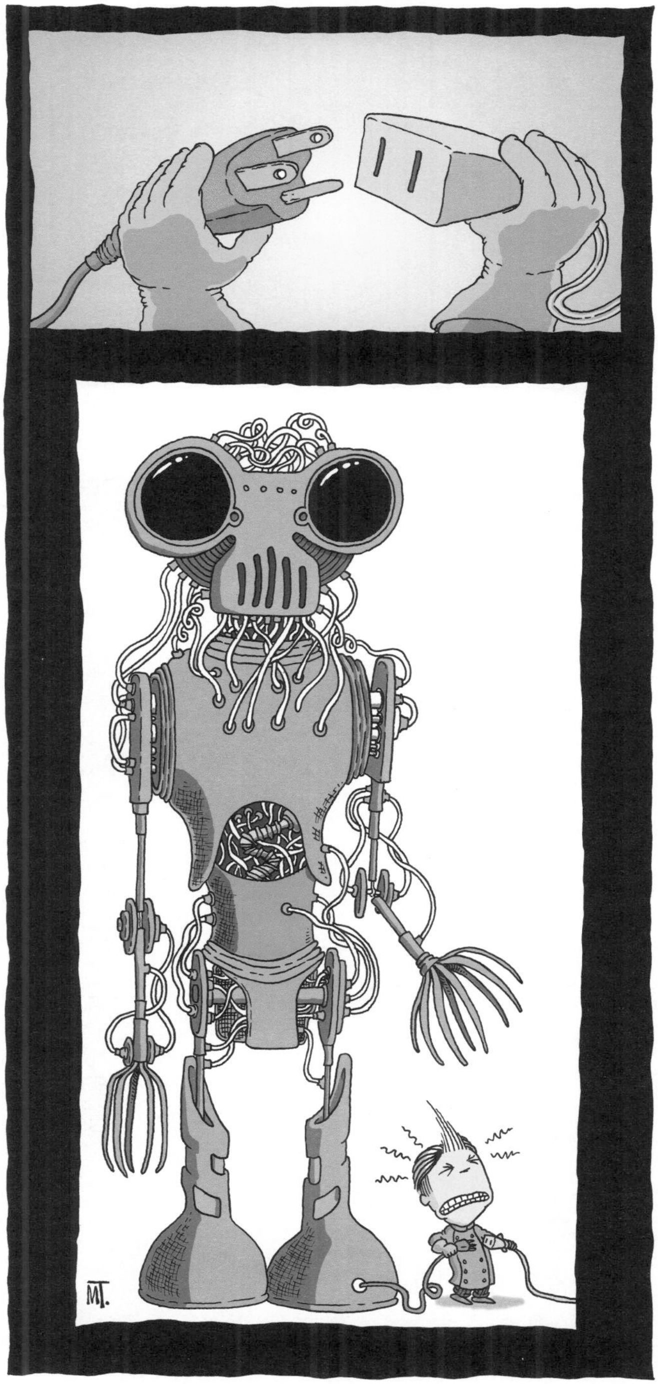
MT.

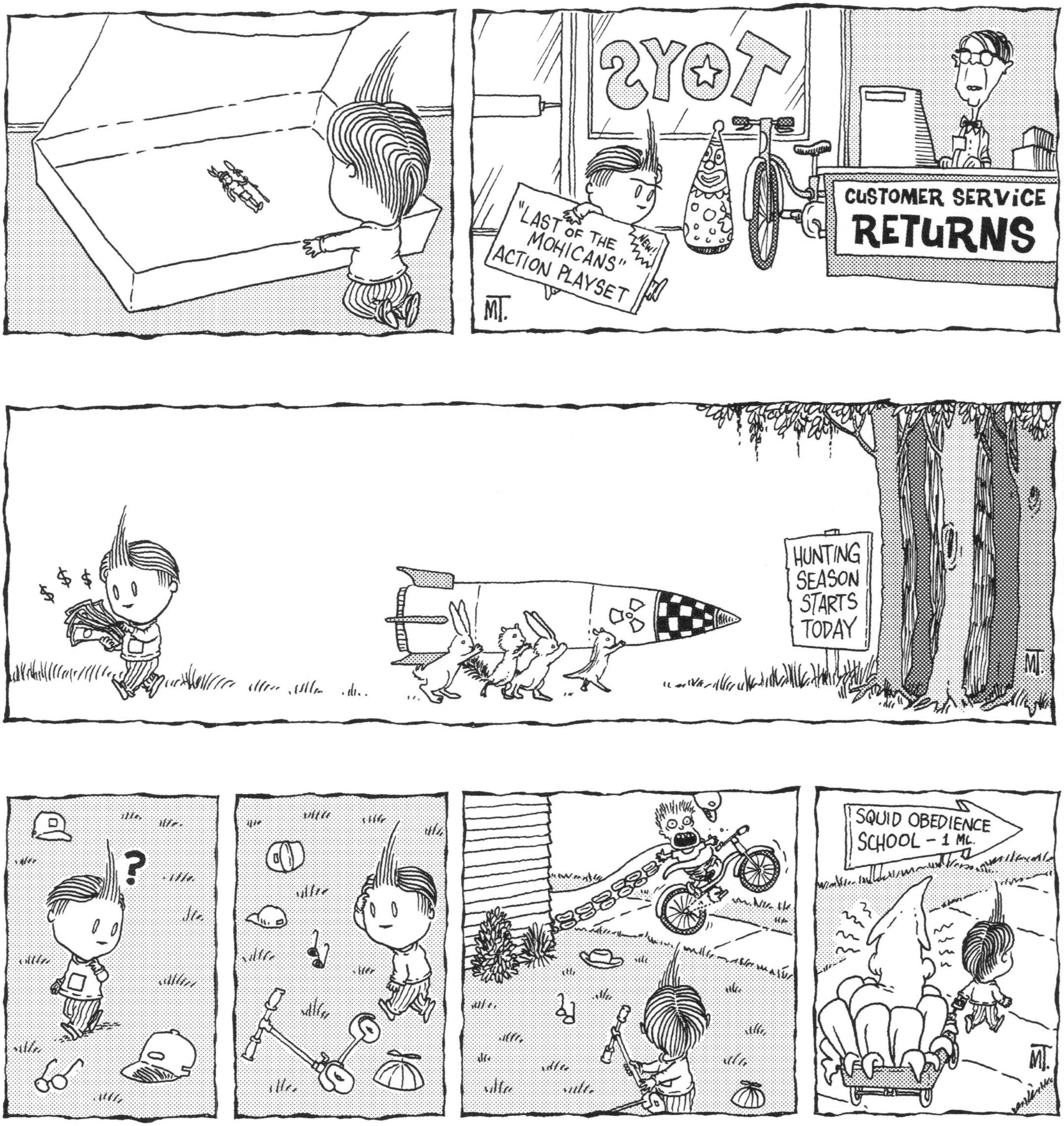
"LAST OF THE MOHICANS" ACTION PLAYSET
NEW!
CUSTOMER SERVICE
RETURNS
MT.
HUNTING SEASON STARTS TODAY
MT.
SQUID OBEDIENCE SCHOOL – 1 MI.
MT.

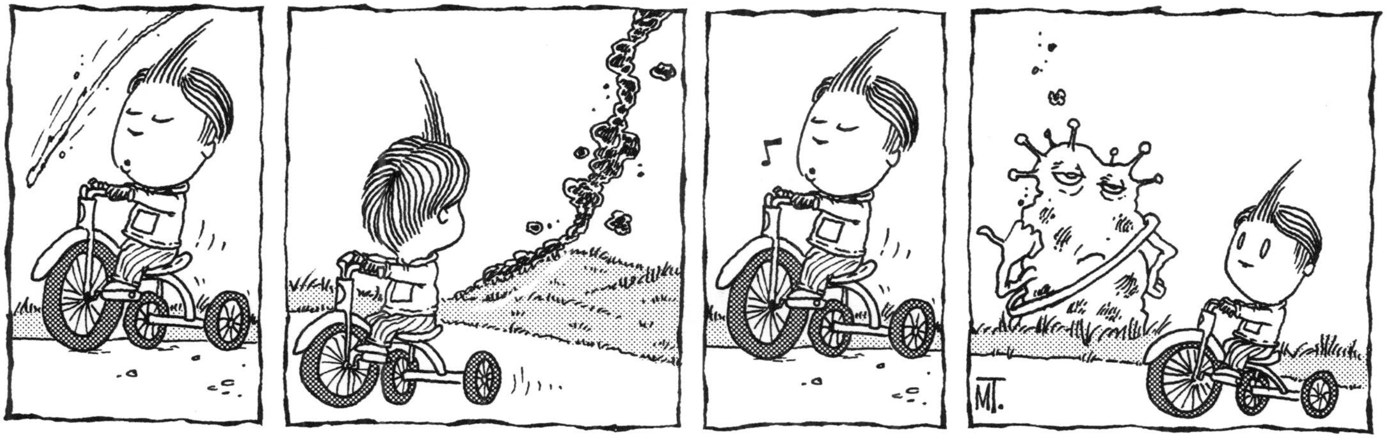

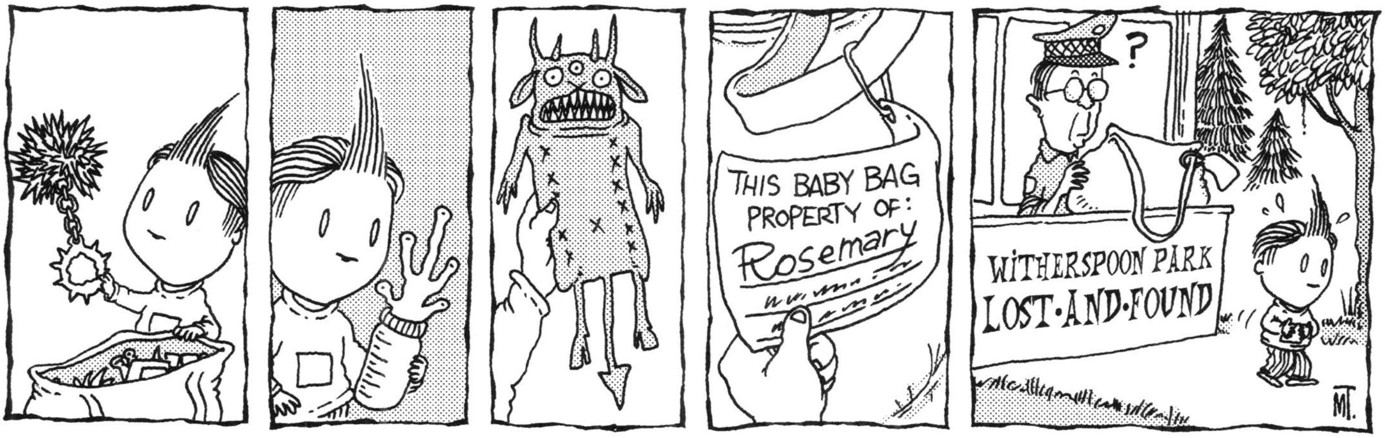
THIS BABY BAG
PROPERTY OF:
Rosemary
?
WITHERSPOON PARK
LOST·AND·FOUND

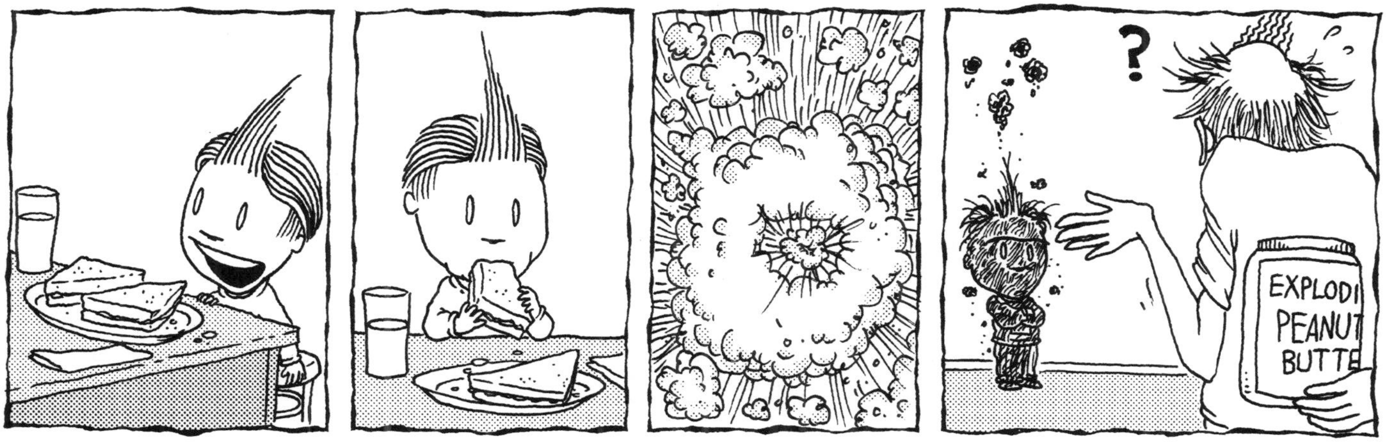
?
EXPLODI
PEANUT
BUTTE

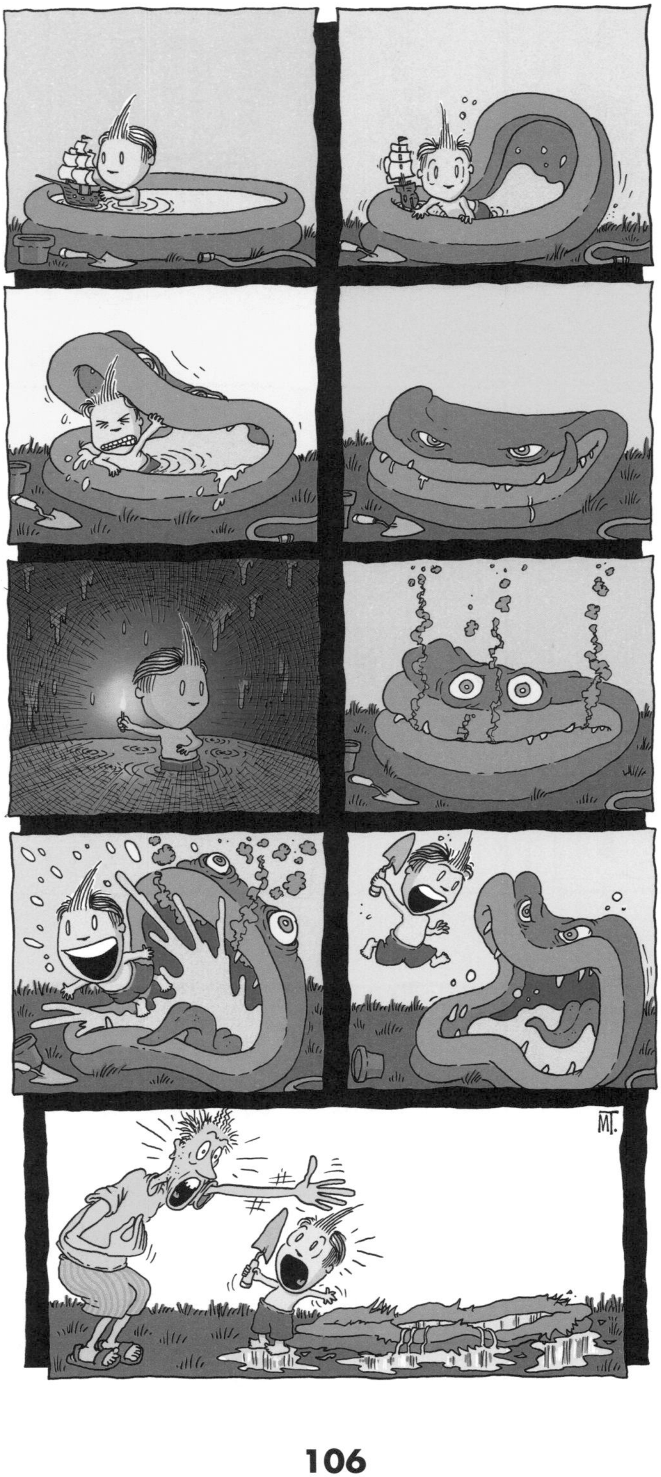
MT.

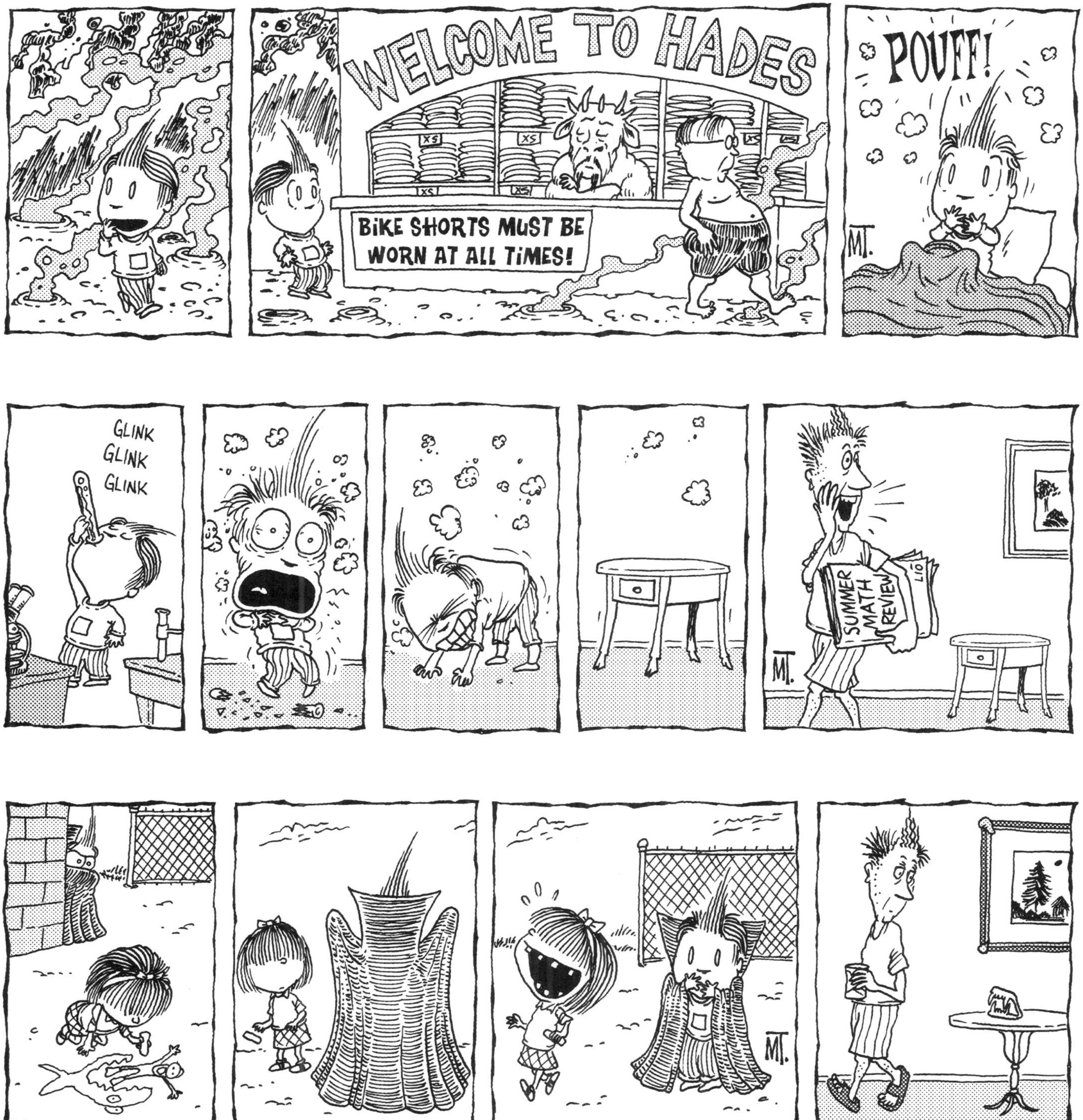
WELCOME TO HADES
XS
BIKE SHORTS MUST BE WORN AT ALL TIMES!
POUFF!
MT.
GLINK
GLINK
GLINK
SUMMER MATH REVIEW
MT.
MT.

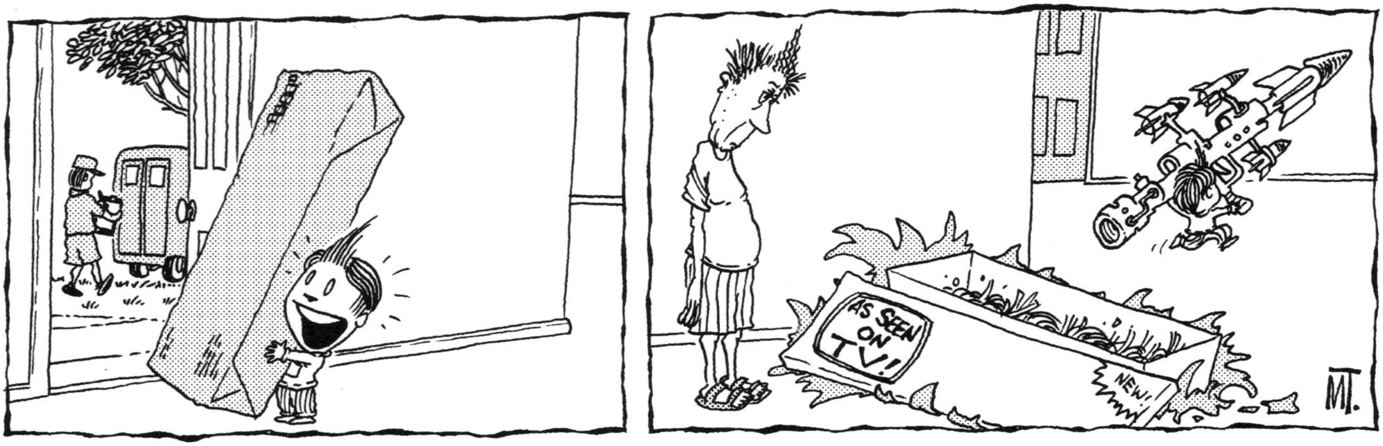
AS SEEN ON TV!!
NEW!

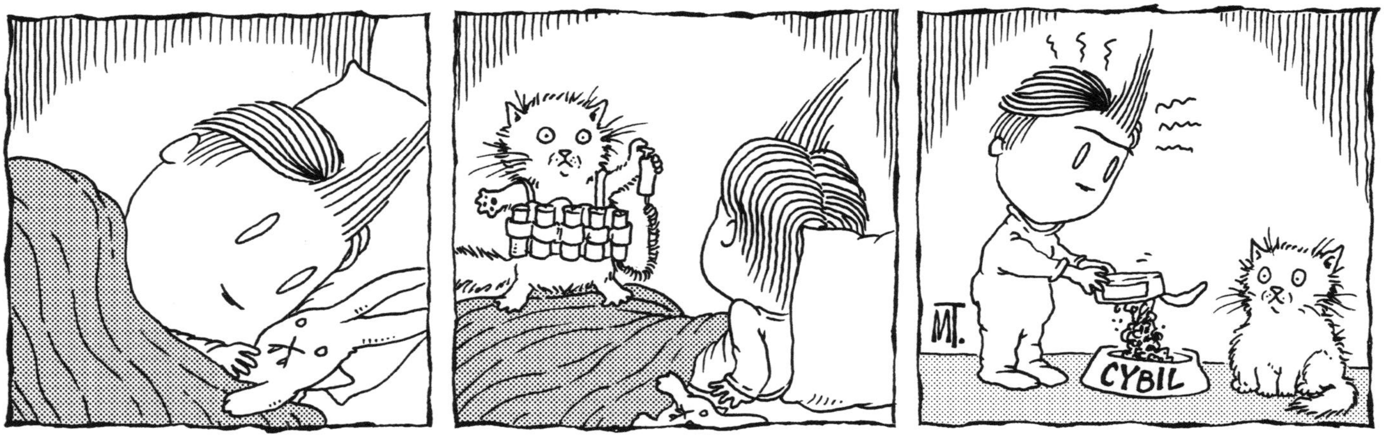
CYBIL

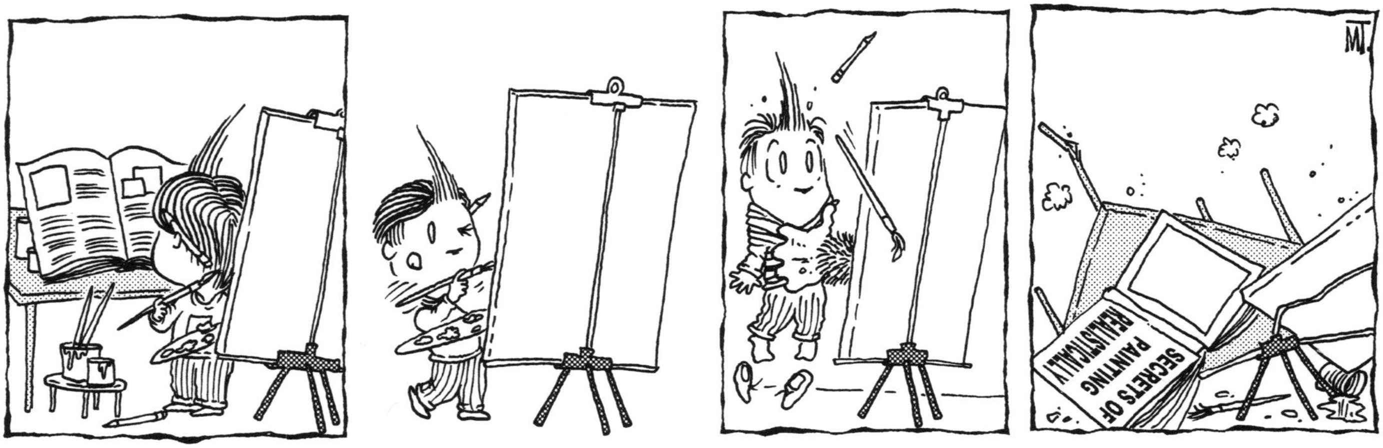
SECRETS OF PAINTING REALISTICALLY

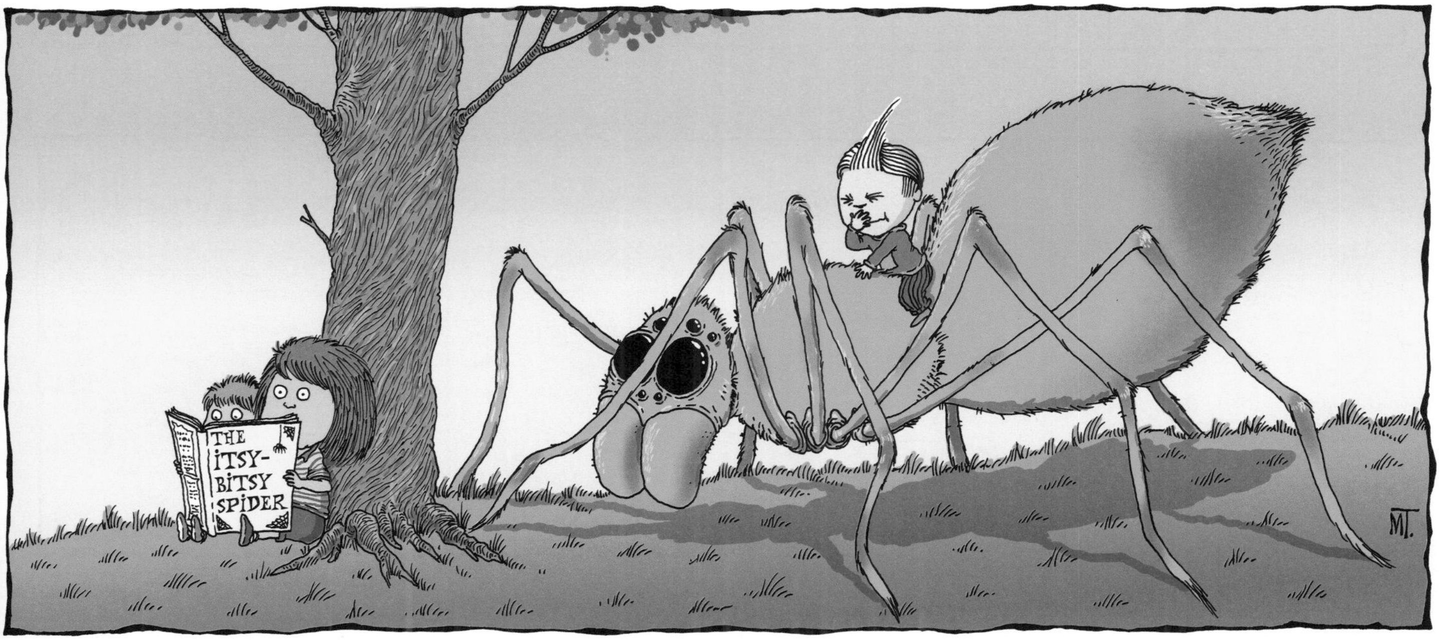
THE
ITSY-
BITSY
SPIDER
MT.

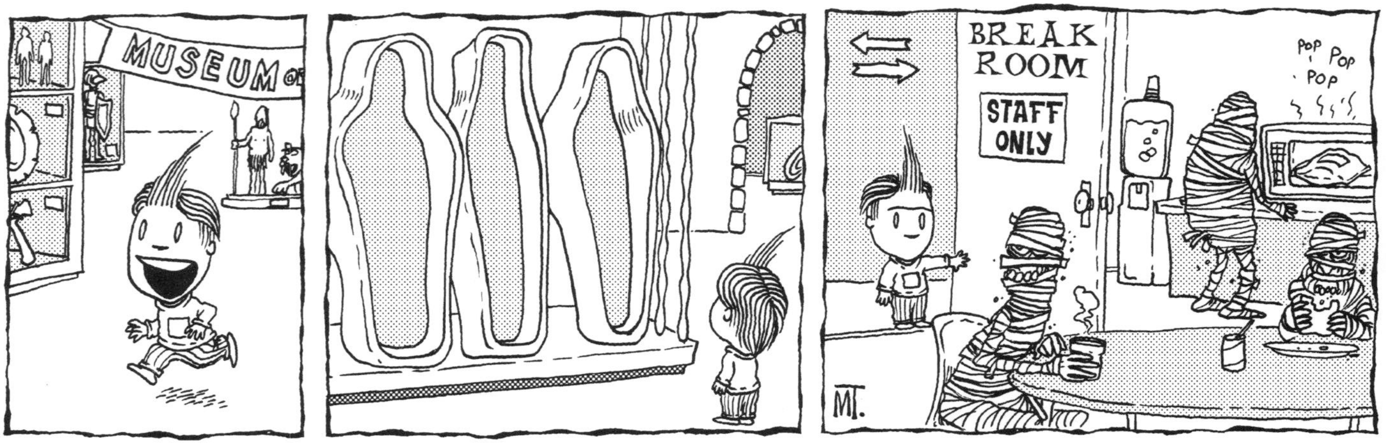
MUSEUM
BREAK ROOM
STAFF ONLY
POP POP POP
MT.

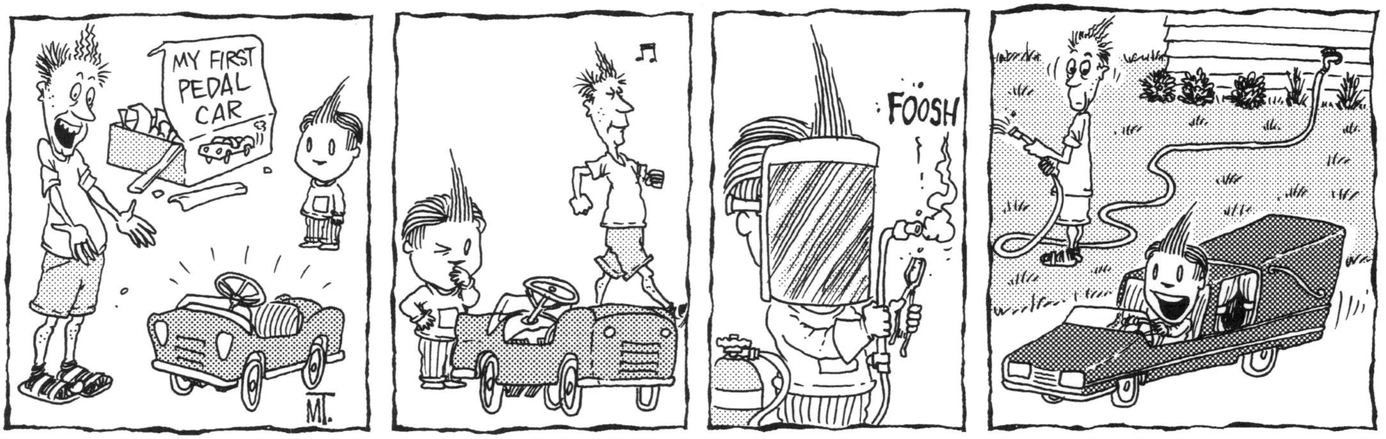
MY FIRST PEDAL CAR
MT.
FOOSH

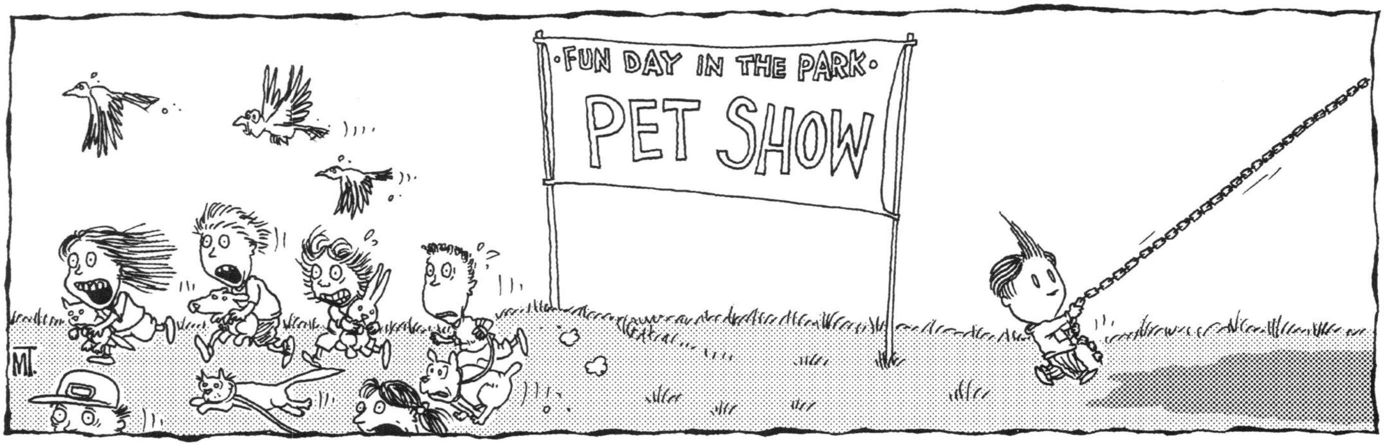
FUN DAY IN THE PARK
PET SHOW
MT.

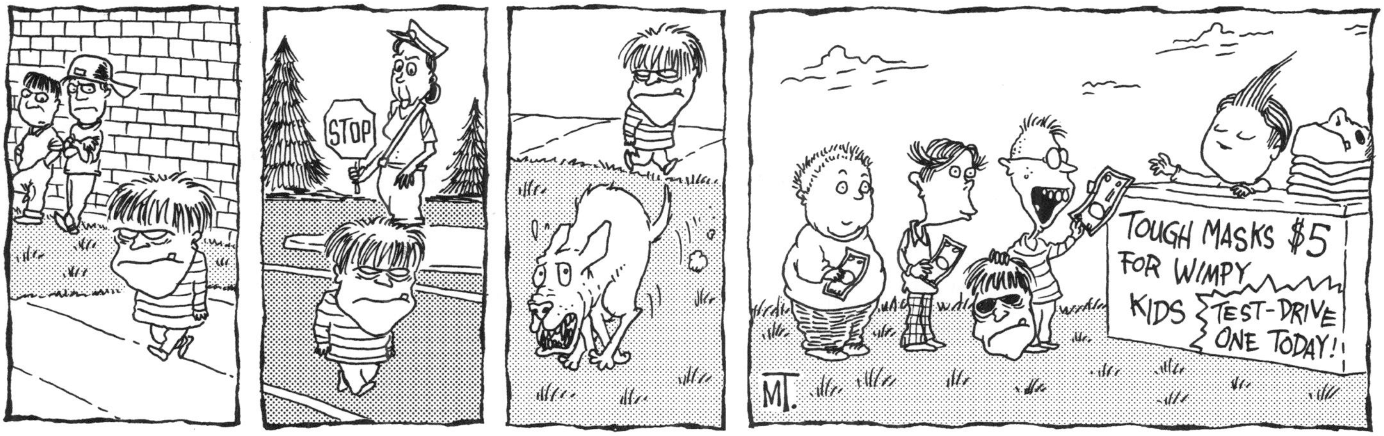
STOP
TOUGH MASKS $5 FOR WIMPY KIDS
TEST-DRIVE ONE TODAY!
MT.

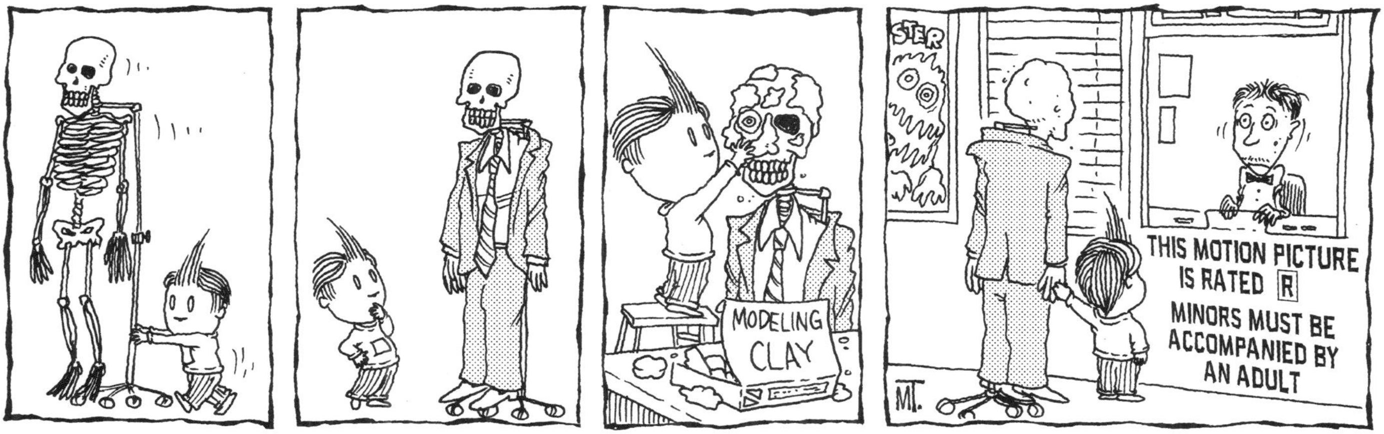
STER
MODELING CLAY
THIS MOTION PICTURE IS RATED R
MINORS MUST BE ACCOMPANIED BY AN ADULT
MT.

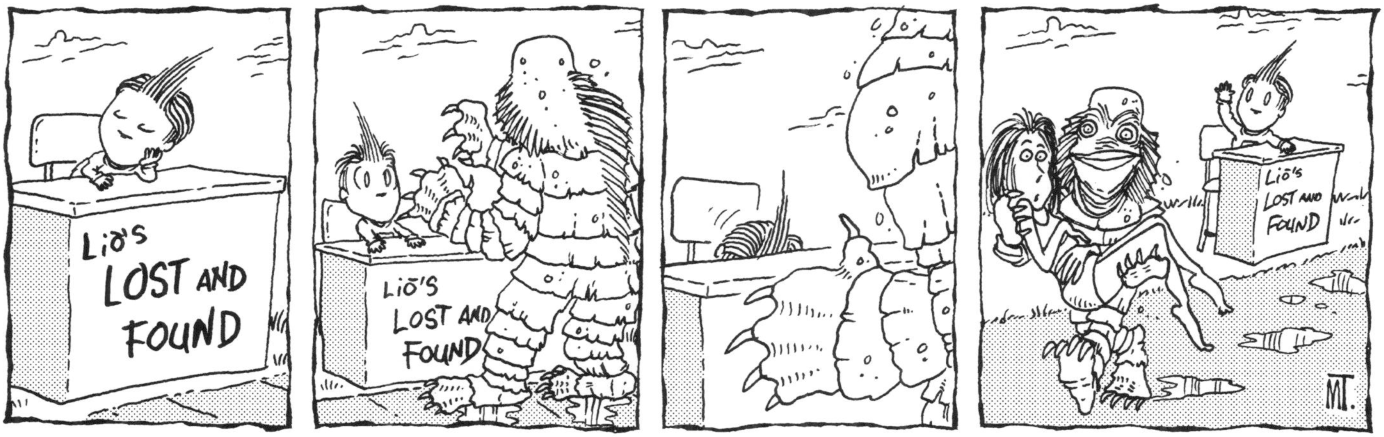
Liō's LOST AND FOUND
Liō's LOST AND FOUND
Liō's LOST AND FOUND
MT.

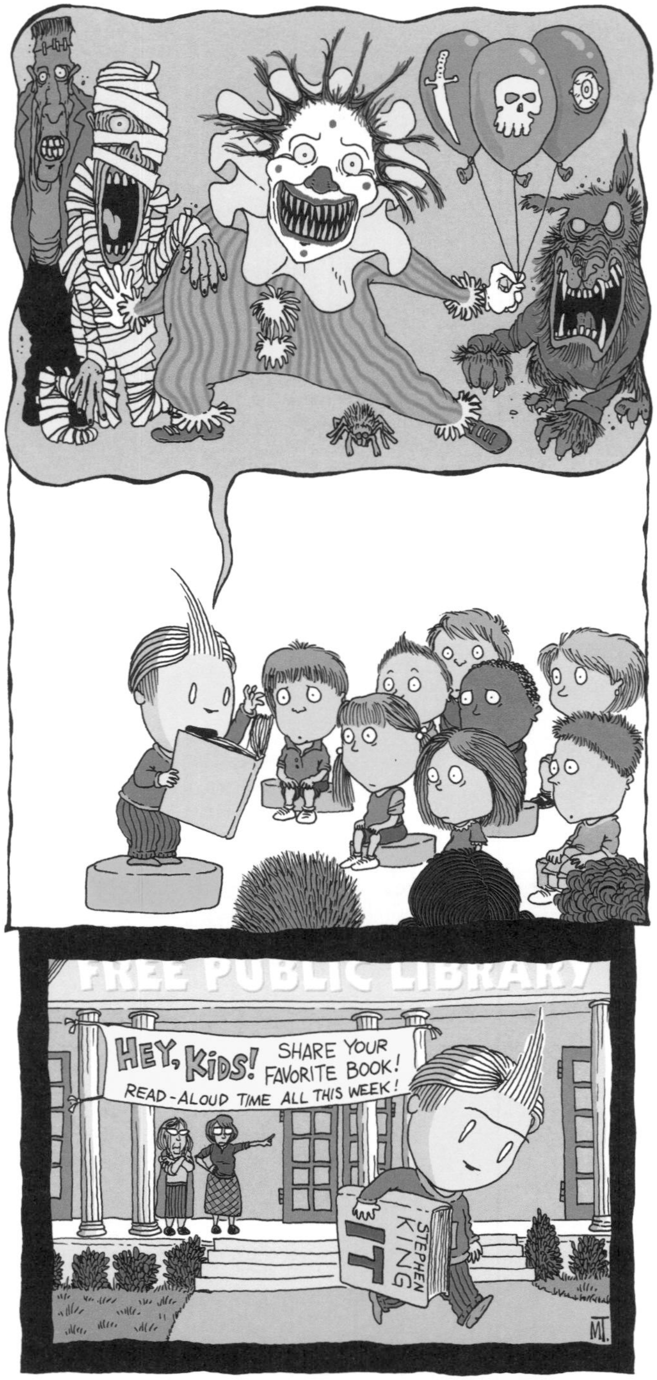
FREE PUBLIC LIBRARY
HEY, KIDS! SHARE YOUR FAVORITE BOOK!
READ-ALOUD TIME ALL THIS WEEK!
IT
STEPHEN KING
MT.

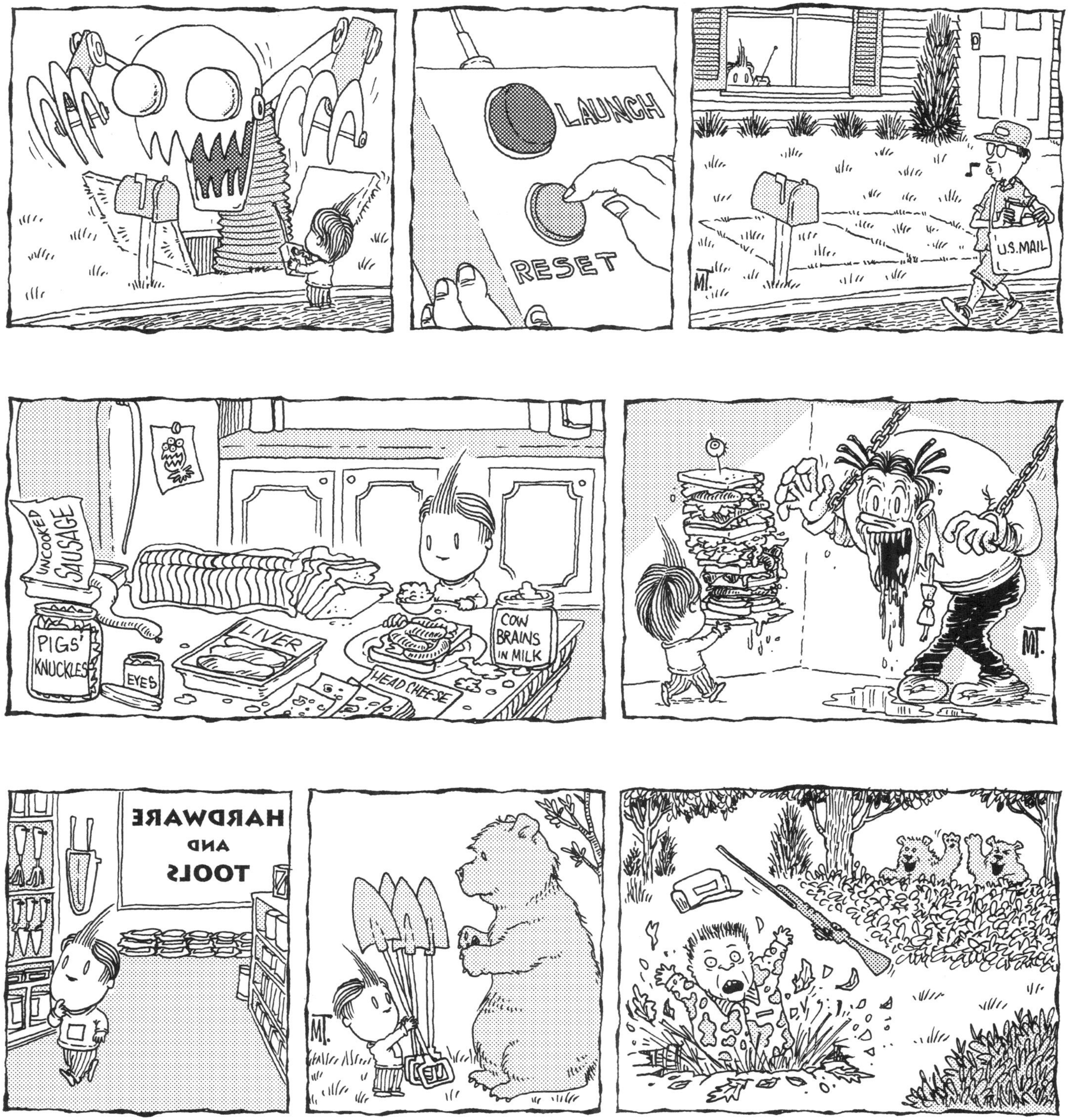
LAUNCH
RESET
U.S.MAIL
MT.
UNCOOKED
SAUSAGE
PIGS' KNUCKLES
EYES
LIVER
HEAD CHEESE
COW BRAINS IN MILK
MT.
HARDWARE
AND
TOOLS
MT.

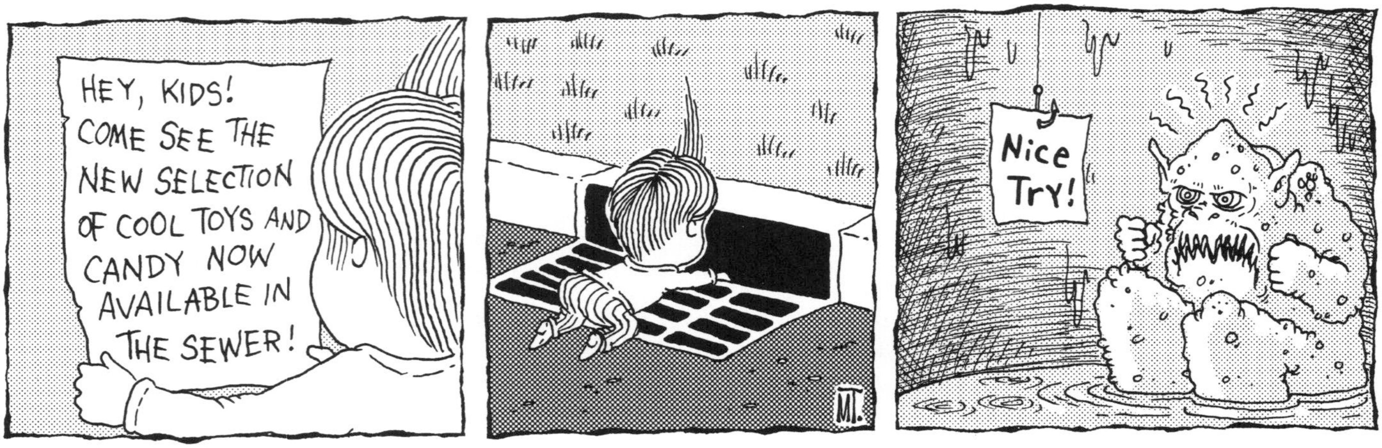
HEY, KIDS! COME SEE THE NEW SELECTION OF COOL TOYS AND CANDY NOW AVAILABLE IN THE SEWER!
Nice Try!

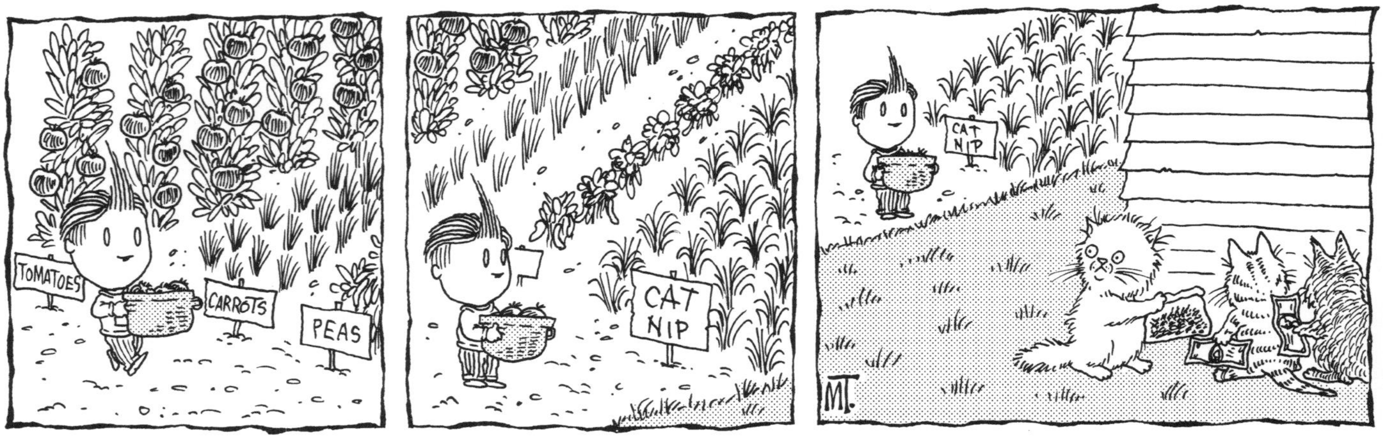
TOMATOES
CARROTS
PEAS
CAT NIP
CAT NIP

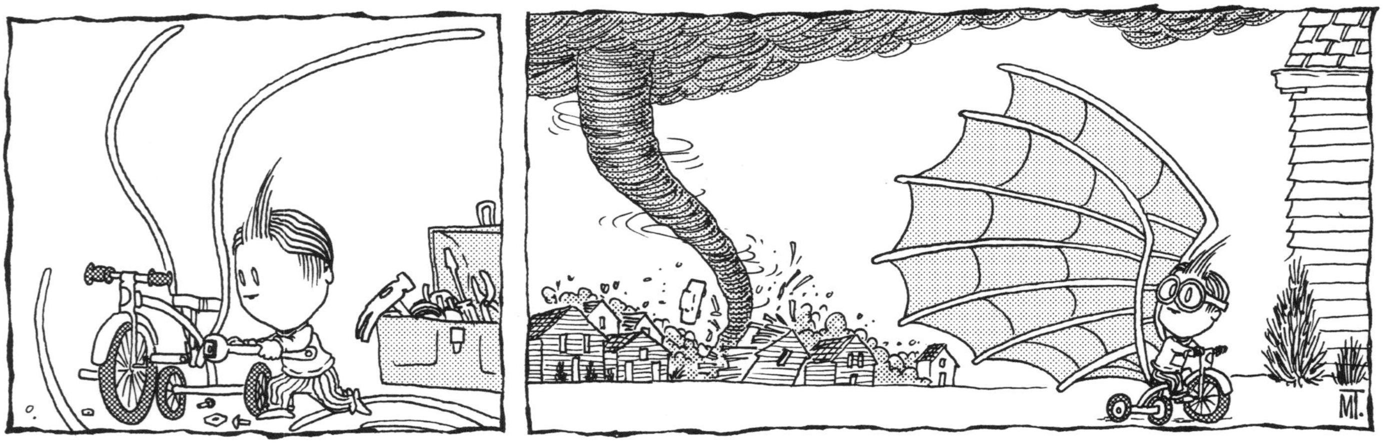

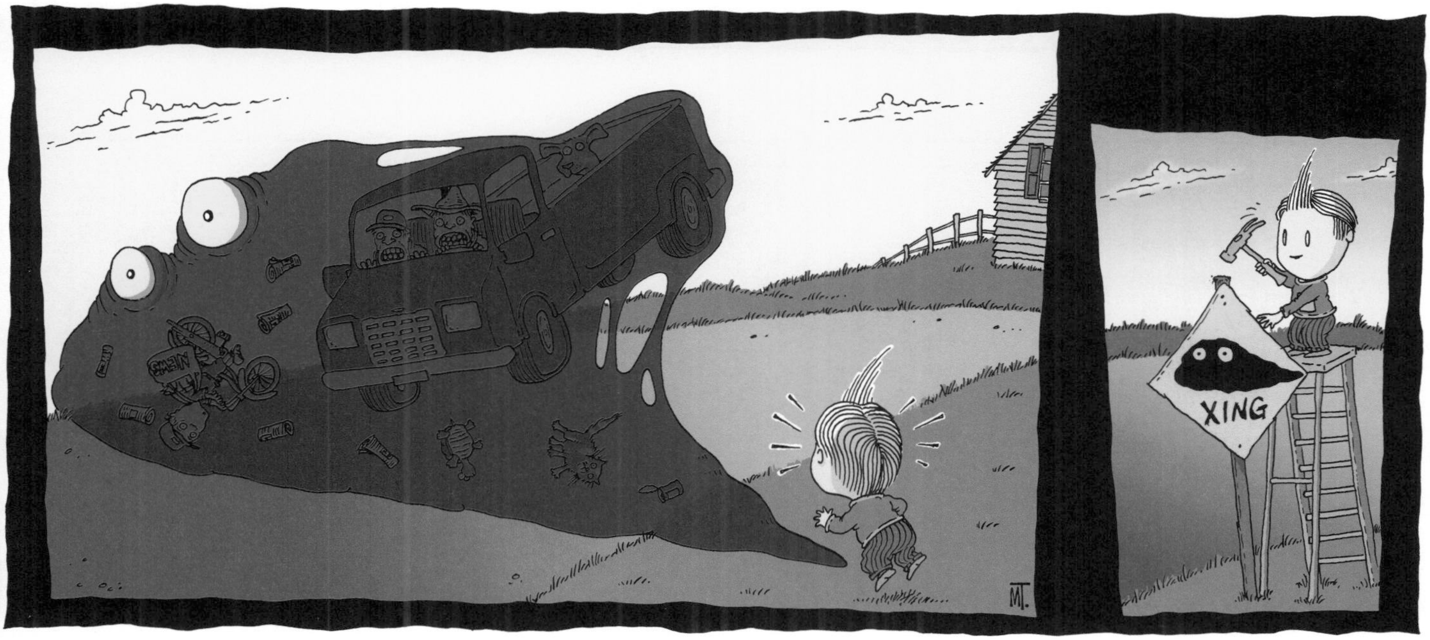
XING

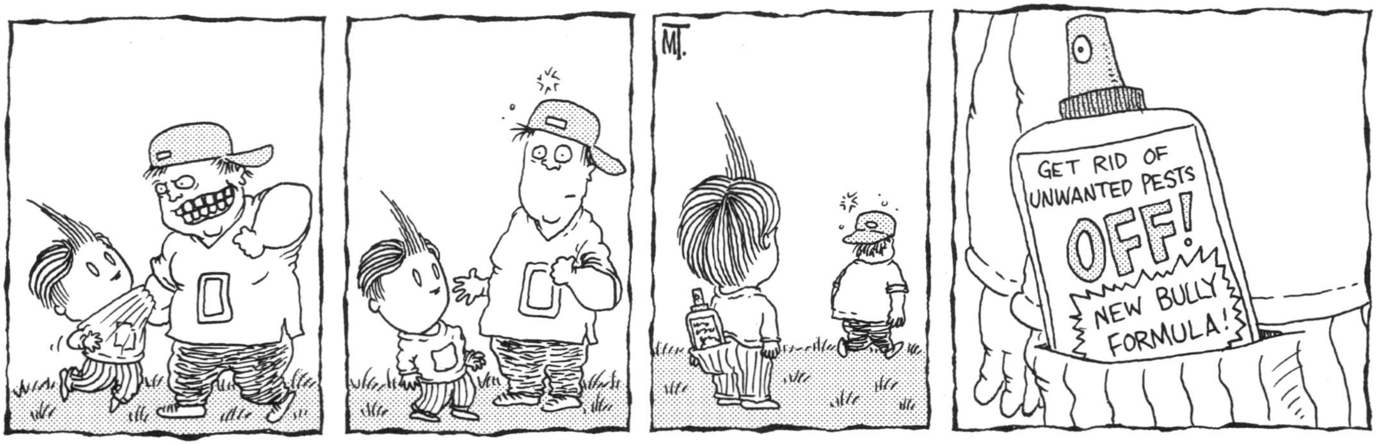
GET RID OF
UNWANTED PESTS
OFF!
NEW BULLY
FORMULA!

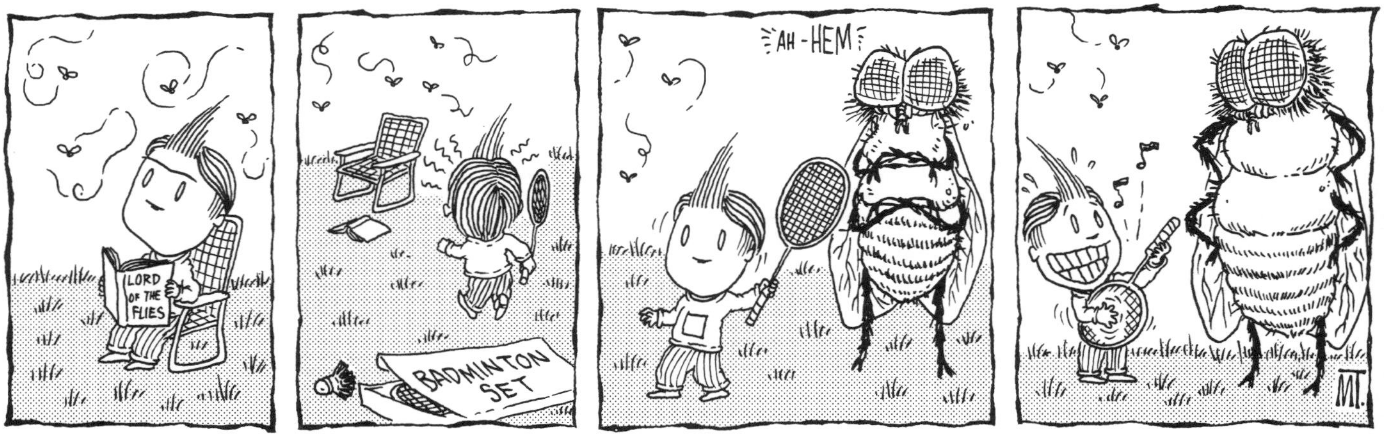
LORD OF THE FLIES
BADMINTON SET
AH-HEM

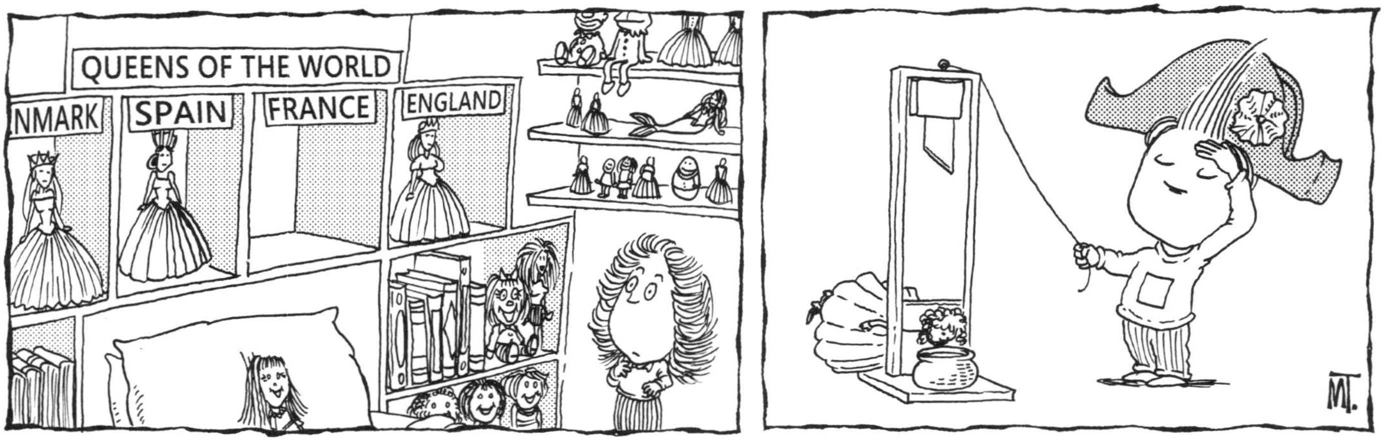
QUEENS OF THE WORLD
NMARK
SPAIN
FRANCE
ENGLAND

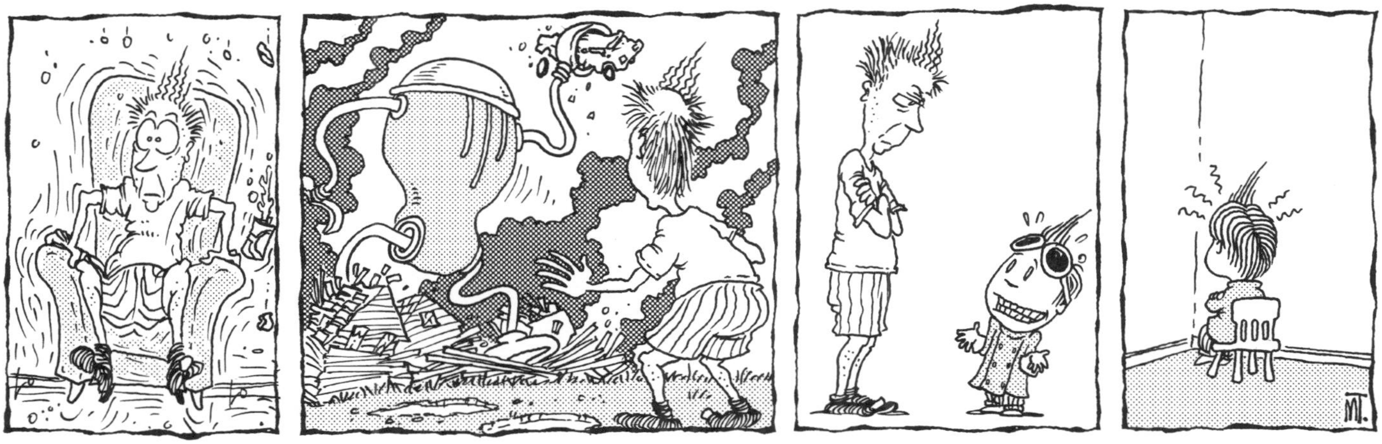

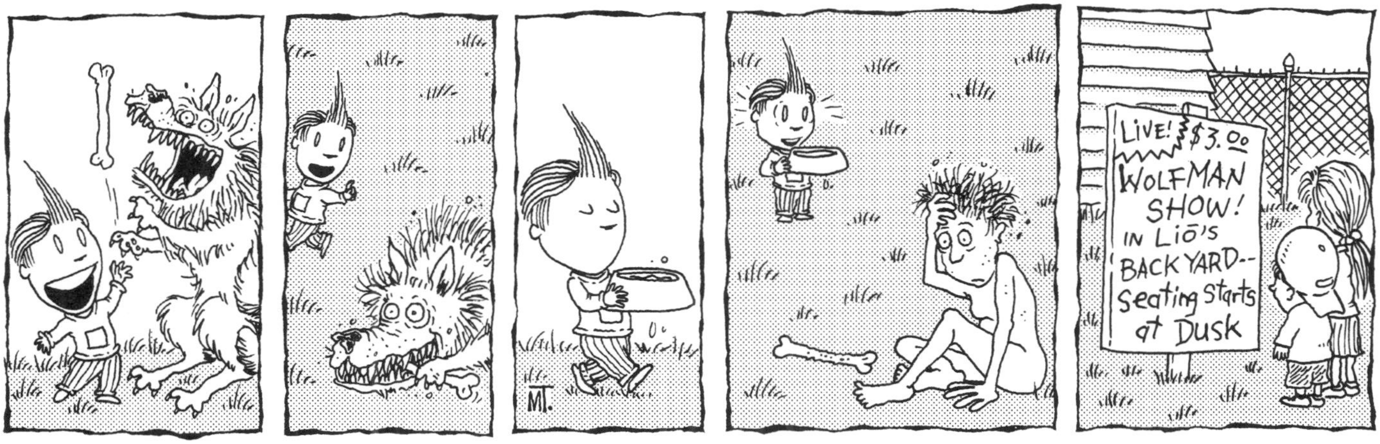
LIVE! $3.00
WOLFMAN SHOW!
IN LIO'S BACK YARD--
Seating starts at Dusk

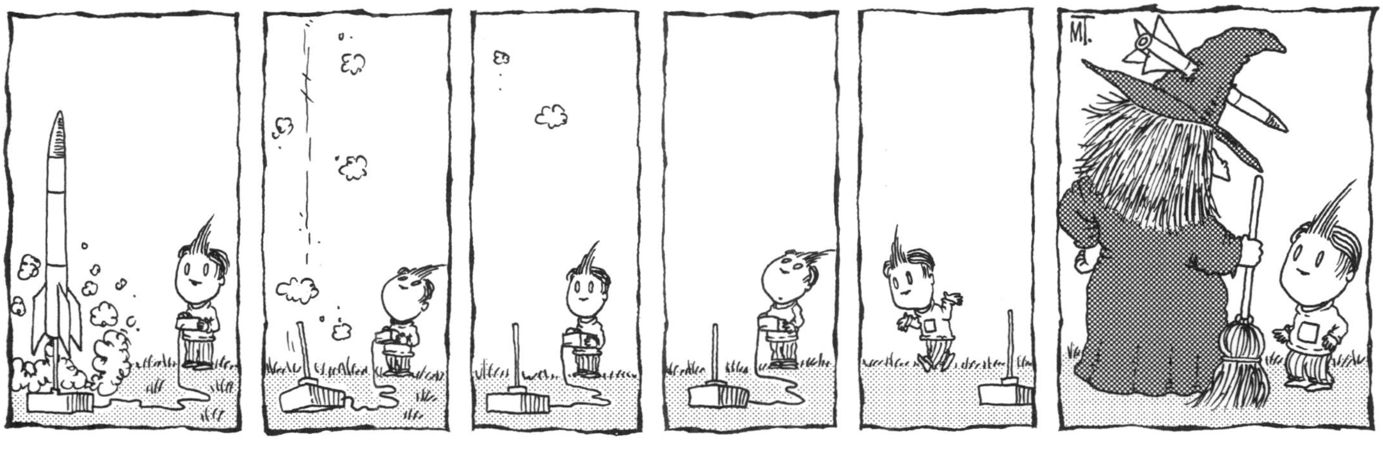

MORE COWBELL!
SOFT & CHEWY
Little Kids
25¢
MT.

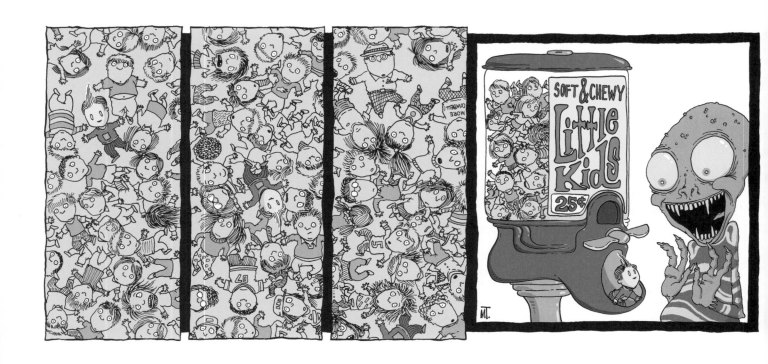

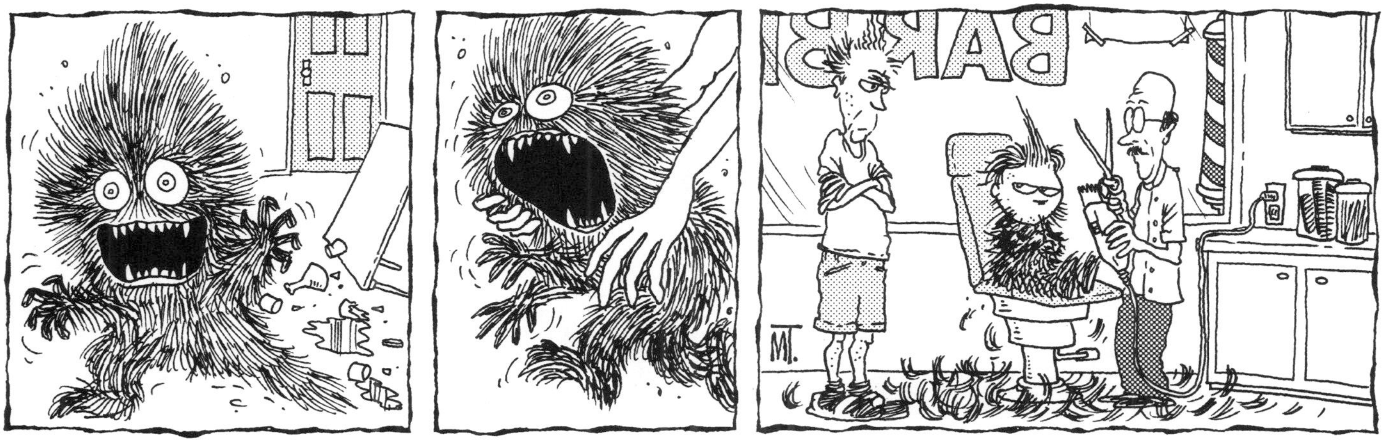

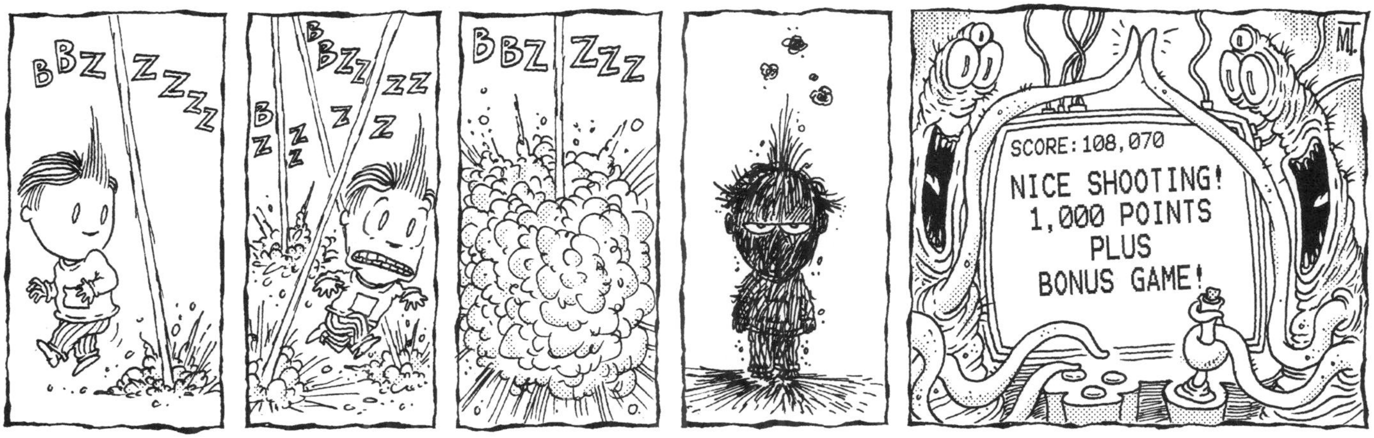
BBZ
ZZZZ
BBZZ
ZZ
BZZ
ZZ
BBZ
ZZZ
SCORE:108,070
NICE SHOOTING!
1,000 POINTS
PLUS
BONUS GAME!

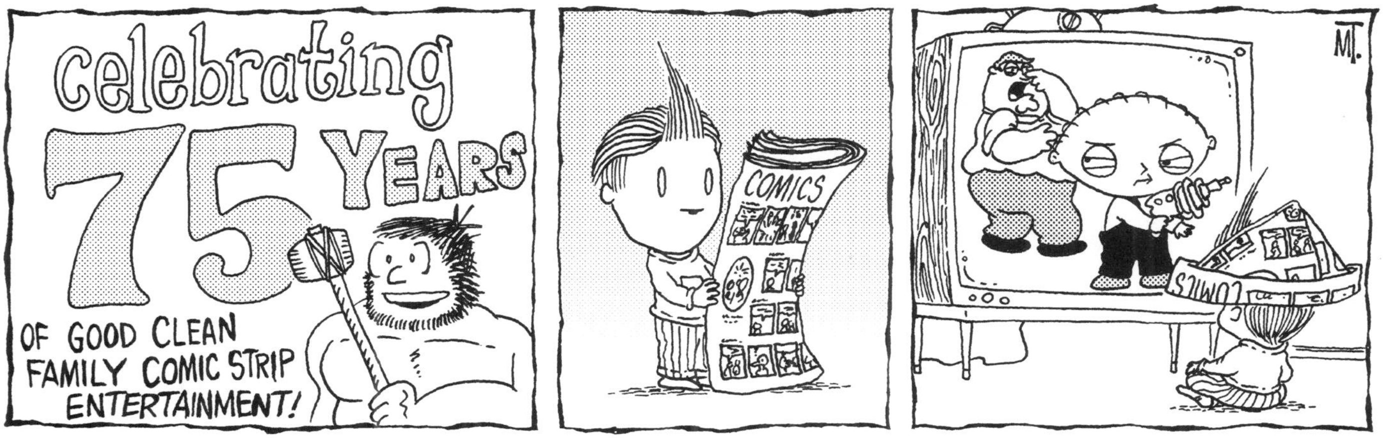
celebrating
75
YEARS
OF GOOD CLEAN
FAMILY COMIC STRIP
ENTERTAINMENT!
COMICS
COMICS

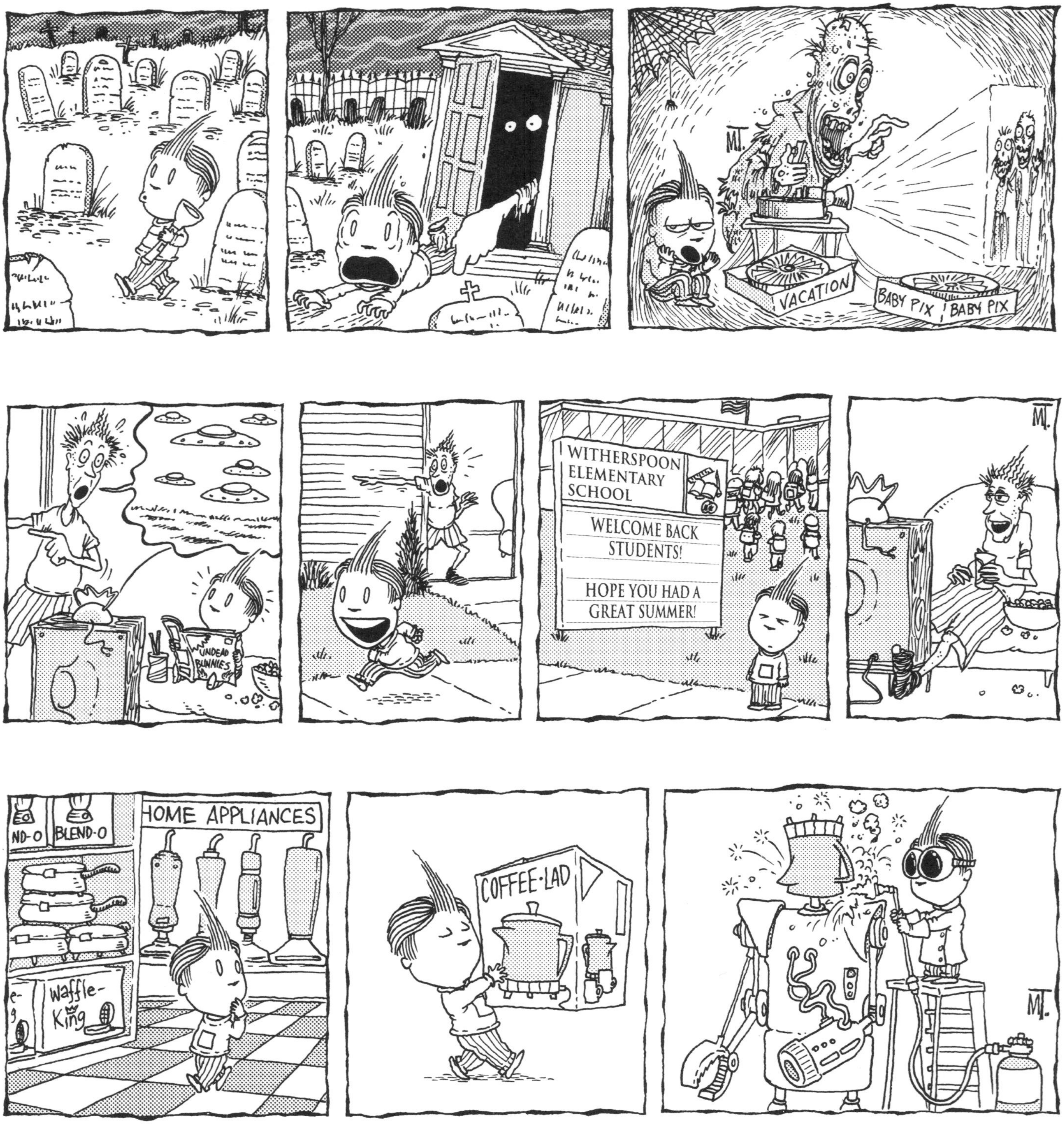
VACATION
BABY PIX
BABY PIX
UNDEAD BUNNIES
WITHERSPOON ELEMENTARY SCHOOL
WELCOME BACK STUDENTS!
HOPE YOU HAD A GREAT SUMMER!
ND-O
BLEND-O
HOME APPLIANCES
Waffle-King
COFFEE·LAD

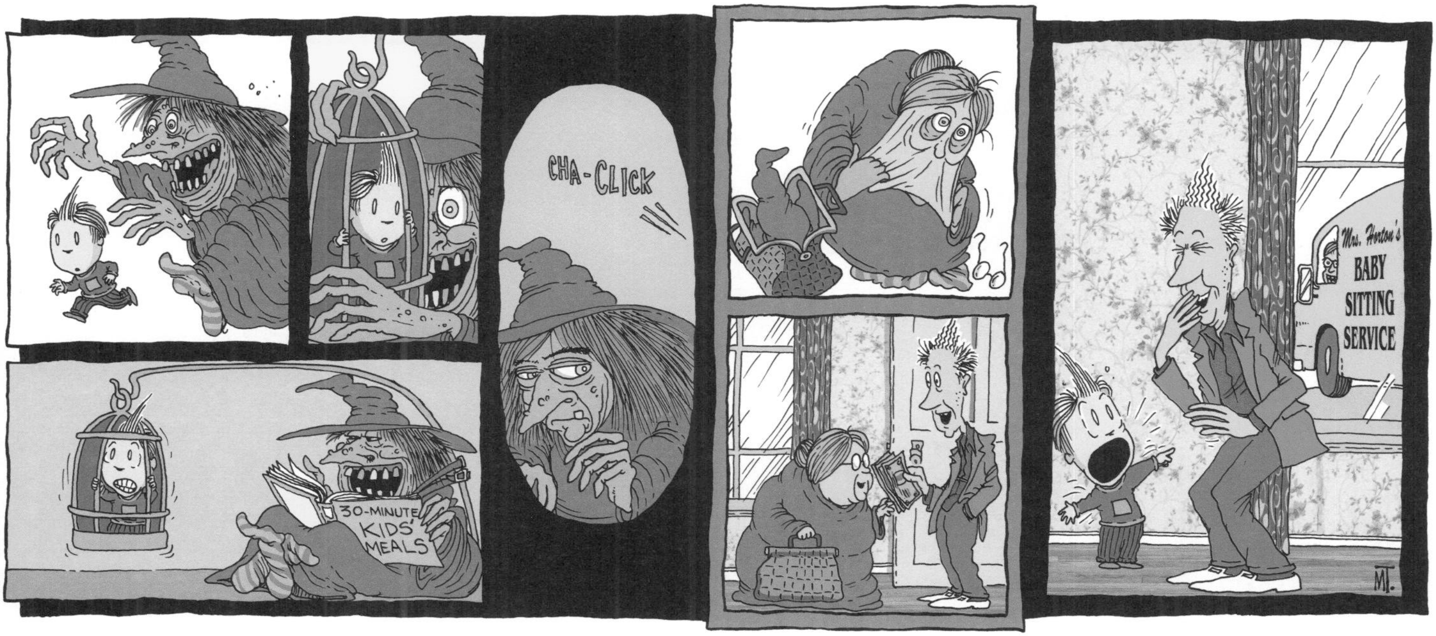
CHA-CLICK
30-MINUTE
KIDS' MEALS
Mrs. Horton's
BABY
SITTING
SERVICE
MT.

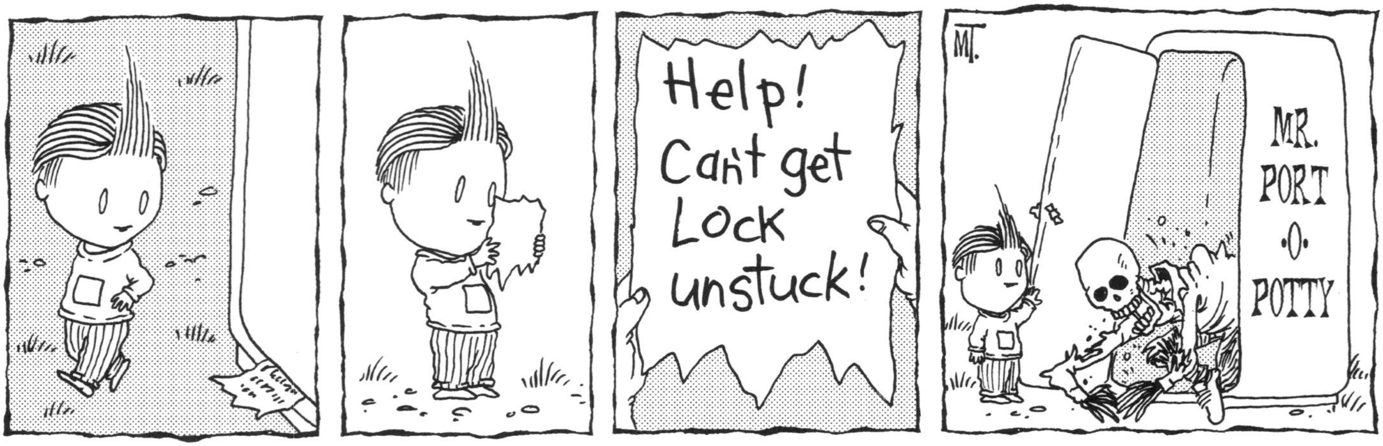
Help! Can't get Lock unstuck!
MR. PORT-O-POTTY

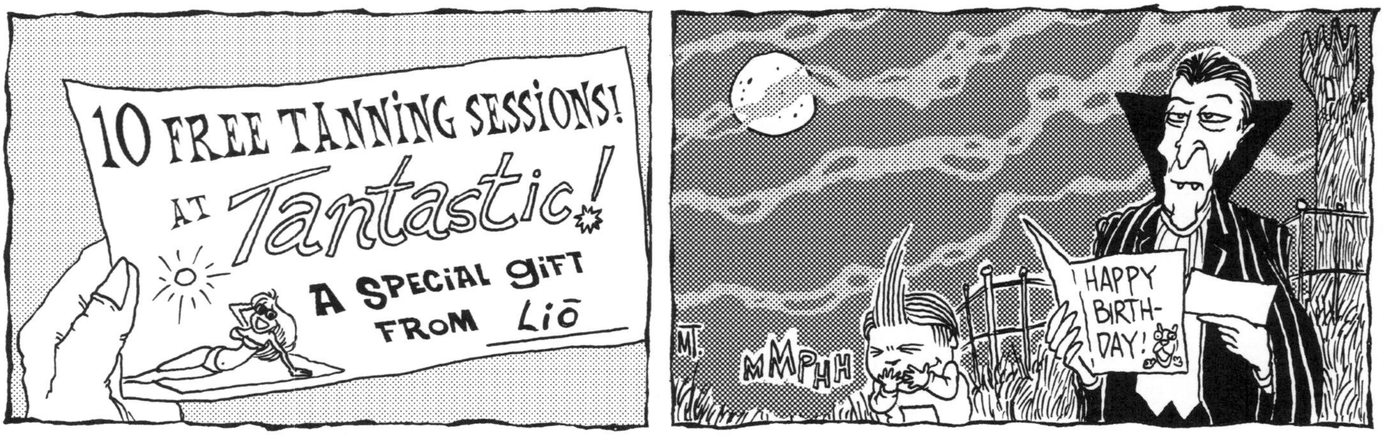
10 FREE TANNING SESSIONS!
AT Tantastic!
A SPECIAL GIFT FROM Liō
MMPHH
HAPPY BIRTH-DAY!

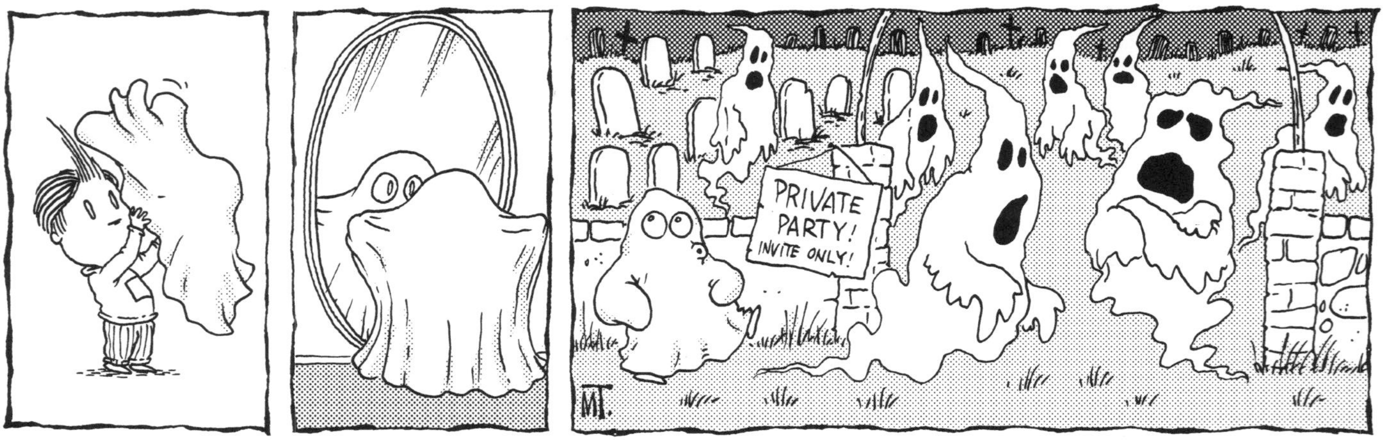
PRIVATE PARTY!
INVITE ONLY!

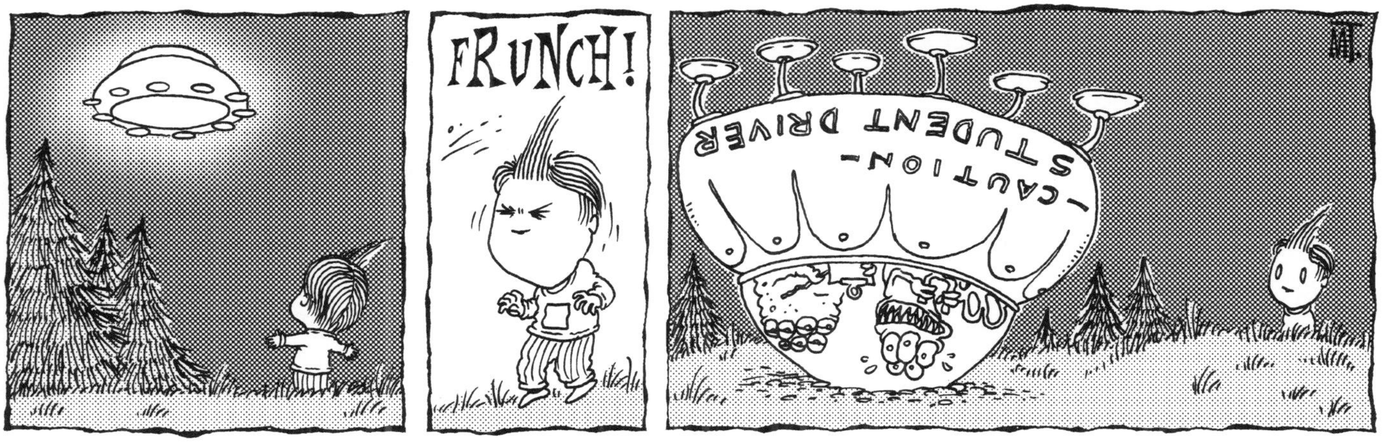
FRUNCH!
-CAUTION- STUDENT DRIVER

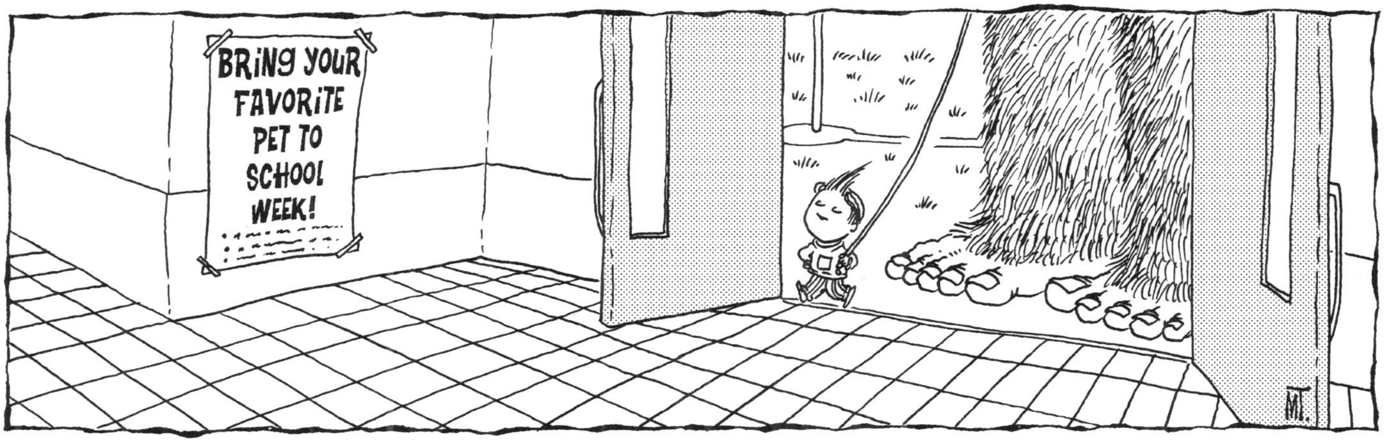
BRING YOUR FAVORITE PET TO SCHOOL WEEK!

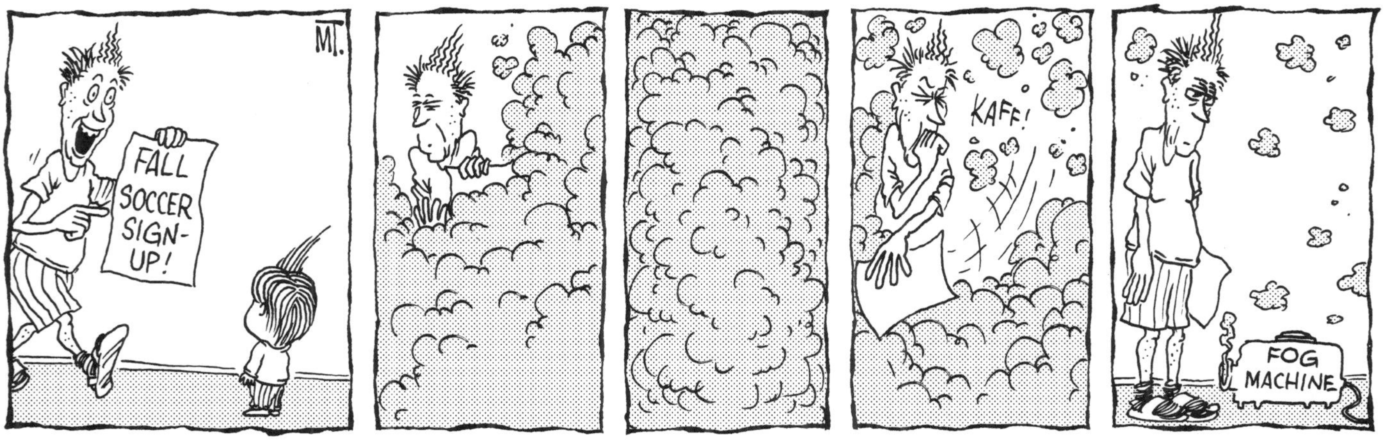
FALL SOCCER SIGN-UP!
KAFF!
FOG MACHINE

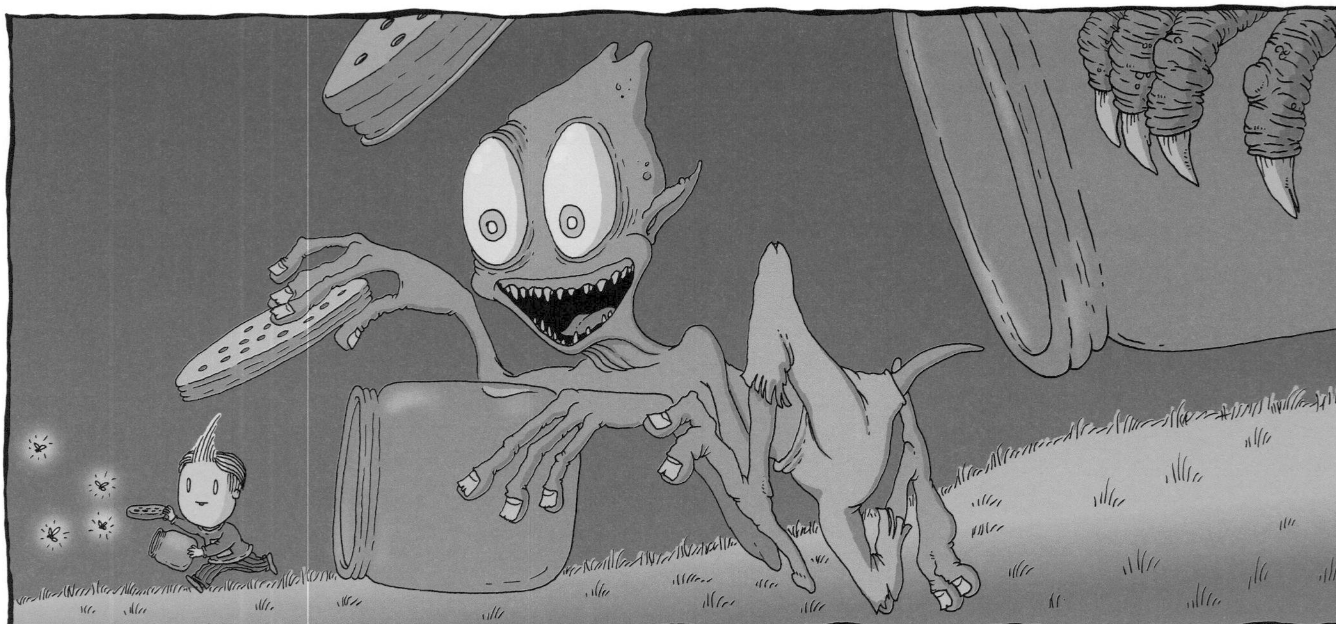
MT.

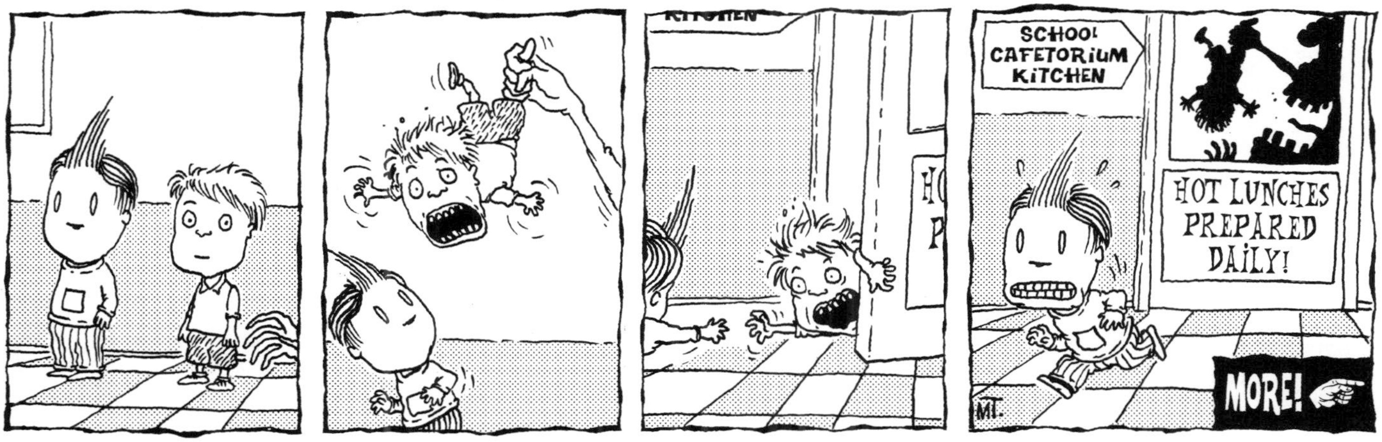
SCHOOl CAFETORiuM KiTCHEN
HOT LUNCHES PREPARED DAiLY!
MT.
MORE!

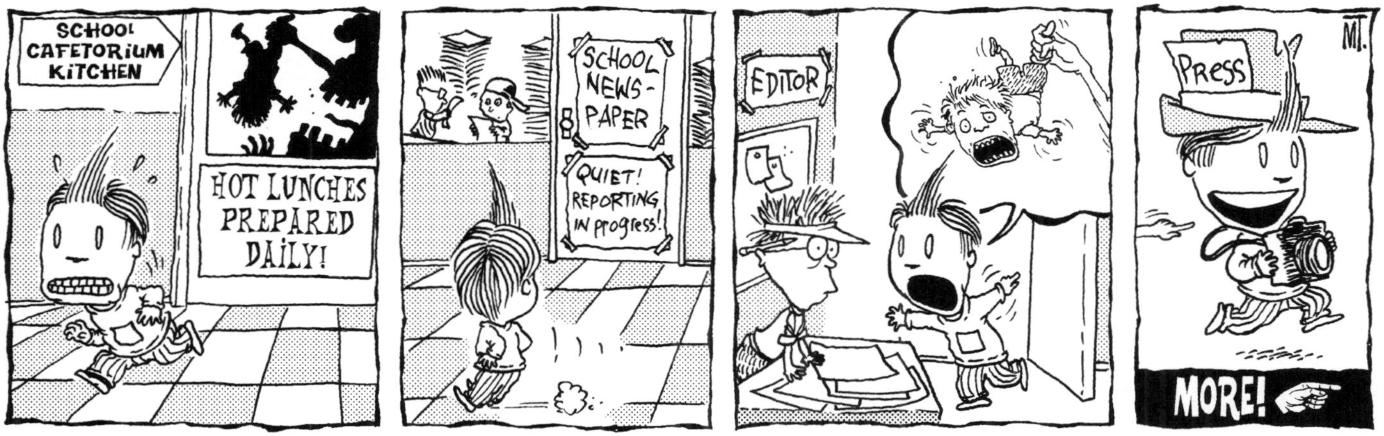
SCHOOl CAFETORiuM KiTCHEN
HOT LUNCHES PREPARED DAiLY!
SCHOOL NEWS-PAPER
QUIET! REPORTING IN progress!
EDITOR
Press
MT.
MORE!

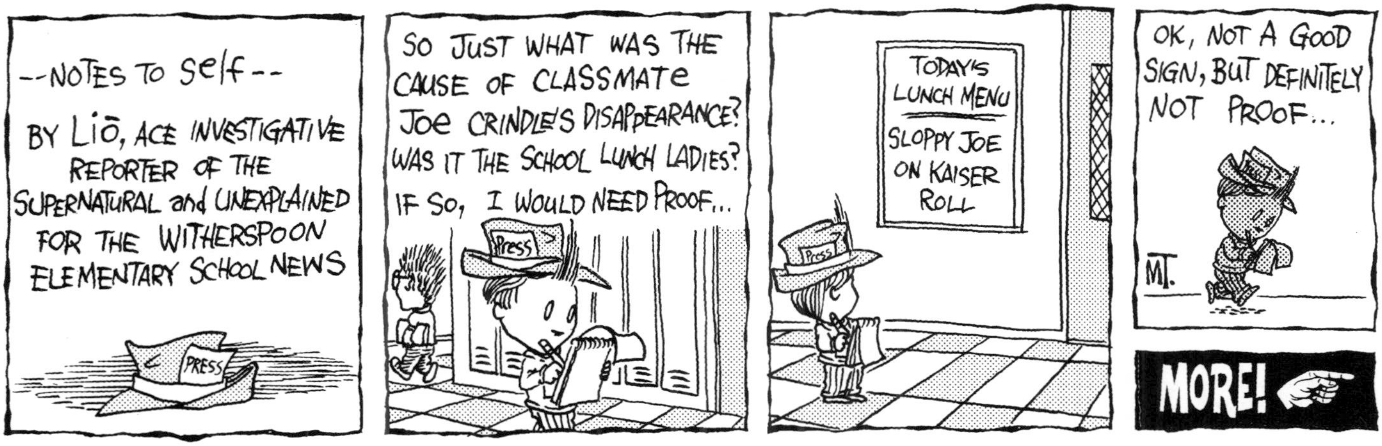
--NOTES TO Self--
BY LiŌ, ACE INVESTIGATIVE REPORTER OF THE SUPERNATURAL and UNEXPLAINED FOR THE WITHERSPOON ELEMENTARY SCHOOL NEWS
PRESS
SO JUST WHAT WAS THE CAUSE OF CLASSMATE JOE CRINDLE'S DISAPPEARANCE? WAS IT THE SCHOOL LUNCH LADIES? IF SO, I WOULD NEED PROOF...
Press
TODAY'S LUNCH MENU
SLOPPY JOE ON KAISER ROLL
Press
OK, NOT A GOOD SIGN, BUT DEFINITELY NOT PROOF...
MT.
MORE!

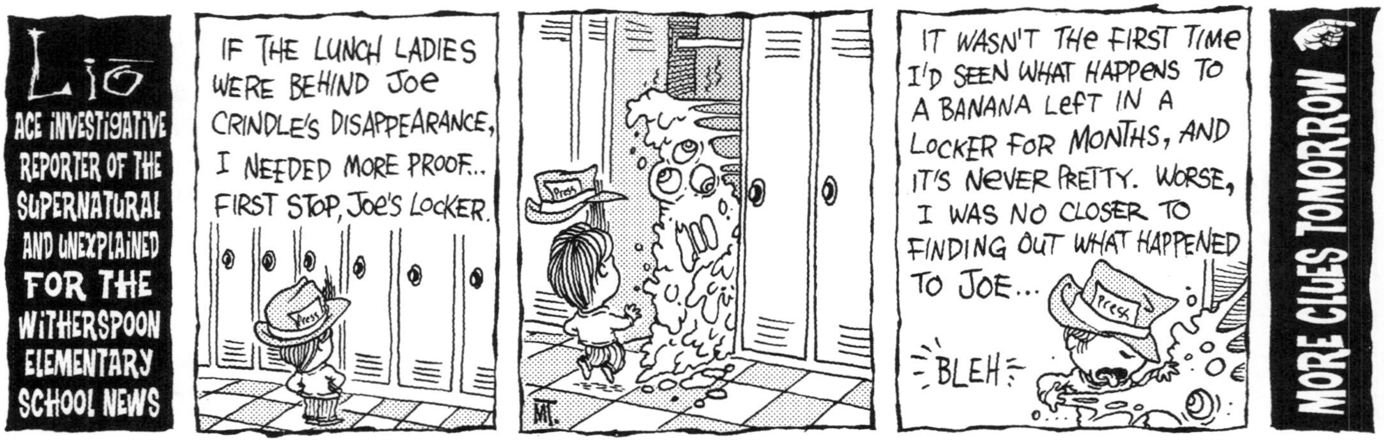
Liō
ACE INVESTIGATIVE REPORTER OF THE SUPERNATURAL AND UNEXPLAINED FOR THE WITHERSPOON ELEMENTARY SCHOOL NEWS
IF THE LUNCH LADIES WERE BEHIND JOE CRINDLE'S DISAPPEARANCE, I NEEDED MORE PROOF... FIRST STOP, JOE'S LOCKER.
Press
IT WASN'T THE FIRST TIME I'D SEEN WHAT HAPPENS TO A BANANA LEFT IN A LOCKER FOR MONTHS, AND IT'S NEVER PRETTY. WORSE, I WAS NO CLOSER TO FINDING OUT WHAT HAPPENED TO JOE...
BLEH
MORE CLUES TOMORROW

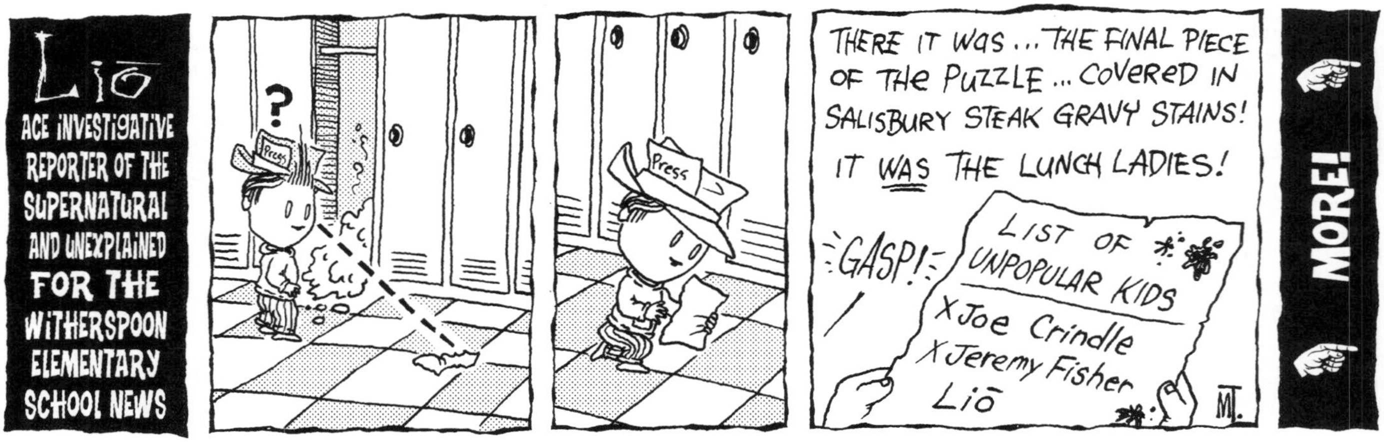
Liō
ACE INVESTIGATIVE REPORTER OF THE SUPERNATURAL AND UNEXPLAINED FOR THE WITHERSPOON ELEMENTARY SCHOOL NEWS
?
Press
THERE IT WAS... THE FINAL PIECE OF THE PUZZLE... COVERED IN SALISBURY STEAK GRAVY STAINS!
IT WAS THE LUNCH LADIES!
GASP!
LIST OF UNPOPULAR KIDS
X Joe Crindle
X Jeremy Fisher
Liō
MORE!

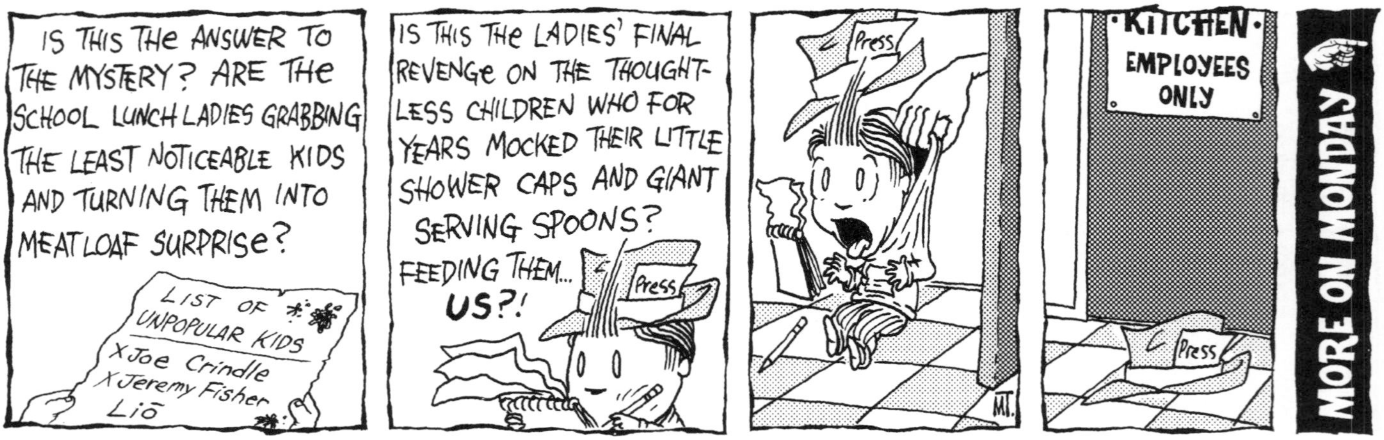
IS THIS THE ANSWER TO THE MYSTERY? ARE THE SCHOOL LUNCH LADIES GRABBING THE LEAST NOTICEABLE KIDS AND TURNING THEM INTO MEATLOAF SURPRISE?
LIST OF UNPOPULAR KIDS
X Joe Crindle
X Jeremy Fisher
Liō
IS THIS THE LADIES' FINAL REVENGE ON THE THOUGHTLESS CHILDREN WHO FOR YEARS MOCKED THEIR LITTLE SHOWER CAPS AND GIANT SERVING SPOONS?
FEEDING THEM... US?!
Press
·KITCHEN·
EMPLOYEES ONLY
MORE ON MONDAY

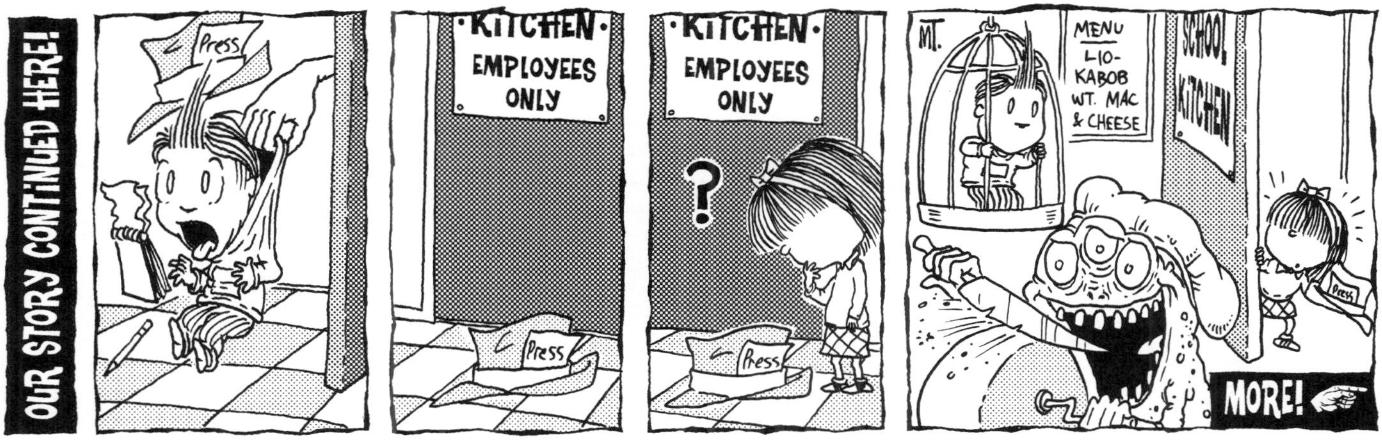
OUR STORY CONTINUED HERE!
Press
·KITCHEN·
EMPLOYEES ONLY
Press
·KITCHEN·
EMPLOYEES ONLY
?
Press
MT.
MENU
LIO-KABOB WT. MAC & CHEESE
SCHOOL KITCHEN
Press
MORE!

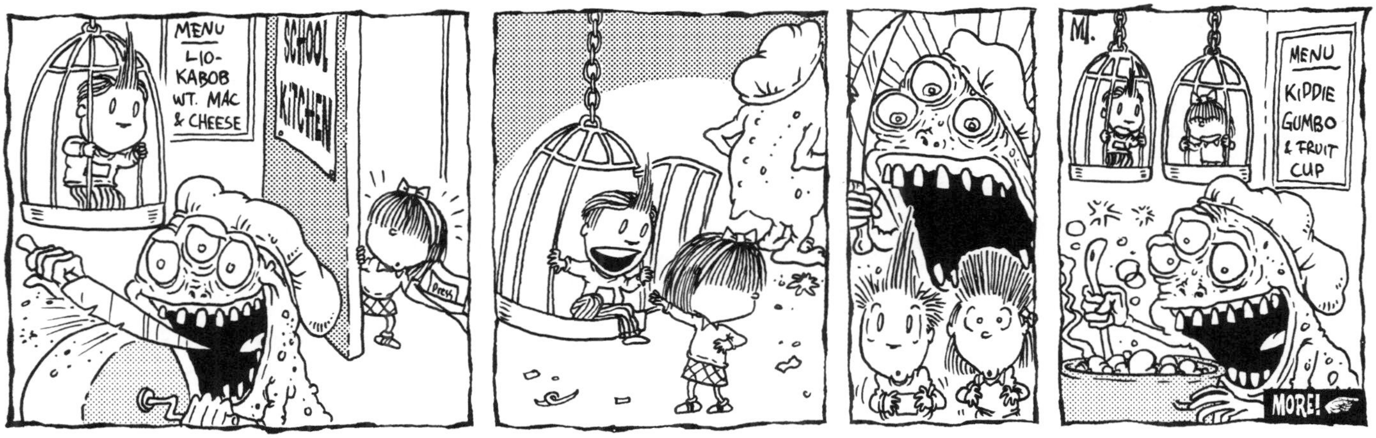
MENU
LIO-KABOB WT. MAC & CHEESE
SCHOOL KITCHEN
Press
MT.
MENU
KIDDIE GUMBO & FRUIT CUP
MORE!

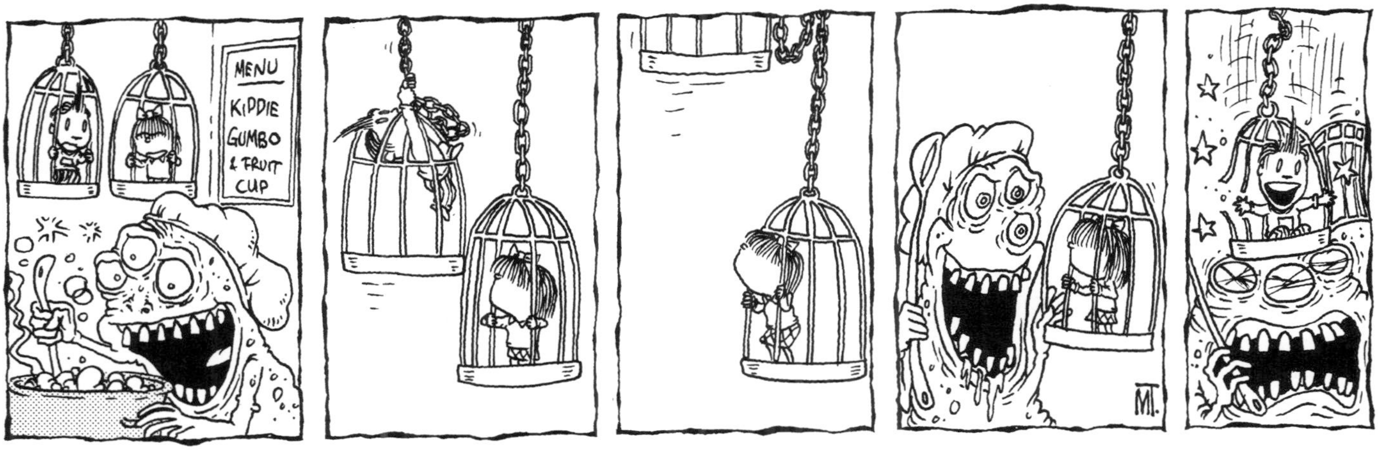
MENU
KIDDIE GUMBO & FRUIT CUP
MT.

PPFFFFT!
MT.
MORE!

EDITOR
Witherspc
School
News-
Paper
Press
WITHERSPOON ELEMENTARY NEWS
LUNCH LADIES SERVE STUDENTS -- AS LUNCH!
Press
?
Press
MT.
SIGH
Cartoonist
FIN.